MONEY TALKS

Also by Gail Vaz-Oxlade

Debt-Free Forever
Take Control of Your Money and Your Life

Never Too Late
Take Control of Your Retirement and Your Future

It's Your Money
Becoming a Woman of Independent Means

Money-Smart Kids
Teach Your Children Financial Confidence and Control

Money Rules
Rule Your Money or Your Money Will Rule You

Saving for School
Understand RESPs, Take Control of Your Savings,
Minimize Student Debt

MONEY
TALKS

When to Say Yes and How to Say No

GAIL VAZ-OXLADE

Collins

Published by Collins, an imprint of HarperCollins Publishers Ltd

First Edition

HarperCollins Publishers Ltd
2 Bloor Street East, 20th Floor
Toronto, Ontario
M4W 1A8

www.harpercollins.ca

Library and Archives Canada Cataloguing in Publication

Vaz-Oxlade, Gail E., 1959–
Money Talks: When to Say Yes and How to Say No / Gail Vaz-Oxlade.

ISBN: 978-1-44343-407-2

Printed and bound in the United States
RRD 9 8 7 6 5 4 3 2 1

To Alex and Malcolm, who have taught me so much about being a better me.

CONTENTS

INTRODUCTION

Why are we so unwilling to talk about money? It's part of our everyday lives and yet, despite its ever-presence, most discussions about money manage to keep the real issues at arm's length. Experts are happy to share how to make more, how to save on taxes, how the economy is doing. But when it comes to real money talks—to the nitty-gritty of telling the truth about money and behaviour and how they intersect—personal money matters seem too private to discuss. Witness all the money makeovers where participants are pictured holding something in front of their faces. They'll only cough up the deets if you can't tell who they are.

Have you ever bailed out someone you love? Y'know, "Sure, I'll lend you ..." or "Never mind, you can get the bill next time." Did you think to yourself—or say to someone else—"Geez, she's just terrible with money. I wish she'd get her act together"?

People will moan about bailing someone out, but they won't hold said someone accountable. It's so easy to just throw some money at the problem. But you know what? It's the "easy" that keeps the problem rooted. And it's the "easy" that keeps you on the hook.

The idea that money is the leading cause of problems in relationships is routinely repeated in the media. More than sex, more than children or in-laws, money is cited as the most common area of conflict.

It's not the money. Nope. It's not.

Money is a medium of exchange, that's all. It's what we use to complete our transactions. So money isn't the problem.

We are the problem. How we behave—what we do with our money and how we communicate about that behaviour—is at the root of most of the challenges we face with, and blame on, money.

There are people who want to maintain power over others. There are people who want to be in control. There are people who are willing to use guilt to get what they want. And there are people who do not want to take responsibility for their own lives. All this—and so much more—is reflected in what we do with our money.

We can use money to demonstrate affection. We can use money to exhibit pride. We can use money as a measure of success or failure. We can blame our lack of money for what we have not achieved. We can look at others' abundance and be jealous of what they have. But the problem isn't the money. Money isn't at the root of whatever it is that's gone wrong or right, no matter how often we may say it is. Our unwillingness to tell the truth, to really communicate how we feel—that's the problem.

So what's the solution?

It isn't easy. And it isn't comfortable. But the only way money will stop being a problem for most of us is if we start talking about it—and talking about it honestly.

When your best friend hits you up for cash and you don't want to give it to them, you can't lie, make some pathetic excuse, or worse, simply hand over the money. You have to tell them the truth. You have to talk about why you won't lend to them. Or if you choose to lend, you have to talk about what your expectations are for repayment.

When your parents say things like, "I'm counting on you in my old age," you can't just nod, smile, and go home thinking, "Now what am I going to do?" You have to talk about it with them. You have to explain why that's not going to work for you. Or, if you're able to help them, what you'll each need to do to make it work.

When your children say, "Can you buy me . . ." you can't respond with the rote "Do you think I'm made of money?" or "Money doesn't grow on trees!" You have to use those requests as opportunities to talk about money: how you get it, how you prioritize spending, and how to make it work hard for you. Pat answers teach diddly-squat. Really talking about money means engaging, being truthful, and constantly reinforcing that money is simply a tool.

I know how hard it is to talk about money. Believe me, I know. And that's why I've written this book.

As I've worked with people on television and spoken with people from coast to coast, it's become clear to me that the common sense that should be applied to money is often derailed by an emotional twist. It's hard to deal with the disappointment of our loved ones. It's hard to watch friends struggle financially and not acquiesce to their requests for help. It's hard to stay true to our own goals when there are so many demands being put on our wallets.

Sometimes we are unwilling to face our reality. We choose to believe that bad things won't happen to us and so we don't take the appropriate precautions. We don't want to know what we're spending and where because that would mean facing up to the fact that we can't just whip out our wallets and buy a round if the rent is due. We don't want to appear poor or as though we have less than our peer group, so we spend money we don't have to buy things we really don't need.

People ask and we say yes. "Of course I'll lend you some money until Friday." Or "I'm not such a jerk that I'd let my sister get evicted from her apartment because she spent her rent money on other stuff." Or "Sure, boss, I'll let you defer paying me because, really, I need this job more than you need me."

We don't want to say no to friends and family or to co-workers (really, another collection for a gift?) or to bosses, so we say yes. And then we quietly kick ourselves and deal with the consequences of not being able to come up with the language we need to make our values and what we really want to say clear to others.

It can be hard to come up with the words to bridge into a money talk. Jumping in without thinking through what you'll say might leave you struggling to find the right words to express what you're thinking and feeling. Almost no one has the ability to say the right thing without giving it a little forethought.

Since no one talks about money, we have no models on which to base our own forays into these conversations.

Money Talks models many of the conversations you wish you could have with your mate, mother, best friend, or son. In dozens of scenarios, in which you may recognize yourself or someone you love, are ideas for how you can deal respectfully and lovingly with whoever it is that's asking you for financial help. And I give you some guidance on when to say yes and how to say no.

Do you have a bully in your life? Wish your brother would grow the hell up and stop counting on you to save his ass? Want to tell your BFF that dreaming is only the first step in making a better life? I get hundreds of letters every year from people who can't figure out how to get their sister off their couch, their mother to stop hitting them up for money, or their mate to recognize that saving is part of having a solid financial foundation. The letters' common theme is "Gail, how do I get through to them?"

So that's what this book is all about: how to tell your mate, your father, your best friend, or your grandmother that it's time for a change. It's about helping you see your own situation through stories that reflect what you may be experiencing. It's about empowering you with the language to negotiate effectively. And it's about showing you that for each problem there are steps you can take and words you can use to come to a solution.

Here we go.

Part One

PRESSING EMOTIONAL HOT BUTTONS

Emotions are powerful things. They can make your heart soar—think love, awe, and pride. They can turn your mood on a dime—think criticism and what that does to the rest of your day. They can make you crayzee—think jealousy, envy, and anger. There are a bunch of emotions that make people do things they would never do if they were thinking straight.

Marketers know you're more likely to buy a product if they can find and push your emotional hot buttons. They collect data, analyze behaviour, and develop strategies to part you from your money. Far less scientific, but no less successful, family and friends also know how to push your buttons.

There's your sister, who makes far less money than you and is always leaving her wallet at home because, well, there's nothing in it anyway. As the "richer" sister, you pony up. There's your mate, who knows you want to fix up the master bathroom and promises he'll do it as soon as he finishes building that deck with the hot tub you'll never go in. There's the parent who, having been widowed recently, plays the "I don't want to be too much trouble," card even as she demands your constant attention.

Psychologists recognize that there's a huge difference between what you know in your mind and what you feel in your heart, and it is in this gap that emotional hot buttons are wired to make you twist and squirm. Sure, you *know* you can't always be at your mom's beck and call, but that doesn't stop you writhing with guilt (and subsequently fuming with anger because you were made to feel guilty) if you're not there when she needs you.

An appeal to your emotions—to your heart—will almost always elicit a response, particularly if you're not aware that your buttons are being pushed. It's hard to not get caught even when you do know that someone is poking at you. But if you don't realize that you're being played, you're a goner.

Think about who knows your hot buttons and how often they push those buttons to get what they want. Do you even want to know how many of your decisions are being made from an emotional place, or are you happy to just keep jumping through the button pusher's strategically placed hoops?

If you see yourself in the following stories, know that you have plenty of company. Also know that you are allowing your buttons to be pushed. Yes, you. Disconnect the switch and you retake control. Keep salivating like Pavlov's dog and you're at the whim of the button pusher.

1 • SAVE ME!

When Suzie and Donny divorced, Donny declared bankruptcy and left Suzie holding two young babies and a bag of debt. Suzie moved home to her parents' house to rebuild her life. Always a responsible worker, Suzie was doing her best to get the debt paid off, but with built-in babysitters and a pent-up desire to see friends she hadn't seen in almost four years—as long as she'd been married to Donny—Suzie started to parent less and hang out more. Her mother and father didn't want to say too much because they loved having the grandkids under their roof and they knew Suzie was just blowing off steam.

Six months later Suzie was still partying and her mom started to wonder when Suzie was going to come to her senses. When her mom approached her to talk about how long she and the kids would be staying, Suzie got really angry. She didn't realize she was being such a burden. Didn't her mother understand how hard this was? Was she trying to get rid of her? Suzie's mom backed right off.

A year passed. Life at her parents' house was comfortable. The kids could swim all summer and Suzie could see her friends a couple of times a week. To give herself more entertainment money, she stopped putting her heart and soul into getting the debt paid as fast as possible. Suzie's dad told Suzie's mom that it looked like Suzie and the kids were there to stay. They'd rescued Suzie and as the Protective Parents Rule holds, when you save a life, you become responsible for that life.

As parents, it's hard to watch our children go through tough times. We want to help in any way we can. But the dynamic can change so quickly from helping to enabling. And if there are no ground rules, old roles reassert themselves. "You can't tell me what to do!" seems petulant coming from a 15-year-old, but from your 30-year-old it's absolutely true!

Whenever we choose to help the people we love, be they children, parents, or best buds, it's important to lay down the ground rules for the help we are extending. It may not be the very first thing you do, but there comes a day when you must have that conversation.

You'll walk a fine balance between expecting some contribution and not being seen as lording it over your poor pal. Laying down the ground rules ahead of time will go a long way in setting the tone for the length of your togetherness.

"Suzie, we have a date Thursday for dinner and a check-in on how you're doing and where you are with your plan, right?"

But what if Sue attempts to blow you off? Stay calm and respond with, "We made a deal at the beginning of this, and this is your end of the deal. So, are we having a meeting or are you finding a new place to live?"

Emotions may run high. Don't bite. Stay cool and stick to your guns even when you hear, "You're a bitch. Just because I need some help doesn't give you the right to treat me like a child."

Respond with some version of "I'm not treating you like a child. I'm treating you like the person you said you'd be when we made this agreement. If you change the rules, that's fine, but that means things change on my end too. Think about it and let me know tomorrow if Thursday works for you." Then walk away. Go weed the garden. Go to the grocery store. Don't stay where you can get drawn into a fight. Give the other person some time to think.

Victim/rescuer is one of the most common relationship dynamics I've seen. He runs up his credit card bills and you pay them off. She spends her money on manis and pedis, and when rent time comes you pony up for the whole thing. This might be your partner. It might be your BFF. It could be your kid or your mother or your Uncle George. If you are constantly coming to the rescue, you're playing your part in helping the other person remain a victim.

When Jack met Paula he was blown away. Tall and lanky, he towered over her petite frame. He loved how it felt when she turned her face up to look into his eyes. He knew immediately that this was the girl for him and he was determined to win her.

Jack had beautiful eyes, a dark blue that took Paula's breath away. And they always seemed to be dancing, full of light and life. He was such a great guy too. He'd bring her flowers, shower her with compliments, and tell her that she was the reason he had been put on the earth.

Jack had all kinds of money. For seven months he wooed her, taking her to concerts, giving her small gifts, and making her feel like a princess. When they were out with friends, he'd pick up the tab. And if anyone had a little too much to drink, he was quick with a twenty to send them home in a cab.

Paula had always had a steady job. Even in high school she worked weekends and summers, saving up for the things she wanted. She finished university with no debt, and when she landed a job that paid $60,000 a year, she thought she'd fallen into money. Her family hadn't had much, so she'd learned at a young age that if there was something she wanted, she was going to have to work for it. No problem.

Jack came from a family with much more money and he was used to the finer things. The first time Jack asked Paula to lend him $500, she thought nothing of it. He was a little short, he said.

Jack took Paula to Negril, Jamaica, for a winter vacation their first year together. It was just after that trip that the transmission on his truck went, and she felt it was the least she could do to lend him the money. She never gave a second thought to the fact that he'd yet to repay the $500 he'd borrowed.

Jack and Paula got engaged two years after they met. He presented her with a beautiful ring nested in a bouquet of yellow roses, her favourite. She said yes and they started to plan the wedding.

One Tuesday morning Paula was surprised when Jack showed up at her workplace and asked her to go for coffee. She told him to meet her down the street at Dan's Diner and finished clearing her calls. When she got to the diner, Jack had her favourite tea, made just the way she liked it, waiting for her. He was turning his mug of coffee around and around. She knew something was wrong.

"I'm in trouble," he said. She waited. The mug rotated. "I'm a little behind in my rent and if I don't get caught up I'm going to have to find another place to live."

"How'd that happen?" Paula thought it was a reasonable enough question.

"It's a long story," said Jack.

Paula hesitated. "How much do you need?"

"Enough to cover three months—$3,750," said Jack, staring into the black coffee.

"Oh, Jack, how did you fall so far behind?"

He looked up then, sad, embarrassed. "I wouldn't ask you if there was anyone else."

"Okay," said Paula, resolved to solving the problem at hand. "We'll take it out of the money I've set aside for the wedding hall and you'll just have to catch it up before we make our next deposit payment."

"Absolutely," said Jack. "I'll take on some extra shifts and we'll have that money back in no time."

"Before or after you pay me back for the transmission?" was what should have gone through Paula's head. Instead, she was happy to see him so relieved and was glad she could help.

Being in love with someone doesn't mean it's your job to bail that person out. Strong relationships need two partners who are working towards the same ends. If it always falls to one to do the thinking, solve the problems, come up with the money for the next bailout, the relationship won't be a healthy one.

But what if you're already in a relationship with a financial idiot?

Again, it's about setting expectations and making clear what's important to you both. Here's what I wish Paula had said:

"Jack, I love you. And I want to be able to share your life. But I'm not going to be the one who bails you out because you can't figure out how to handle your money. I can help you make a plan. And I'll support your efforts to make things right. But I'm not going to keep giving you money."

"But where am I going to live?"

"Babe, we're planning to get married and you can't keep a roof over your head? How am I supposed to be able to believe you've got my back?"

"It's just temporary."

"You mean like the transmission was temporary?"

"You won't let me forget that, will you?"

"Why would you want to? Didn't it happen? Listen, I've got to get back to work. You think about what I said. If you want me to help you figure out a plan, I'm happy to do that. But I'm not going to just keep handing you money. I love you."

Tell your loved one you're happy to support them in coming up with a plan. Remind them that you love them. Then leave. Dude needs time to think. It may take a few hours or a few days. Stay busy and out of the way. After a few days, if you haven't heard back from buddy, raise the issue again by asking what he has decided to do.

If your next thought is, "What if he or she dumps me?" stop and think for a minute. If your future (or current) life partner would dump you over this, you should count your blessings to be out of that relationship. Why would you want a person in your life who will constantly be in need of bailouts? Sure, it seems simple enough when it's only a couple of hundred dollars at a time. But what about when there's a mortgage payment due and your home is on the line? Or when you're six weeks from maternity leave and you find out the money you set aside must go to pay off a credit card you never knew existed?

Be brave. We can't help whom we fall in love with. We can help if we let them turn us into doormats.

AVOID THE ROLE OF RESCUER

Allowing anyone—mates, friends, parents, children—to cast you in the role of rescuer is a dangerous game. It means you're willing to take on the responsibilities they should rightfully be assuming for their own lives. If you're faced with a body that needs help, you can offer to assist without getting caught in the role of saving them. You should

1. Decide for how long you are prepared to extend the help. If you let your kid, your sister, your best friend settle in and get so comfortable you end up stuck with your new roomie indefinitely, know that YOU did that. Make it clear that whatever you're doing to help is temporary and has a predetermined end date. Name that date.

2. Determine and agree upon the specific conditions that apply to any help you may be offering. Reciprocity is the key to keeping the relationship balanced and you out of the role of rescuer.

   What are your expectations while you are helping? Do you want to see a debt repayment plan? How will the person you're helping contribute while getting back on their feet? If it can't be money (they are asking for financial help), it can be other things. They can cook, clean, and do errands. There are all kinds of ways for your son, your cousin, or your mother to show appreciation for the fact that you're going above and beyond to help out. Do NOT let this person you love enough to help take that help for granted or you're sunk.

3. Ask for a periodic progress report to ensure both people are on the same page throughout the process. The schedule for review should be agreed upon from the beginning. Make sure you both stick to it to so there's no sense that it is just for show.

4. Create clear consequences for your loved one breaking the agreement. There should be no doubt that failure to follow through means you'll stop whatever aid you are giving immediately. You've already given them a second chance. No third chances.

2 • YOU OWE ME

Ashleigh was a princess, no doubt about it. Tall with long, dark hair and a smile that would charm the stripes off a zebra, Ashleigh was used to getting her own way. All her life she'd demanded—and received—whatever she wanted from her parents. When she asked for a new car for her 16th birthday, they obliged with a cherry red Toyota. When she begged for a puppy—a fluffy little thing—promising to do everything necessary for its care, her parents agreed. A year later Ashleigh still loved to play with Biscuit, but she didn't do walks, feedings, or poop cleanup. Eww!

Ashleigh's parents tried to teach her about money by putting her on an allowance, but when teenage Ashleigh blew through her money and asked for more, they gave it to her. After all, she was a good girl. She was popular and did well at school, and was loving towards her parents. Sure, her mother was always on her to clean up her room, but that was pretty normal. As for all of the clothes with the tags still on, well, Mom had some of those in her closet too.

When she headed off to university, Ashleigh's parents insisted that the limit on her credit card be no more than $500. But each time Ashleigh ran the card to the limit, they'd pay off the balance. Finally, in the middle of her second year of university, her father read her the riot act.

"Ashleigh, this is ridiculous. We're paying off your credit card every week or two, and you're going out and running it right back up again."

"I only use the credit card when I don't have any money in my bank account," said Ashleigh, so sweetly butter wouldn't melt in her mouth.

"Ashleigh, darling" her mother said gently, "we give you $800 a month and we pay your rent. You really should be able to manage on that."

"I try, Momma, I really do, but there's always something."

"Well, you're going to have to try harder," said Ashleigh's dad. "As of today you may only use the credit card for emergencies. If you put anything else on it, I'll reduce your next month's $800 deposit accordingly."

"You can't do that," Ashleigh screamed. "You can't just cut me off like that. I didn't ask to be born. You brought me into this world and got me used to living like this. You can't just stop now."

Ashleigh went back to university ticked. On the way, she bought two new dresses to make up for the lousy weekend she'd had at her parents' house. Total: $475. She smiled to herself. She'd wait and see if her mother paid it off next week.

Princesses aren't born, they are made. And you don't make a princess by giving her loads of stuff; you do it by having no expectations. When Ashleigh's parents gave her an allowance without the expectation that she'd limit herself to spending only that much each week, they taught her to live beyond her means. And when they repeatedly paid off her credit card, they taught her she didn't have to make choices, she could have everything she wanted.

From the moment babies are born they demand that their needs be met. As children get older, it is imperative that parents learn to set boundaries within which they expect their kids to operate. It is not reasonable to buy multiple items and not use them. Unworn clothing and shoes with the tags still on are flashing signs that impulse control is a problem. Spending money and asking for more denotes an inability to prioritize spending. And making but not keeping commitments demonstrates a lack of responsibility.

So why do parents have such a tough time holding the line with the children they love so dearly? All kinds of reasons: guilt over a broken family or time spent at work; as compensation for their own feelings of failure as parents; inability to curb a selfish child's behaviour; or the desire to avoid a scene.

Ashleigh's mom paid off the credit card, just as Ashleigh expected she would. And Mom continued to do so, despite her husband's objections. Ashleigh graduated, got married—her parents paid for a lavish affair—and bought a home with her new husband, with a 20% down payment courtesy of Mommy and Daddy.

Ashleigh knew she should be independent. She made a good income. But her parents were so willing to help and it was so easy to let them.

When Ashleigh decided she wanted to renovate the basement of her three-year-old home, her parents gifted her $20,000 towards the reno. Ashleigh couldn't resist spending just a little on herself. She went shopping. Five thousand dollars later she said, "Whoops," and her parents gave her another $5,000 to complete the basement renovation.

What's at the root of Ashleigh's sense of entitlement? Her parents' unwillingness to say no. As her enablers, they perpetuate Ashleigh's reliance on them. Sure, they love her, but they're not doing her any favours.

It's easy to fall into the role of enabler. We don't just do it with our children. (When you lend someone money and they try to pay you back but you say, "Hey, it's fine, don't bother," you're being an enabler.) But children are often the recipients of our greatest generosity. While paying off your adult child's credit card may seem like a gift, it isn't. You're actually saying loudly and clearly that you don't believe this adult has the ability to take care of him or herself. Is that really what you want to be saying?

If you genuinely fear your adult sons or daughters are unable to handle their lives without your intervention, who will save them when you're dead? No amount of money you leave them will be enough. Theirs is not a problem based on a lack of money. Their problem stems from not knowing when enough is enough.

Ashleigh said she felt awful about taking advantage of her parents. "I know I shouldn't," she said, "and I know there are things they could be doing with the money they're giving me." But did she stop asking for "a little help"? Not on your life.

In her most recent predicament, Ashleigh owed $26,000 on her company credit card. She'd racked up that balance by being a sport and treating all her friends who do not make as much as she does. Fifteen hundred dollars after a night of clubbing, $800 per dinner out with the girls, and a plane ticket for her best friend who couldn't afford the getaway the Fabulous Four—they'd been friends since elementary school and still vacationed together once a year—had planned.

But Ashleigh was in a bind. She'd been offered a new job with a substantial increase in pay. The problem: she couldn't leave her existing job until that credit card balance was paid off because it was a company card. She considered asking her husband to bail her out, but he'd done that eight months ago, the last time she'd run up the credit card. So she'd have to ask her parents again.

When Ashleigh told her mom and dad what she wanted them to do, her father finally put his foot down. "You're 31 years old, Ashleigh. When are you going to take responsibility for yourself?"

"Now," she said, plaintively. "I promise I'll pay you back. And with the new job and the raise it won't take that long. Please, Daddy."

"Absolutely not."

Ashleigh turned to her mother and looked at her imploringly.

"Sorry, sweetheart. Daddy says no and I agree with him. You're going to have to figure your own way out of this box."

Ashleigh got angry. "This is your fault. If you hadn't kept giving me everything I wanted, I wouldn't be in this mess."

Ready to stop enabling your adult child? First, you need to be able to distinguish between helping and enabling. Helping means you're doing something your adult child cannot do for herself. Enabling means doing something for her that she should be doing on her own.

If your daughter has a baby and you show up to help during the early days, that's great. If you end up changing all the dirty diapers while you're there, not so much. If your son asks you to give him some guidance as he makes his budget, that's helping. If he asks you to make him a budget, that's not your job.

Don't fall into the trap of confusing your sense of your child's ineptitude with lack of ability. Just because you think they can't cope doesn't mean that they actually can't cope. That's what got you into this enabling mess to begin with. If other adults are handling their own lives, living within their means, coping with challenges, so too should your child.

Helping means giving assistance. Enabling means removing all power and responsibility. So when Junior graduates from school and asks to move home for six months while he makes a plan for the rest of his life, as long as he's paying his way (with money or effort), you're helping. If you let him stay indefinitely and he's not paying (with money or effort), you're enabling.

Start by losing the feeling of guilt. Hey, it doesn't matter how great or crappy you were as a parent, there comes a time in every adult's life when they must accept responsibility for themselves. You may have contributed to your child's sense of entitlement, but you don't have to keep reinforcing it.

Set a time to talk to your offspring to make it clear that the gravy train has stopped. Stay calm as you tell your adult child that while you love him and will help him by being emotionally supportive, you will no longer be giving him any money.

If you need help accepting that as a parent there comes a time when your financial responsibility ends, seek that help. Unless you are wealthy enough to set up a trust that will support your child until she dies, you must allow her to learn to stand on her own two feet.

Ask your adult child to figure out solutions to his problems for himself. Say you are happy to be a sounding board but offer no solutions. Ask questions. Lots of questions. You want to help your adult child see holes in her plans or see options she may not have considered. A conversation with Ashleigh might sound like this:

"So, you need to get that work credit card paid off before you can take the new job, is that the problem?"

"Yes, exactly."

"What options do you have for paying off the credit card?"

"I can't ask Marc. I did that just a few months ago."

Avoid rolling your eyes or saying things like, "Oh, Ashleigh!" Just nod.

"So, what are your options?"

"I suppose I could apply for another card and transfer the balance to me solely?"

"How long do you think it would take you to pay off the balance?"

"I could do it in about four years, I think."

"And what do you imagine you'll end up paying in interest costs by the time the balance is paid off?"

"A lot?"

"Are there any other options?"

"I guess I could get a line of credit."

"Do you think you'll qualify for a line of credit?"

"I should. I have the house and a great credit rating."

"Are you going to tell Marc? Because you'll need his agreement to tie the line to the house."

"Oh, I didn't think of that."

"Can you think of any other options?"

As much as you want to say, "Sell the damn Chanel handbag," you can't. It's not your job to come up with solutions.

You might say, "Do you have anything you can sell to come up with some money so you don't have to borrow quite so much?" Your job isn't to make the decision for her (that's how you both got into this mess), it's to help her identify her options.

Priya and her mom, Aditi, had been on their own since Priya was six. Aditi busted her butt to put a roof over their heads, sometimes working two jobs when things got lean. By the time Priya was 15 she was working too. Aditi just couldn't afford to buy Priya clothes and the other things she wanted. Priya started walking dogs in her neighbourhood so she'd have some money. When they ran short of milk and eggs Aditi would send Priya to the store, saying she'd pay Priya back later. She never did.

Just before Priya headed off to university—she'd gotten two scholarships and $9,000 in student loans—Aditi sat her down to tell her that things were really bad. She was losing some hours at work because, well, everyone was losing hours at work. That meant she wouldn't be able to keep up with the minimum payments on her credit cards. It turned out she had five of them.

"Oh, Mom. Five credit cards!"

"How do you think I've kept it together all these years?" her mother asked. "There was never enough money for rent, food, and all the other things we needed." She pulled an ashtray towards her as she lit another cigarette. "You think it was easy stacking shelves until six in the morning?"

"I had no idea you were in this much debt," said Priya. "You took that vacation to Cuba last year. I thought things were okay."

"You don't think I deserved a vacation?"

"That's not what I'm saying, Mom. I just didn't know."

"Well, it really wasn't your business."

"But it is now?"

"Don't you take that tone with me after all I've done for you. I know you've got money in the bank, and if you just lent me $1,000 I'd be able to make up what I'm missing from work. It's not like I'm planning to sit around doing nothing. I'm a hard worker."

Priya agreed. Her mother had done everything she could for her, so how could she say no? Besides, she planned to work while at school; she'd just make up the difference with a few extra shifts.

Priya worked hard. She did well at school. And she was proud of herself for graduating from nursing school with less debt than many of her classmates. She hadn't been able to work as much as she'd expected because of her course load, but she'd been diligent about making what she did earn go as far as it could. The debt was a little bigger than she'd hoped because there were times each semester when her mother seemed to hit a wall financially and Priya had to bail her out.

Three years into her nursing career Priya met Kumar. They decided to move in together a year later so they could save money on rent and accumulate a down payment for a home. When they had about $10,000 saved, Aditi called in a panic. She was going to be evicted if she didn't come up with the rent money she owed.

"Mom, I told you that place was going to be too much for you to handle. The other apartment was fine. Why did you move somewhere more expensive?"

"What, you and Kumar get to live in a nice place and I'm supposed to live in a shoebox?"

"That isn't it. Kumar and I got a great deal on this apartment. We have two incomes."

"Right, and I'm just the woman who put a roof over your head for 18 years. Don't you think it's time you help me out a bit?"

Priya agreed. She told Kumar she needed to use some of the down payment money to bail her mom out. Kumar was not happy.

"We sacrificed a lot to save that money," he said. "Your mom goes on vacation, buys all the clothes she wants, and goes to the casino with her friends. When was the last time you bought yourself something that wasn't a uniform for work?"

Priya sighed. Kumar was right. How much longer would she have to bail her mother out? This had been going on since she was 15. Twelve years later and the end to the bailouts was nowhere in sight. But how could she say no to her mother? After all her mother had done to take care of her, how could she watch her mother stumble and fall without helping? She felt her neck tighten and her back stiffen as she considered what life would be like when her mother couldn't work anymore. Did her mom think she and Kumar would step in to support her later?

If your parent has ever said,

- "After all I've done for you."
- "This is the thanks I get?"
- "You should be ashamed of yourself."
- "You're so ungrateful!"
- "I took care of you."
- "Where did I go wrong?"

you are the victim of parental guilt.

Guilt is pure manipulation. Some parents lay it on so thick you can cut it with a knife.

I grew up in a household that used guilt as a two-by-four. It became such a thing that I'd actually call out, "Guilt trip!" when it was being laid on thick. Overexposure to anything inures you, so over time, I became immune. And as I raised my own children, I inoculated them against guilt. Sadly, there are lots of parents who use this form of manipulation to get their children—young and old—to do what they want. From "You don't love me," to "I sacrificed my life for you," parents who use guilt to manipulate are selfish. They've turned their obligation as parents into a favour they expect their children to repay. It's a twisted dynamic.

I don't think there is anything more manipulative than parents who guilt their children into giving them money. When they pull the "Do you know what I had to sacrifice?" line out of their guilt-induction armoury, here's what you have to say to yourself: "When my parents had me, they made a choice (religious or not). They also assumed the legal responsibility to support me until I was of age to support myself. They were not being generous. They were obligated to meet their responsibility to care for me until I could care for myself."

You might hear the phrase "I didn't have to . . ." attached to a lot of the things your parents did for you. In some cases it might be true. They didn't have to buy you skates or sign you up for dance lessons. But they did have to put a roof over your head, food in your belly, and clothes on your back. That was part of the job of being a parent. And in choosing to be a parent—accidentally or not—they chose to take on the job.

As the owner of a beautiful puppy, is it reasonable for me to expect that Tabitha owes me for her feeding and care? Or is providing those things my choice in assuming the responsibility of bringing Tabitha into my life?

As the mother of two beautiful children, is it reasonable for me to expect that Alex and Malcolm owe me for their feeding and care? They were no more involved in the decision to be brought into my family than Tabitha was, were they?

So what do you do if you're caught in a dynamic where your parent is playing victim and you're expected to be the rescuer? When do you say yes to requests for financial help? And how do you say no?

There may be times in your life when a parent genuinely needs help and you are in a position to give it. A parent who becomes ill may need financial and emotional support. A parent who is unable to care for him or herself may need to be brought into your home or put into a nursing home. And there may be times when a parent hits a wall financially, despite their best efforts to be fiscally responsible, and you are in a position to help. If you can do so without putting your own financial position at risk, then the choice to help or not is yours. In all likelihood, if your parent has been loving and supportive, you will want to help.

Families pull together in tough times, sharing resources so that everyone has most of what they need. That's what family is for.

However, if giving the aid being requested—or demanded— would make your own financial foundation less sound, you'll have to work up the guts to say no.

And believe me, it will take guts. This isn't about getting angry so you can use that anger to carry you through the conversation. You must remain calm and explain your position very clearly.

"Mom, I get that you're in trouble, but the last time I bailed you out I told you it would be the last time. And it was. I have no more money to help you. I'm happy to sit down with you and help you work out a plan, but there won't be any more money."

Let's look at this sentence again: "I have no more money to help you." This doesn't mean "I have no more money." It doesn't matter if you have a little or loads of money. The important part of the sentence is "to help you." Having said that there will be no more money, there must be no more money.

As your parent rails against your selfishness and cold-hearted refusal, know that allowing yourself to become embroiled in conflict means you can't possibly win. No matter how much you want to say, "Damn it, why didn't you put all the money you were sending up in smoke from your nasty cigarette habit in the bank so you could pay your rent?" don't. People who refuse to look at their actions as being at the root of the consequences they're experiencing won't be shown the way. You have to let the natural consequences teach the lesson. And that means keeping your hand out of your pocket.

You don't owe your parents anything. If you end up helping a needy parent financially, it should be because you love your parent and you can afford to, not because you think you are indebted.

HOW TO SAY YES

Whether it is an adult child who has asked for help, or a parent in need of some financial support, there will be times when it is appropriate to say yes.

1. Decide if aid is warranted. Are you helping or are you enabling? If the child or parent is *unable* (as opposed to *unwilling*) to solve the financial problem, you may need to step in.

2. Determine if you are able to help. Putting yourself at risk to help anyone is dumb, Dumb, DUMB! Blowing out your emergency fund, delaying your retirement savings, or co-signing a loan are all things you should NOT do. While your child's or parent's need may be immediate, and your retirement is a long way in the future, shorting your own savings for the sake of bailing out family (or friends) is not a smart choice. You must figure out if you can actually afford to help. What will you be giving up? If you are deferring wants, no problem. Feel free to give. If you are deferring needs—and saving for the future is a need— you'll have to find other ways to help than with money.

3. Get everything on the table. Talk about a plan to solve the problem. Invite everyone who needs to be at the table together so there are no backroom machinations or secrets that must be kept. Anyone who is asking for help has given up his or her right to privacy. Just as a person must make a full disclosure if they are borrowing money from a bank, so too must they be willing to make a full disclosure to all parties who need to know they are seeking help. That means if you have four children and one asks for help, it isn't done quietly. Everyone knows. And if a parent is asking for help, all of their children must be in on the discussion.

4. Agree on the rules of engagement. Is the help a gift or a loan? If it is a loan, what is the repayment schedule?

What will the consequences be if payments are missed or late? Are you prepared to follow through on those consequences? If you are not, don't bluff. You'll just end up reinforcing that you're a patsy. Instead, give the money as a gift and be done with it. Even if it is a gift, there are rules of engagement: Is this a final gift? How many more times are you willing to come to the rescue? What do you expect (not financially, but behaviourally) from your child, parent, or friend if you give this gift?

5. Consider other ways to help. While handing over money may seem like the only solution, it hardly ever is. Could your child or parent move in with you for a specific period of time while they get back on their feet? Is there some other way you can help them reduce their costs, like taking care of their kids after school to save on daycare costs? How about helping to prepare a resumé, create a budget, or make a debt repayment plan?

What if you said yes on the spur of the moment and later realize that was a mistake? Say so. "I know I said I'd help. And I'm sorry that I misled you. I've thought about it carefully and looked at the numbers and I'm not in a position to give you money [or co-sign a loan]. How else can I help you?"

HOW TO SAY NO
Whether you are a parent dealing with an entitled child or a child dealing with a guilt-inducing parent, there are times when you must say no. It won't be easy. But it will be the right thing to do. Here are some things to think about:

1. There is nothing wrong with wanting to help the people you love, but you can't do it if it'll derail your own money plans. "Mom, I'd love to help you out again, but I can't. We have given up a lot to save for our down payment, and I'm not going to derail those plans. I *will* help you to figure out some other plan, if you'd like." Be prepared for a hissy fit. Stay calm. Don't change your mind.

2. Fear that your child, parent, or friend will end up on the street is not a good reason to put your own financial situation at risk. "I want to be able to help, but I can't do it financially. I can help you find a less expensive place to live." If you can actually afford to give your mother $20 to buy food, then that's a choice you must make. If giving your mother $20 for food means you go without, that's not a choice, that's an action driven by fear.

3. If you think saying no will mean the end of your relationship, you may be right, but the relationship sucked! Some people think it's okay to threaten the removal of their affections if they don't get what they want. That's a sure indicator your strings are being pulled. Any mother, father, son, or daughter (or even friend) who would end a relationship based on the fact that you won't fork over the money requested does NOT love you. It will be hard. You will mourn the loss. But being manipulated by the fear of loss into giving money is emotional blackmail. Don't play that game. "I love you a lot and I'm happy to help you, but not with money. Please let me help you in some other way." Be prepared for the person to storm off in anger or say things that are hurtful. When they've had time to cool off, offer your help again. Keep your hand out of your wallet.

3 • THE BLAME GAME

Patsy and Joe hadn't been together long, but almost from the get-go it was like they were in a competition. Four years into a relationship and three years into a marriage, with one beautiful baby boy and another on the way, Patsy and Joe were up to their eyeballs in debt. And they were each positive it was the other guy who had gotten them into the mess.

"With all the money he spends on his car," Patsy told her mother, "I can never seem to make headway on the credit card balances."

"All the money I spend?" Joe retorted. "What about the fact that you can't walk past a store without checking out what's on sale?"

"Well, if you get to spend all that money on your stupid car, I get to spend money on things I want too!"

It was a never-ending cycle of arguments and tears. Patsy's mom, Vanessa, didn't know what to do.

Vanessa was having tea with her best friend, Monica, describing the latest fight she'd witnessed. "I'm so worried about them," she said, as she poured coffee and put out cookies. "They have a young baby and another on the way, and heavens, Monica, they can't seem to figure out how to get along, never mind get out of debt."

"I know how you feel," Monica said reassuringly. "Peter and Flavia just argue constantly now. Peter blames Flavia for getting pregnant before they were financially stable and now he feels stuck."

"I thought they were doing great," said Vanessa.

"That's how it looks from the outside, what with the new house, the new car, the new baby, and everything else new they've gotten. But I know Peter is very resentful of having to bear the brunt of financial responsibility. Sometimes when they fight, he just disappears for days."

"Oh, that's not good."

"You think? I don't think Flavia got pregnant on purpose, but the 'accident' has had a big impact on their relationship. They both love little Noah to death, but they are almost to the point where they can't look at each other. It's so sad to watch them."

Sometimes money is at the root of a relationship meltdown. But sometimes it is the relationship problems that end up wreaking havoc with the money. Broken promises, broken trust, and a propensity to keep score can all result in money messes. Before the money problems can be fixed, the relationship issues have to be addressed.

This is a case for counselling. If you feel your relationship isn't working, then you must seek help to identify the issues and work to resolve them. If one partner is unwilling to seek professional help—it happens all the time—then you must find someone in the family or within your friend circle to act as a sounding board as both of you work to correct what you've broken.

The friend or family member who agrees to help can never be perceived as taking sides. That will nullify any benefit they may bring to the discussion.

It's important to air what the root cause of the relationship strife may be. You may hear things like:

- "He works so much, and I'm lonely so I go shopping."
- "She said she'd quit smoking and won't, so to hell with it, I'm spending $600 on crap too."
- "He spends his money any way he wants. Why can't I?"

- "She's always out with her girlfriends partying like she's still single."
- "He's always out playing hockey and drinking beer. If I didn't scrapbook I'd go nuts."

At the root of any sense of competitiveness in a relationship is the fact that partners do not see themselves on the same page. They are not working towards common goals. So the best way to eliminate (or at least minimize) competitiveness and the harm it's doing is by getting both parties to work together to achieve something they both want.

The next time Patsy and Joe were at Vanessa's house for a visit Vanessa said, "I have something I want to talk to you two about."

"Is something wrong, Mom?" asked Patsy.

"Yes," said Vanessa slowly. "Something's very wrong. Have you two heard how you speak to each other? You have a young child and another on the way, and half the time you sound like you hate each other."

"We don't hate each other, Vanessa," said Joe.

"But you do fight a lot," said Vanessa.

"Yes, sometimes we fight, Mom," said Patsy, "but all couples fight."

"I don't think all couples fight about the stuff you fight about," said Vanessa, "and I don't see this ending well if you don't get some help."

"You mean a counsellor?" laughed Joe. "I'm NOT doing that."

"Well then, someone else," said Vanessa. "Patsy is about to go on mat leave again. How are you going to keep up with the bills without killing each other?"

"I've been a little worried about that," acknowledged Patsy.

"Well, if you wouldn't spend your life in the malls—" started Joe.

"And if you wouldn't spend your life with your car," interrupted Patsy, "I'd get a little more help around the house, and maybe we'd have some money to get our credit cards paid off. Seriously, Joe, do you know what you're spending on that stupid car?"

"I work hard," said Joe.

"And I don't?" asked Patsy.

"I didn't say that," said Joe.

"No, really? But when you come home from work and tell me you're going to the garage for the next four hours, you're pretty much saying Josh is my kid and my job. I work too, you know."

"You work part-time. It's not the same."

"Really?" The colour rose up Patsy's neck and flooded her face. "I work part-time so that we don't have huge daycare costs. Doesn't that count for something? And then I get home and all the stuff you were supposed to do while you were with Josh is still not done."

"Well, Joshie wants me to play with him. I don't see him enough as it is, with work and stuff."

"Stuff, like all the time you spend with the car?"

"Okay, you two," interrupted Vanessa, "this is exactly what I'm worried about. Patsy, you're three shades of red and Joe, your fists are balled up like you're going to hit the wall. Take a deep breath, both of you."

The three sat at the table in silence. Vanessa watched as tears welled in her daughter's eyes. Joe huffed as he shifted uncomfortably in his chair.

"Joe, I want you to tell me what you really want from Patsy that you don't think you're getting."

"I wish she'd stop shopping and using Josh as the excuse. She's

always bringing home new stuff, stuff he doesn't need. He's a baby."
Patsy started to speak but Vanessa told her to wait her turn.

"Anything else, Joe?"

"And when I get home, we never seem to have any time for each other. She's feeding Josh, she's bathing Josh, she's putting Josh to bed. So I go out to the garage."

"And what's your biggest worry?" asked Vanessa.

"I worry about how we're going to cope when the second baby comes. We're barely managing financially now."

"Okay, so you're worried about the money, you think Vanessa is too focused on Josh, and you'd like to participate more in taking care of him?"

"Well, she's actually better at that than I am," said Joe.

"How will you ever get better at it if you don't get some practice?" asked Vanessa. "With a second baby on the way, can you see how this is going to get harder?"

"Yeah, maybe, although I can't image how it could be harder."

"I can," groaned Patsy.

"Patsy, it's your turn. Can you tell me what you really want?"

"I want Joe to help me with the house and with Josh so I don't feel like I have to do it all myself. I know I'm only working part-time but I feel overwhelmed."

"And the shopping?"

"Sometimes I have to get out of the house or I'll go mad. So I take Josh to the mall to walk around. And then I see stuff. And it's so cute. It feels good when I buy things for Josh."

"And what are you most worried about?" asked Vanessa.

"Imagining how much more trapped I'm going to feel with a second baby. I love Joshie, and I want this baby, but I'm feeling like I'll never see the light of day again."

"So you want Joe to help you more, and you want some time out of the house. We know the mall is a temptation, so you shouldn't go there, right?"

"I guess," said Patsy.

"Good," said Vanessa. "Let's talk about what you could each do differently to give the other person what they want. Then you can work together to stop your spending so you can pay off those credit cards."

Joe and Patsy both nodded. "Okay," said Vanessa. "How soon do you want that credit card debt gone?"

Joe laughed. "Before the baby comes would be best, but that's not possible."

"I dunno," said Patsy. "If you agreed to take Joshie on Saturdays, I could get a few more hours at work and we could put all that extra money on the credit cards."

"But I thought you were exhausted?" said Joe.

"I am, because I get no help Monday through Friday. If you help me with the house and Josh, I won't be so tired on the weekend."

Joe nodded. He could do that.

The three sat at the table and talked and talked and talked. And when Joe and Patsy left that night, they had a plan and a better sense of being in it together than they'd had for a long time.

Helping friends or family members resolve the underlying relationship problems that contribute to their financial woes often can't be done in one conversation. There are all kinds of things that will come out and must be dealt with. But getting them talking is the first step.

WHEN RELATIONSHIP ISSUES GET IN THE WAY

1. Once you've recognized that the issue is the relationship and not just bad money management skills, pick a private place to have a conversation. Neutral territory works best.

2. Explain what you've witnessed and ask if they are aware of how blame is affecting both their relationship and their money management. Offer to help them negotiate some balance so they can work together instead of blaming each other for what's gone wrong. If they agree to your help, ask both people to make a commitment to doing what it takes to improve their relationship. They must both want it to work for the talk to lead to action.

3. Set the rules for the conversation:
   - Both people must be prepared to listen without interrupting.
   - Your job is to summarize and ask questions to clarify.
   - The first step is getting the problem out into the open. Ask each person to describe what they perceive the problem to be.
   - If there are questions that need to be asked for clarification, they must be delivered neutrally, not with condemnation or sarcasm.

4. Ask for examples of the problems each is experiencing. Blanket statements like, "You never listen to me," aren't useful. The situations described must be specific.

5. Ask each person what they think the solutions to each problem might be.

6. Ask them for a financial goal they are both prepared to work towards.
7. Help them to negotiate common ground as they lay out a plan to achieve their goal.

4 • ATTENTION! PLEASE!

Siobhan and Niall had been married for only two years when Niall confessed to his best friend, Jonathan, that he'd gotten himself into a financial fix. They were having Saturday brunch, a ritual they'd started after graduating from university and getting their first jobs.

"I'm not sure what I'm going to do about it," Niall said. "I'm overdrawn at the bank, I've got two credit cards maxed out, and I'm stressed all to hell."

"How'd this happen?" asked Jonathan. "You're the guy who managed to graduate school with practically no debt."

"Well, first it was the wedding. Siobhan wanted more than we had saved for so I put a few things on the cards, meaning to pay them off quickly."

"It was a pretty spectacular wedding," said Jonathan. "You kind of did the rest of us in because you set the standard so high."

"It was ridiculous," said Niall. "Looking back, I should have put my foot down then."

"But it was her day," said Jonathan.

"Yeah, it was her day."

"I thought things were fine. You guys have been travelling a couple of times a year since you got married," Jonathan said as he attacked the plate the waitress had just placed in front of him.

"That's what got me into this mess," said Niall, lifting his over easy eggs onto his toast. He took a sip of coffee and watched as Jonathan cheerily chomped on his food. Niall had no appetite.

Through a mouthful Jonathan said, "What? The travelling?"

"Yes," said Niall.

"Then why do it if it's causing you so much stress? Nobody's holding a gun to your head."

Niall pushed the food around on his plate, "I feel like I have to take Siobhan away to get her attention. Between work and her parents and all her girlfriends, the only way to get her to myself is to go on vacation."

"You're not eating those sausages?" asked Jonathan, pointing with his fork. Niall waved for him to take them. "I don't understand what you're saying. You guys seem to have a great relationship."

"We do, but she's got so much going on in her life that I don't feel like I get her to myself enough. So I book a trip. I try to get last-minute deals to cut the costs, but the cruise was more expensive than I'd planned. It adds up." Niall took another sip of coffee and then bit into a piece of toast.

"So, you're telling me that Siobhan is so busy you're driven to booking vacations to get her attention?"

"Yup, that's pretty well it."

"Damn!" said Jonathan.

People will go to desperate measures to get their mate's attention. From buying expensive gifts to wining and dining beyond their means, men and women do ridiculous things in the name of love.

Andrew buys Kate a cellphone and service package because she says she can't afford one on her own and he wants to be able to text her. She runs up the bill calling her girlfriends instead of just texting as she and Andrew agreed, and he keeps paying it.

Mei insists that Hiroto take her out to dinner at least

twice a week. He works hard and she's a little jealous of all the business meals he has with attractive clients, so she wants her pound of lobster. Hiroto agrees because he loves Mei and if this is what it takes to keep her happy, it's fine with him.

Carrie wants Mick to pay more attention to her. She feels like he takes her for granted because he not only works late but spends two nights every week playing hockey with his boys. And then there's the best friend he's had since high school, Kathy. So every time Carrie and Mick go out together she flirts with the other men in the room. She wants Mick to get jealous and prove to her that she's important to him.

All the eating out, the flirting, the vacations, and the stuff are a substitute for the conversation these people refuse to have. It's a conversation that goes something like this:

NIALL: Siobhan, there's something I need to talk to you about.

SIOBHAN: Sure, hon, what's up?

NIALL: You know all those vacations we've been taking since we got married? We can't afford to do it anymore.

SIOBHAN: What do you mean?

NIALL: I mean that I've been putting them on my credit card and now I'm maxed out. So until I get the balances paid off, we can't do any more travelling.

SIOBHAN: Why are you suggesting vacations we can't afford, then? That makes no sense.

NIALL: I've been doing it to get your attention. I can't seem to get any time alone with you unless we're away.

SIOBHAN: What?

NIALL: Babe, I love you. And I want to be able to spend time alone with you. But between your work and your friends and your parents, it feels like the only time I can do that is when we're travelling.

SIOBHAN: I had no idea you felt that way. You know, there's a pretty simple solution that doesn't involve getting on a plane or a boat. Why don't we pick a night every two weeks when it's just you and me? We don't even have to go anywhere. We can just stay in, cook, watch a movie, or play Scrabble. We can just chat.

NIALL: I'd love that. Thank you.

SIOBHAN: Now, how deep is the hole?

Very often, when someone feels ignored they resort to accusations, putting their partner on the defensive.

- "We need to talk!"
- "You don't make any time for me."
- "You're always on your phone or texting!"
- "You spend more time playing those stupid games than listening to me."
- "We never do anything together anymore."

Women and men alike are unwilling to say to their mates, "Honey, this is what's currently missing. How can we fix this?" Not talking about something that is affecting your relationship is silly when you think about it. If you plan to spend the rest of your life with a body, shouldn't you and that body be able to talk about whatever is bothering either of you? And if you're playing games of any kind to try and get or keep your mate's attention, or if you're resorting to anger, how do you suppose that will end? Not well, I expect.

Giving your mate attention doesn't require a date night every week. From love notes slipped into a packed lunch to Post-it hearts left on the bathroom mirror, there are about a million ways you can demonstrate that you value your mate. If your mate doesn't reciprocate, you might have to point out that what you give, you'd also like to receive.

GETTING THE RIGHT KIND OF ATTENTION

1. Make a date with your mate for the conversation you need to have.
2. Explain how you feel. It may be hard to put into words, so practise vocalizing your feelings until you get the hang of it.
3. If your mate says you're being ridiculous or silly say, "You may think that, but this is what I genuinely feel, so I think we need to talk about it."
4. Don't just come to the table with the problem; offer some strategies or solutions to fix the problem. "So, I was thinking, how would you feel about . . ."

5 · I WANT TO HELP

Babs put her coffee cup on the counter and poured more coffee, adding sugar and milk. "Kev's done it again," she sighed.

"Done what?" asked her sister, Val.

"Spent money we don't have," replied Babs grimly. "He just had to have that new truck." She took a sip of her coffee and then added another splash of milk. "Sorry the coffee is so strong. Kev made it."

"How much is the monthly payment?" Val took a sip of coffee, grimaced, and tipped some into the kitchen sink before adding more milk.

"Too much, which is why I've run short this week. Davey's hockey fees are due and I thought I'd have the money, but I can't find a way to come up with it. Would you consider paying them as his Christmas present?"

"Now, in September? Do you think Davey's actually going to remember come Christmas?"

"Don't worry, I'll remind him," laughed Babs.

"How short are you?"

"The whole thing . . . $760," said Babs apologetically.

"Then maybe Kev should tell Davey that he can't play hockey this year because Daddy got a new truck."

Babs' eyes grew narrow. "You think Davey should have to give up hockey because Kev's a jerk?"

"I think Davey should have to give up hockey because you can't afford it," replied Val matter-of-factly.

"You're a hard-ass."

"Really? The last two times you needed to be bailed out, I was happy to help. Do you borrow from anyone else in the family?"

"That's none of your goddamn business. If you don't want to pay for Davey's hockey just say so."

"I do want to pay for Davey's hockey because he's a good kid and I love him. But you know you and Kev are headed for trouble, right?"

"No one else seems to think so, so I don't understand why you're so high and mighty. Y'know, ever since you and Brian started dating you've been kind of uptight."

"Listen, if no one else is telling you that you're spending your way into a divorce, that's only because they're afraid you'll have a hissy fit. And leave Brian out of this. You barely know him."

"That's because you don't bring him to family get-togethers. What, are you ashamed of your family?"

"Don't change the subject, Babs. We're talking about you and Kev and your crappy financial decisions."

"Not anymore we're not," said Babs picking up Val's keys and handing them to her.

Val put down her coffee mug, took the keys, and left.

As she got into her car she thought about how Babs and Kev were headed for financial disaster and perhaps even divorce. Oh, the kids. A breakup would be so hard on them. Even though every time she'd tried to talk to Babs she'd been dismissed, she'd have to try again. She had to for her niece and nephews.

It's hard to watch the people you love destroy themselves and their families because they're crap with money. You want to help. But you're not sure where to start or how far to go. Knowing what you should and should not talk about can be very tricky territory. What if your attempt to broach this difficult subject is unsuccessful? If it doesn't work, it could affect your relationship; you might become *persona non grata.*

Often the toughest part about trying to help is getting the person with the problem to admit that something is wrong. If they think they're fine, you might just have to wait until things get worse. You can't help people who won't acknowledge the mess they are in. If you can show them, through examples of things they've done, how their behaviour is creating a problem, you're more likely to get them to hear you. If they acknowledge that things aren't all that rosy, you might offer your help as a money mentor.

Consider tiptoeing into the talk using a side door: Ask your dear one if she's seen that TV show about couples who are having money problems, and then tell her it's fun and make a date to watch an episode with her. Or talk about a relevant book you've read or a conversation you've had with a friend. Whatever it takes to open the door.

"Hey, Babs," Val might say. "Remember my girlfriend Goldie?"

"Uh-huh," replies Babs, only half listening.

"She and her husband are thinking of getting a divorce. She says they fight so much over money that she's just going to pack up and leave."

"Doesn't she have kids?" Babs is paying attention now.

"Yup. But she figures she'll make him pay child support and nothing much will have to change. She's in for a shock."

"Why do you say that?"

"She thinks they don't have enough money now. Once he sets up a place of his own, how will he have enough money to run two households?"

"Can't they sort out their problems?"

"I'm sure they could if they'd even talk about it. They're a little like you and Kev. You know, you blow up and then it kinda goes away until you blow up again."

"Yeah."

"So, have you and Kev talked about the truck he bought and how you feel about it yet?"

"No, I'm not sure he'll listen. He's talking about fixing up the basement now. Wants a place where he can have some privacy."

"Do you have the money for that?"

"Nope, and if he does that, I swear I'm gonna book that trip to Disneyland with the kids."

"And how do you think this is going to end if you both just keep spending money neither of you have?"

"What?"

"Well, if you both just keep on keeping on, how do you think things will end?"

Telling someone that they are screwing up their life—and, perhaps, their children's lives—and that they can't manage their money isn't going to go over like a chocolate sundae. You could very well be told to mind your own beeswax. And you could be censured by other family members or friends for having the audacity to try and tell someone else how to live their life.

Proceed with caution. **Love, not judgment, must always be the source of your motivation.** And you need to be well armed with concrete examples to illustrate the points you're trying to make.

"I don't know if we're really that bad," Babs said, as she reached for the coffee pot and poured the leftovers down the drain.

"Hey, sis, you know I love you like fire, but the last time you and Kev went at it, it was over the ATV he bought. You were furious enough to pack up the kids and take them to Great Bear Lodge for the weekend. Remember?"

"Yeah, I was pretty mad."

"How much did that end up costing you and Kev?"

"More than we had," Babs said, rinsing out the pot.

"And how many times has that kind of thing happened in the last year?"

"Hmm, I guess it's been a couple."

"Or four?" laughed Val, ticking off on her fingers the other three blow-ups. "And that's not including the truck."

"You're keeping count?"

"Shouldn't you be too? I don't want to see you and Kev fall apart. Those kids love you both and I love you both. I really think you should take a good, hard look at what you two are doing."

Ask questions, lots of questions. Your goal is to get your dear one thinking about the answers. Just telling them what they're doing wrong will feel like you're being intrusive. Asking them to think about how something will turn out is a better way of directing the discussion.

- If you both keep spending like this, where will that lead?
- Where does saving for the future fit into your plans?
- If you were to get sick or lose hours at work, how would you manage?

- How long do you think it will take you to pay off what you already owe?
- Have you figured out how much you're spending in interest? What else could you be doing with that money?
- I know the vacation is very exciting, but how will you feel when you get home to the balance on your credit card?

The toughest part of knowing that your friend, sibling, or parent is making a mess of their financial lives may be when a request for a bailout comes. You'll be in a quandary. Help and you will be enabling your loved one to continue down a slippery slope. Don't help and you will be a selfish, mean, horrible, no-good person who can just stand by and watch the kids go hungry.

Whether you pony up some money or not, if you really want to help you must address the root of the problem your dear one is creating for him or herself. It's not an easy job. And it may not be a job you want to take on. So here's a question for you: Can you just stand by and watch them self-destruct?

If you can't, it's time to open up the conversation and do more than *wish* you could help.

Before you talk, make sure you're clear on YOUR role in the conversation. It will be easy to get drawn into a communication that disintegrates quickly if you aren't clear on what your role is. Take a few deep breaths and imagine how you want the conversation to go. First, imagine it as a successful talk. Then imagine it with things going off-track and what you'll do to get it back on track. Are you planning to be loving and firm? Will you be physical (hugging, touching)? Will you be kind no matter how harsh your words have to be? You can find a balance between saying the tough things your dear one has to hear, and saying them in a way that clearly denotes that you love them and want the best for them.

No matter how much visioning you use to prepare yourself, don't expect things to go smoothly in every encounter. And don't think that one encounter will cut through years of crappy behaviour. **Make sure you're ready for what you're taking on when you step onto the path of helping someone else see his or her reality.** It's a very bumpy path, and you've got to be ready for the slippin' an' a slidin' that's in store. If you truly love the person, you'll find the strength and the wisdom to make it work.

HOW TO REALLY HELP

1. Get yourself into the right headspace to talk. Envision your actions, and those of your dear one, with all the twists and turns you might encounter. Know the role you want to play.

2. Open up the conversation using a third-party example: an article you've read or an example from your life—anything that doesn't directly attack the person you want to help.

3. Use specific examples to describe the things the person is doing that are having a negative impact on their money and their relationships. "Remember when your account was overdrawn because you had to have that new area rug you fell in love with?"

4. Ask questions designed to get the person to think about the consequences of their actions. "How do you think it feels to be the person you're hitting up for money because you spent all yours on a wonderful vacation?"

. . .

When I was working with people on television, one of the things that helped me help them was my ability—for the most part—to keep my emotions at bay. I've had so many letters and tweets from people asking why I didn't do physical harm to some of the people I worked with. I didn't even want to.

While I had a vested interest in those people—I wanted them to succeed—they didn't know how to push my emotional hot buttons, so they (again, for the most part) couldn't get to me. (I can count on one hand the number of times I lost it. But, hey, that made for good TV.) I knew it was important for me to remain calm, stay focused on the problems, and look for solutions. We would all win if I could do that.

That's not to say that people didn't lose it with me. But their losing it, while it also made for good TV, didn't help in getting us closer to solutions. So I'd have to wait them out. Shooting over several weeks for each episode meant that I could walk away and leave them to think about what I'd said, what I'd asked them to do, and how that would impact their money. And most times that walking away—the cool-down period—helped tremendously. When the emotion had had a chance to dissipate, the sensible things I'd been saying could take hold.

I've done this in my own life too. My daughter and I—who are both strong personalities—have a policy of taking some time to let the emotion pass before we respond, particularly when one of us has just pissed the other off royally. Just the other day I was looking at some work she had done. After I gave her some advice she responded with, "We're done talking about this now, okay?" Her eyes were flashing.

"Okay," I said.

After a few minutes she said, "I have to tell you something."

"Sure."

"This is really hard for me, and I don't need you to tell me what I'm doing wrong right now."

"Okay," I said. I knew this was hard for her but in my enthusiasm to help, I had jumped in with both feet. "I love you," I said.

"I love you too, but I need a few minutes more."

"Done," I said, as I picked up my knitting. A few minutes later she leaned her head against mine. We were fine again.

Learning to take the emotion out of an interaction is key to being able to clearly communicate what you're trying to say. The emotion is like mud: it'll stick to every word, shrug, and facial expression.

. . .

Unplanned conversations—those that take place on the spur of the moment in response to something that has just happened—can end up disintegrating because they're often fuelled by anger or frustration. Putting a little time and space between whatever has created the upset and your response can help. While a planned conversation may not be a cakewalk—things you say may still illicit an emotional response—taking time to think about the impact of both your words and your messages can help you prepare for those responses.

Of course, you don't always have the opportunity to push Pause on a conversation. If someone is using emotions like guilt against you, identifying the emotion and stopping your reaction to it is your best defence.

When someone says or does something that makes your blood pressure rise, ask yourself what it is EXACTLY that pushed your button. Look at your response from all angles and develop a strategy for not responding to the emotional poke. That doesn't mean ignoring the poke—although sometimes that's the best route. If something someone has said or done has made you angry, you have to acknowledge that anger and understand why you feel that way. But then you have to set aside the emotion and deal from your head.

For goodness' sake, don't let their button pushing draw you in somewhere you shouldn't be. Know that each time you step in to take responsibility or solve a problem for another, you are robbing that person of a lesson they need to learn in order to grow. So instead of seeing yourself as the altruistic problem solver, know that you are a thief, robbing your lovie of the experiences, the problem solving, and the decision making they need to become all they can be.

When people ask for help, you have to decide if that help will truly aid them or if it's simply a request to be saved from doing the hard work themselves. In the case of the former, helping lets them move to the next level of understanding. In the latter, they stay where they are. The big clue is if it is only a matter of weeks or months before they are asking for exactly the same kind of help again. Having missed the lesson, having learned nothing, they're doomed to keep making the same mistakes over and over. And you helped them stay stuck.

Part Two

CHANGING THE GAME

People hate change. We believe, beyond a shadow of a doubt, that where we are now is where we are always going to be. Our ability to resist change, to insist that things are as they are and there's nothing we can do about it, to push back against what's coming next, is Herculean.

Can't imagine changing jobs, moving house, or leaving a mate? You're suffering from what psychologists have termed "recency effect." Whatever our most recent experience has been carries far more weight than anything else. When the stock market has been going up, Up, UP, we think it will always continue to go up. When we've been in a relationship for a period of time—especially if we have become dependent on our mate—we think independence sounds impossible. When we have been buried in debt for what feels like forEVER, we think we will always be in debt.

Think of the times you've been unwilling to accept a change in your circumstances. Perhaps you lost a job or had your hours cut at work but kept spending like everything was fine, just fine. Or maybe you found out that your mate was doing things that worked against your joint goals, but you didn't want to rock the boat. Did you work really hard to maintain the illusion of constancy, of keeping everything the same, rather than try to deal with accepting a new reality? What contortions did you put yourself through to stay the course?

Rest assured, you are not alone.

We're hard-wired to hate new. In one study, two groups of participants were offered chocolate and asked to rate it. The first group was told the chocolate was being introduced by a relatively new company. The second group was told the chocolate was made by a company that had been making chocolate for more than 70 years. You know what? The people who thought their chocolate recipe was 73 years old rated their chocolate as tastier than the group who thought the recipe was new. Same chocolate.

Change is hard.

One of the reasons we hate change so much is because stepping off the path we know feels impossibly wrong. It means we have to rethink everything we thought was well organized and in hand. Change means we're going to have to discard what we've always done and come up with new patterns. We'll go through trial and error, we'll fail, blunder, misstep, until we figure out the new, and the whole time we'll be hissing and spitting about things changing.

Another reason we hate change is because we anticipate that the thing we must change to will be worse than what we're living with now. That's the thinking behind the old saying "Better the devil you know," right?

Just because it's uncomfortable to change doesn't mean you can justify holding on to what's no longer working. If you keep on keeping on just because you're unwilling to face a new reality, ask yourself how that's working for you.

If you think managing change in your own life is tough, try introducing change into someone else's life. It's like trying to walk up a mountain with a hippo on your back. But walk you must. Especially if you love that person and know that the course they are on is detrimental to their—and your—well-being. It takes real guts to step in and tell a body that things have to change. And how you do it can make all the difference in the world.

6 • THE DEAL HAS TO CHANGE

When Tommy and Carlie got married and had their first child, Jack, they both believed that Carlie should be a stay-at-home mom. Things were great for the first two years. Carlie was always out and about with the baby. And when Tommy got home, the house was neat as a pin and dinner was ready.

When Jack was three, Tommy lost his job and was piecing together just enough money to make ends meet by working four part-time jobs. Carlie wouldn't budge on going back to work. Daycare costs would eat all her income, so what was the point?

Tommy finally got a new job. Carlie got pregnant with Grayson. Three years later, the baby of the family, Danni, came along. Over time, as their expenses kept going up, Tommy and Carlie remortgaged their house twice to consolidate their line of credit debt. It seemed that no matter how much Tommy made, it wasn't enough. The kids needed clothes. There were the family vacations. And Carlie was house-proud so everything needed to be updated. When Tommy watched her walk through the door with shopping bags full of new bedding and dishes, he'd cringe.

Now Tommy and Carlie have been married for almost eleven years and they are out of credit. Tommy is out of patience with Carlie's unwillingness to get a job. She's furious that the rules have changed and he's angry that she's spent him into a debt hole yet again.

People make deals all the time. But it's naive to think that as life changes the deals won't have to change too. That being said, how the deals change has to be negotiated carefully. If one person is heavy-handed about implementing a new deal, the other person may grow resentful, even retaliatory.

The first thing to talk about is what's changed. When you made the deal, things were one way and now they are another. It doesn't matter what the deal was about—who would stay home with the children, how long you'd let your adult son live at home while he found his feet, how much you'd give your mother a month to help support her—if the plan no longer works you must revise it.

Ignoring the problem and hoping for the best isn't going to end well. It will make the problem worse in the short term. And over the long term it reinforces the idea that nothing has to change. So it's time to say something.

"Carlie, we may have been able to support our lifestyle on one income when we just had Jack, but we've been living way beyond our means for a long time now."
"What do you mean, living beyond our means?"

Don't expect you won't get some push back.

"Well, you know we've consolidated our line of credit to the mortgage twice."
"That's just because you don't make enough money."

That's [heavy sarcasm] what you want to hear. Your job is not to respond angrily.

"You're right, I don't make enough to pay for everything we're buying.

And now we're all out of credit too. We can't keep spending like we have been. And we have to find a way to get this debt paid off. So, we have two choices."

Choices are a great way to help people see what's at stake.

"You can find a way to help financially or we can sell the house, pay off the debt, and start again. We'll just come out even, so we'll have to rent for a few years until we can rebuild a down payment."

When you deliver the downside choice you shouldn't be surprised if the other person freaks. You've been thinking about the implications of your situation for some time. Buddy may not have given it a second thought, blissfully ignorant of the consequences. So a freak-out is completely natural. Do not get drawn into the emotion.

"Hey, I know you're upset. I'd like to sit down and go through the numbers with you so you can see for yourself. Do you want to do that now, or do you want to wait until the kids are in bed?"

You're not asking if you'll go over the numbers; you're giving a choice for when you'll go over the numbers. That's better than asking a question that could lead to a no.

As you explain the numbers, make sure you've got it all laid out as clearly as possible. You don't need to have all the solutions to the problem, just all the facts. You should come up with the solutions together so that the other person feels like part of the process and is committed to following through.

If you haven't armed yourself with all the details and laid the situation out so clearly that even an eighth-grader could understand it, things won't go well. The case you're making has to be crystal clear.

Once you've shared the details, give your mate some time to assimilate the information before you ask for solutions.

"I know that's a lot to take in. I'm going to leave this with you so you can think about it for a while. I need to go get Grayson from his sleepover. When I get back, you can let me know when you want to sit down and see what we can come up with together."

Be prepared for pushback and negotiation.

"If I go to work, don't think I'm going to come home every night and make dinner."

"No, you'll be as tired as I often am. We'll find a way to make our meals more practically so we're not starting from scratch every night."

"You're going to cook?"

Don't take the bait when an insult or disbelief shows up to the party.

"Things are going to have to change. I know that. I'm prepared to do my share."

"I haven't worked in 10 years. How am I supposed to find a job?"

Acknowledge how the person is feeling. Empathize. But keep the issue front and centre so it doesn't get lost in the swirling emotional fog that's very likely to blow in.

"I know you think it'll be really hard. But we have to do something. So, if not work, then we need to put the house on the market. But there is no more money."

Talk about how much income the family needs to make the new deal work. Is part-time work an option? Could your mate start an at-home business?

"With Danni in school full-time now, is there something you've always wanted to do? You used to talk about becoming a nurse."

"That'd take forever. You say we need money now."

"Yes, we do. Let's look at how much we need now. But let's also look at how we can help you get back to school for nursing if that's still something you want to do. We have a whole life together. We need to look at both what we need now and what we want for the future."

Since you're moving from never having talked about change to embracing change short term and into the future, you should expect to have several discussions. Some will get heated. As the initiator of change, your job is to stay cool until your buddy catches up emotionally. Once you're pointed in the same direction, you'll be unstoppable!

DEALS SOMETIMES CHANGE

Faced with a situation where a deal must change, take these steps:

1. Identify why the deal must change. What has changed and how is that impacting the original agreement and necessitating a new deal? Answer the question, "What will happen if the deal does not change?"

2. Acknowledge how difficult change can be and empathize with the person's anger about the deal changing. Acknowledging the emotional response is the first step to moving past the emotion.

3. Present the facts. Work together on creating options for how the deal will change and be prepared to negotiate a solution that is acceptable to both sides.

4. Once you've agreed on a new deal, be very specific about the details so both parties are absolutely clear on what needs to be done and by when. Nail it down.

7 • ROLE REVERSAL

Bethany was successful. After she graduated she was actively recruited by a number of high-tech companies. She chose carefully, worked hard, and progressed quickly. Three years later she was head-hunted into an assistant vice-presidential job at the ripe old age of 29. She was going places.

When Bethany met Karl, he was just finishing his apprenticeship as a plumber. They met on a canoe trip and hit it off immediately. They liked the same things: being outdoors, being active, pizza, hockey, and good wine. Karl came from a big family and Bethany soon met and fell in love with his parents and siblings. As an only child, she enjoyed the rambunctiousness of his huge family.

The first sign that there might be a problem was when Bethany asked Karl if he wanted to move in with her. She had a beautiful two-bedroom loft and he was always there anyway. She thought it just made sense. He could get his school debt paid off faster if he wasn't also laying out money for rent. Besides, she hated the house he shared with four other guys. It was dirty and there was always some fight or party going on.

Karl hesitated when she brought it up. "Here, to your place?" he asked.

"It would be our place," said Bethany.

"No," he said adamantly. "It's your place. Give me a few weeks to think about it."

In the meantime they continued dating. Karl slept over at Bethany's four nights out of seven. They joined a mixed dragon-boat team and were planning a vacation together the following winter. When Bethany showed Karl where she thought they should go he got really quiet and changed the subject.

She broached the holiday discussion again a few days later and Karl said, "You know, Beth, maybe this isn't the best idea."

"What do you mean? I thought you wanted to go away."

"I thought so too. But, babe, I can't afford the places you're showing me."

"I'll pay," said Bethany. "I've got a pretty healthy savings account, so it's not a problem."

"Not a problem for you, maybe," said Karl hesitantly. He got up from the couch and walked into the kitchen. She followed him. As he bent into the fridge to get bottle of white wine he said, "Maybe we should talk about this next weekend."

"No," said Bethany, a little more forcefully than she'd intended. "I think we should talk about it now." Karl poured two glasses of wine and handed one to Bethany without looking at her. He followed her back to the couch.

"Does it bother you that I make more money than you do?"

"It's not just that," said Karl. He was clearly uncomfortable. But he'd fallen hard for Bethany and he supposed they were due for this talk. "It's that you're probably always going to make more than me."

"Plumbers make good money," said Bethany.

"Not as much as vice-presidents with stock options and bonus packages," retorted Karl. "There's no way I'm going to be able to compete with your income."

"We're competing?"

"No, not competing, but, Beth, I'm the guy and I'm supposed to take care of you."

"What a neanderthalic thing to say," said Bethany. "Really? You man, me woman," she mocked in a deep voice as she beat her chest.

Karl's colour rose. "You think it's easy watching you pay for dinner?

And I know you're just being kind, but you're even re-dressing me."

"I thought you liked those clothes."

"I do," he said, a little sorry he'd raised the clothes as an issue. Bethany had offered to buy him a new suit for a wedding. He'd been grateful at the time not to have to show up to her friends' reception in his old sports jacket.

"You know what?" said Karl, getting up and walking over to Bethany. "I love you. We can't resolve this now, and I don't want to fight." He leaned forward and kissed her. She kissed him back. She didn't want to fight either. But she also didn't want to apologize for her career. She let it go. Again.

Once upon a time men brought home the mastodon and women cooked it on the spit. That's changed. Now many women earn more than their partners and the role reversal is wreaking havoc with their relationships. While many men find it perfectly acceptable to flaunt their high status, some women feel like they have to dim their lights to accommodate their partners' egos. Other women actually hold their higher incomes over their partners' heads. Neither scenario bodes well for a strong, long-lasting relationship.

In the "she makes more than he does" power struggle, common sense flies out the window. Instead of working together to accomplish goals, couples draw battle lines to defend their territory and carve out places that give them back status. Men refuse to do "women's work." Women take on all the housework, child care, and family care to avoid further emasculating their men. Burnout is inevitable.

If you do not want resentment to consume your relationship, coming to terms with income role reversal is important. Societal pressures to conform are hard enough when you're on the same page; they can be devastating if you're not.

What does your salary actually say about you? Are you measuring your worth by how much you make, how much your partner makes, and how society perceives your success? And if you lose your high-status job, choose to change your career to one where you make less money, or stay home to take care of your children, does that make you less than you were when you were making the big bucks?

Societal messages are there, no question, but to buy into them to the detriment of your relationship is disastrous. What will you do when the babies start coming? How will you and your mate choose to split mat-leave benefits? Will she stay home for a year and sacrifice her higher income? Will he be willing to take on the role of primary caregiver so the family can benefit from her higher income? Will you be willing to split maternity/parental leave so she can get back to earning while he gets his opportunity to bond? How will you each get out of your stereotypical roles to make things work for your family?

Bethany raised the issue of the vacation a few weeks later. Karl had had some time to think about it and said, "I think there are some things we need to talk about before we get any deeper into this relationship. I'm crazy about you, Beth, but I'm uncomfortable with the differences between us."

"Would you be less uncomfortable if we were living together and pooling our money?" asked Bethany.

"I'm not sure that would fix it for me," said Karl. "If everyone knows you make more, then everyone knows I'm not taking care of you."

"But you take care of me in ways other than with money," Bethany said. "When my kitchen sink needed to be replaced, you did that for me. Isn't that taking care of me?"

"You could have hired anyone to do that," said Karl.

"You know what plumbers cost?" Bethany joked. He smiled. "Can't you see that the things you do for me that make my life easier are worth as much as the money I bring into the relationship? When my car broke down, you came and got me, arranged to have the car towed, and then fixed the problem. That was worth way more than dinner out. And when my mom fell, you showed up and stayed with me through her hip operation. There's no amount of money that can replace that."

"I did those things because I love you," he said as he took her face in his hands and kissed her.

"And I'm taking you on vacation because I love you," she responded softly, kissing him back.

Maybe part of the problem is that there is no rule book for when she makes more than he does. The old rules have been around for eons and everyone knows what they are. But the new rules have yet to be established.

Just because a woman earns more doesn't mean she wants other aspects of the relationship dynamic to change. She still wants to feel protected and be taken care of. She wants to be given gifts as tokens of love (they don't have to be expensive, just well considered). And she doesn't want her contribution to the family coffers taken for granted (as in, "We can't talk about money because my income makes you feel like less than a whole man").

Just because a man earns less doesn't mean he wants to feel like less of a hero in the relationship. Men with fragile egos—don't we all have fragile egos when we tell the truth?—want to feel strong and in charge. He might want to pay for things. And he definitely won't want to be made to feel like he has less motivation or ambition just because his job has a lower pay scale.

You must set your own rules for your dynamic. You can create a joint household account to which both of you contribute proportionate to your income. If you enjoy eating out, sports, or other forms of entertainment that can run to big bucks, include those activities in the joint expenses. If doing the transaction makes him feel better about his role in the relationship, have a credit card that he uses to pay for dinner, which can then be paid off from the joint entertainment budget.

The point of establishing your rules is to make sure awkward situations don't arise. Talk about who will pay for what when you're out socially. Who will manage the family expenses, and how often will you talk about them together so you both know what's going on? If you're unwilling to come right out and say, "Gee, babe, I feel like a loser," how will you signal that you're embarrassed or concerned so that you can talk about the issue quickly and avoid resentment and frustration?

Not all men have a problem with a woman who makes more than they do. Some men glory in the success of their mates; they want women who are financially independent. And there are some women who won't date men who make less than they do because of the stigma (and bruised egos) involved. But for most people, it is the relationship, not who makes more money, that matters most.

From time to time, many of us must come to terms with changes in dynamic as the financial baton gets passed from one partner to the other. Changes in careers, the birth of children, unemployment or underemployment, illness, or the start-up phase of a new business can all bring a switch in who makes more money.

Ultimately, it is mutual respect and unconditional personal regard that will dictate whether a relationship works or not. No man who truly respects his partner will want her to hide her light. No woman who truly respects her partner will diminish him. Honouring and expressing our pride and joy in our partners has absolutely nothing to do with money.

ESTABLISHING THE NEW RULES

1. Recognize that clinging to traditional roles and trying to keep the old rules in place won't work.
2. Talk about how you feel about money. How will you share it? Who will pay for what and how? Establish a budget to which you each contribute in a way that is comfortable for you both. How will bills be paid and by whom? Outline how much (in dollar amounts) can be spent with and without consultation. Can one of you independently buy a $50 treat? A $1,400 electronic toy? A $5,000 vacation? Where are you drawing the lines?
3. Each of you must maintain your own financial identity, so don't choose to do everything jointly in the name of togetherness. Support each other as you work to achieve goals, but maintain individual bank and credit accounts, along with savings.

4. Talk about how you will fairly share the work to be done at home. No one working full-time wants to come home and be responsible for all the laundry, cleaning, cooking, and child care. Get past what your gender has typically been responsible for and figure out how, as a team, you're going to get it all done.

5. Celebrate each other's work. Talk about your challenges and successes with genuine interest. Can't work up a "Great job" for the installation of yet another bathtub? Then why the hell should he care if you just closed another $2 million deal? If you aren't able to share your frustrations and celebrate together, you shouldn't be surprised when someone gets sad.

6. Don't pull power plays or abdicate: "I make the money, I'll decide" or "You make the decision, it's mostly your money." In previous generations, money makers also got to be decision makers. The new rules won't allow that dynamic to exist in a healthy relationship.

7. Keep talking. Money issues won't resolve themselves. You have to keep coming back to them to work them out. And new ones will constantly crop up. Talk about what you're doing and how you feel about it, and negotiate your way to common ground. If things get emotional, take a walk to get some fresh air. Come back to the discussion fresh, balanced, and committed to a positive outcome.

8 • WHEN PRIORITIES CHANGE

Lorraine worked at a high-tech firm for 15 years making a damn fine income. Earning more than most of her friends, she often treated when they went out. Then the hammer fell at work and Lorraine was downsized. It was seven months before she got work again. Thank goodness she had an emergency fund. She's not making as much as she used to, but she's got enough to meet her basic needs and start rebuilding her emergency fund. Thing is, while her career went into free fall a couple of her girlfriends got promotions that came with nice raises. Now they want to do more things—expensive things—and Lorraine simply can't afford it. A couple of times she did go out, but when the credit card bill came in she realized what an idiot she'd been.

You've decided that you want to change how you deal with your money. Problem is, every time your friends call, your desire to not spend takes flight. Out you go, spending money you should not.

Up until now you had been the life of the party. You would pick up the tab when out for dinner. You'd suggest weekend adventures and foot the bill for anyone who balked. And you gave the very best presents.

But things have to change. Having dug yourself a helluva debt hole, it's now or never. Or your income has changed and you simply can't afford what you used to be able to pay for easily. Problem is, you don't know how to tell your friends and family.

The truth will save you. Tell the truth and deal with what comes next.

When the phone rang, Lorraine answered, expecting it to be her sister. But it was Megan, who had been trying to reach her all week. "Hey, you, where have you been? Did you get my messages?"

Damn. Lorraine had been avoiding Megan because she didn't want to talk about the trip their friends were planning. "Hi, Meg," said Lorraine. "Sorry, it's been busy. You're calling about the reunion, aren't you?"

"Yes, we need to decide if we're going to double up on hotel rooms or go with singles."

Lorraine took a deep breath. "Sorry, hon. I'm afraid I can't go."

"Oh no! Don't tell me it's work again."

Lorraine was tempted to take the easy way out. She hitched up her knickers and decided on the truth. "It isn't. To be honest, it's money. Even with this new job there are things I just can't afford to do anymore. Like the expensive dinners out. Or this trip."

"Oh." Megan was a little surprised. "Okay," she began hesitantly, "but if things were tight why didn't you just say so?"

"I was embarrassed."

"You're an idiot," said Megan laughing. "We're your friends. We don't care how much money you make."

"We always used to go to nice places together."

"And you treated all the time. Now it's our turn. Are you going to let us reciprocate or are you going to get all snobby and weird about it?"

Lorraine burst out laughing. The laughter turned to tears. Her unspoken fear had been that she'd lose her friends if she couldn't keep up.

"Oh, you dork," said Megan. "I'll call the girls, and we'll all come to your house for dinner on Wednesday so we can work out a plan. Don't cook, we're bringing Chinese."

If you have friends who judge you based on your ability to keep up socially, they're not really your friends. This realization may be hard to deal with, but you'll have to find new people to call friends. Real friends will love you for richer or poorer. And real friends won't judge you, no matter how much you're judging yourself. But if you don't tell the truth, they won't have the real information to work with and will continue to make assumptions about what you can afford. So tell the truth.

When Andy decided to buy a home, she knew things were going to have to change. While she was saving her down payment, she put herself on a strict budget and gave herself a small allowance for social spending. But that meant she didn't have money readily available to do all the things she had always done with her friends. The dinners out, the bars, the visits to the casino would have to go. A couple of times she tried to convince her girls to come to her apartment for a movie night but they were having none of it. "I'm not staying cooped up after my hellish week at work," said her BFF, Karen. "I'm going to dance and drink my face off tonight." Andy stayed home alone.

A couple of days later Karen stopped by Andy's to return a dress. "You missed a great night," Karen said as she hung up the dress in Andy's closet. "Mickey was beyond wasted and Leah and Jason finally hooked up."

"I'm sorry I missed the fun," said Andy as she put the kettle on.

"Why did you?" asked Karen.

"Well," said Andy, "you know I want to buy my own place. I can't save a down payment and still go out all the time. So I'm staying home until I have enough saved."

"That could be years," said Karen. "You're just gonna hole up here forever?"

"I have a little money in my budget for some fun. But I can't blow through it all in one night. I've got to pace myself so it lasts all month."

"When am I going to see you, then?" Karen whined.

"Well, you could get up and go running with me on Saturday mornings. We can come back here for breakfast. I'm buying myself a good brewer to make up for all the coffee I'm not buying out."

"How about Georgia's wedding shower dinner next week? Are you skipping that too?"

"No, but I plan to eat at home and just have an appie and dessert with you guys so I don't end up spending a hundred bucks on dinner."

"You're really serious about this."

"I am. I've always wanted to buy a house. It's time to make it happen."

Getting friends to understand that things have changed for you financially—whether you've changed jobs, gotten divorced, are digging yourself out of debt, or saving towards a goal—can take more than a couple of conversations. Old habits die hard, and friends usually want to keep on keeping on. You'll have to be firm in your resolve. And you'll have to be patient as you explain how your priorities—and financial focus—have shifted.

COMING CLEAN ON YOUR NEW PRIORITIES

1. Trust that the people you love who love you back only want the best for you.

2. Be prepared to tell the truth, the whole truth. Sugarcoating the reality leaves your friends in the dark.

3. Explain what's changed and why.

4. Ask for your friends' support and for ideas on how you can continue to socialize without sacrificing your financial stability or your goals.

5. Set aside a specific amount for socializing. It may be $25 a month. It may be $200 a month. It all depends on your goals and your resources. Whatever you decide, stick to it.

6. Opt out if your friends regularly play at expensive outings you can no longer justify spending your money on. Choose less expensive activities to do together. Or you can consciously limit what you plan to spend by taking what you plan to spend in cash when you join them. When the money is gone, that's it!

9 • YOUR KIDS VERSUS MY KIDS

James and Jennifer had been married for about two years when it became obvious that their blended family faced some unique challenges. James's two boys, Kyle and Jamie, lived with their mother during the week and spent weekends with James. Jennifer's daughter, Lily, spent Fridays and Saturdays with her dad. The family was in full force on Sundays, when the house felt like it was packed to the rafters.

James wanted to get a bigger home. Jennifer was reluctant. Since James was paying $1,200 a month in child support, she didn't think they could afford a bigger house. James wanted to count the child support Jennifer got—about $2,700 a month—as part of the family income. While Jennifer acknowledged that some of that child support was to offset their family cost of living and had allocated $700 a month for that, she wanted to keep most of the money focused on Lily's needs.

"Mark is paying that child support for Lily, not for me. I'm already paying my half of the mortgage and living costs. I don't think we should have to use Lily's money to get a bigger house."

"The boys have to share a room when they're here, while Lily gets her own room. You think that's fair?"

"The boys are here two days a week, Lily's here five. And she's the only girl."

"Still, you waste all that money on things like Montessori and piano. We could buy way more house with that money."

"Mark and I both want Lily in Montessori, so he pays for that. I can't ask him to give me more money so I can spend it on a bigger house."

"It's just not fair. The disparity between what Lily gets and what my boys get is huge."

"You know this is more of a problem for you than it is for the kids, right? They all eat well, we never exclude anyone, and we're careful to make sure everyone in this house is treated fairly. You're just mad because I won't use Lily's money to buy a bigger house."

From there the heavy rain blew into a hurricane, ending when James slammed the door and screeched out of the driveway.

Jennifer called her sister, Jessica. She described the fight, how unreasonable she thought James was being, and how frustrated she was.

"This isn't our first fight over this," said Jennifer. "It happens every time James feels like he's not doing enough for the boys. Last week his ex called and said the boys wanted to play hockey but it was expensive. She'd only sign them up if James gave her an extra $200 a month. And if he didn't, she'd tell them that Daddy wouldn't pay for their hockey."

"Seriously?" asked Jessica. "That's awful."

"She pulls that crap all the time, using the boys and what they want as a sledgehammer. He's already upped the amount he's giving her by $200 a month above the court-ordered child support because Kyle needed a tutor and Amanda wouldn't take it out of the existing child support."

"Well, maybe she really can't afford it. You get almost double for Lily what she gets for her two boys together."

"I know. Which is why, when he agreed to pay the extra $200, I used $200 of Lily's child support to balance out our family budget. But I'm not prepared to keep doing that."

"So, what are you going to do?"

"I don't know. I just don't know."

I've had more than one parent say to me, "What makes my child worth $___ while someone else's child is worth twice or three times that?" It's a tough question to deal with, in part because it's the wrong question. The amount parents receive in child support has nothing to do with the worth of the child and everything to do with the parent's income and ability to pay. Yes, there are people who circumvent the system, but that's not today's discussion.

When James agreed to pay $500 a month for each of his boys, that amount was based on his income at the time. The same was true for the $2,700 a month Jennifer's ex-husband, Mark, was paying. The disparity was based on each father's income and ability to pay.

Negotiating common ground about whose kids should get which family resources can be tough when one child appears to have so much more than another. And it isn't good for children to hear their parents arguing about the children's "worth" because, really, their worth has nothing to do with how much child support is being paid.

Regardless of how fair Jennifer feels her use of child support for the family's benefit is—assigning that $700 of child support to the family budget—James won't come around as long as he feels like she's not using the money in the same way he would. That's the nature of many money conflicts: "I think you're doing this wrong!"

So, what's the solution?

As parents we have to decide how the money will be divvied up for our children. It can be a tough call to make. If we let discussions dissolve into drag 'em out fights, nothing will be resolved. Talking about how the family's resources—and child support if applicable—will be allocated has to be a priority, and it needs to be done when there are no emotional triggers at work.

When Richard and Christina got married, Christina knew that Richard was coming to the relationship with some serious baggage. He had two children, Brian and Bailey, with his ex-wife, Tiffany. He'd let Tiffany and the boys stay in the family home because he felt so guilty about how he'd disrupted their lives. Christina thought he was a great dad and completely understood his need to ensure his children's lifestyle did not suffer because of the divorce. But when Tiffany kept coming back for more money—for private school and sports fees—Christina got frustrated with Richard's willingness to acquiesce.

Things grew even more complicated when Christina and Richard had twins: Benji and Rachel. Now Christina wanted Richard to focus on making sure the two newest additions to the family were also protected.

At 48, Richard knew life insurance was important to Christina so he took out a 20-year term policy, which cost him $275 a month in premiums. But it wasn't enough. Christina kept harping on the fact that his older kids had used up their fair share of resources and it was time to make sure the twins got theirs. Richard felt like he was being pulled in a dozen different directions.

"I don't understand why you agreed to pay the full shot for Brian and Bailey's university when you know we can't do that and put the twins in private school."

"The twins don't have to go to private school to get a good education," said Richard.

"So, it was fine when Tiffany insisted that Bailey go to a private school, but our kids don't get that option?"

"The twins are two years old," said Richard. "They aren't going to any school right now."

"Brian went to camp for a month every year. Bailey went to private school. And every time Tiffany calls and says she needs more money you just cough it up. I'm carrying more than my fair share of the twins' expenses because of it."

"So, because I have a fresh set of kids I should just dump the old ones?" Richard was furious.

"No," said Christina, equally furious, "that's NOT what I'm saying. I'm saying you need to think about making sure all the kids are cared for equally well. You won't be working when Benji and Rachel are ready to go to university. But because we're paying so much for Brian and Bailey, we don't have any extra money to save for the twins."

"I'm sorry we don't have extra money to save," Richard snapped back. "But I've got four kids to think about, not just two, like you. I've got to make sure everyone gets what they need. And right now Bailey and Brian need money for university. I'm giving it to them."

Balancing kids' present needs with their future needs is another major stumbling block for blended families. Yes, camp is important. But so, too, is saving for post-secondary education. While the demands of the present always seem to take precedence—older children may have more significant financial expenses, like college—when there are significant age gaps between children, the future of the younger kids must also be a priority.

Be clear on what you're trying to achieve by setting up provisions for the future. Yes, insurance premiums take cash flow today, but they protect long-term income in the future. Yes, saving for educational costs takes from cash flow today, but it frees up money that'll be needed down the road, particularly if incomes go down because of retirement.

Christina took a deep breath. "I know that your kids—all your kids—are important to you." She took Richard's hand in hers and led him over to the couch, signalling for him to sit. "And I want you to know that I don't expect you to ignore your older kids' needs."

"I hear a *but*," said Richard.

"Well, have you thought about how we will pay for Benji and Rachel to go to college or university when it's time?"

"That's why we have the RESP [Registered Education Savings Plan], right?"

"Yes, it is, but with the $100 a month we're putting away right now that's still not going to be enough. So, I guess I just want to know what you think we should do to be most fair to all the kids?"

Richard looked at Christina. She had a point. He wouldn't be working by the time Benji and Rachel were heading off to school. "Okay," he said, "I see your point. What if we boost those monthly contributions? And we can plan to downsize the house when I retire so that we have enough money to help the kids with school."

Addison and Mike met about three years after Addison's divorce. When he proposed, Addison was over the moon. But she was determined not to make the mistake she'd made in her first marriage, relying on her husband to make all the financial decisions. Addison and Mike each had two girls from previous marriages, so they decided to keep their money separate. They'd each contribute proportionately to the family's shelter costs and food but handle everything to do with their children separately.

Everything was going great until Addison's ex, William, started missing child support payments. Will's mom was very ill and Will was helping her financially. Addison didn't want to bust his chops because she knew how hard this was for him, but she was running short on her share of the family money and it looked like she might have to pull her girls out of summer camp. She decided to talk to Mike about it.

Mike felt like Addison was asking him to foot the bill for camp. "I have two girls of my own to take care of," he said when she tried to talk to him about how best to handle the shortfall in funds. "Will's first responsibility is to his children. It's not my job to pick up the slack."

When Mike's daughter, Leila, enrolled in college that fall, it turned out she'd be at school just minutes away from Addison and Mike's house. So she asked if she could come and live with them for a few months while she settled in and found a place of her own. Addison balked. While she was fond of Leila, with her stepdaughter came more communication with Mike's ex, whom she couldn't stand. Her instinct was to say no.

"You're kidding me, right?" asked Mike. "You really expect me to tell Leila she's not welcome?"

"It's my home too," responded Addison.

"For which I pay 60% of the mortgage and carrying costs," retorted Mike.

When you remarry and blend two families, you get a mixed bag. Drawing borders around groups within the family isn't the way to make blending work. And thinking that there won't be times when you may have to support more than you bargained for in terms of family (yours, theirs, or ours) is unrealistic.

Regularly talking about the money, what is and isn't working, and what may need changing short and long term is key to avoiding big blow-ups. If you are both open and honest about what you're thinking (what you're afraid of, what you're worried about, what you think needs changing) you're less likely to be sideswiped by a fight.

No matter how well you plan, life will throw a spanner in the works. Your ability to talk through the changes you must make, to come up with solutions that will work in the here and now, is vital to staying blended. And if you are determined to keep score—"You didn't, so I'm not going to"—you might as well give up now.

Your focus must be on creating the best future you can for yourselves as a couple and for your blended family. That means getting on the same page about your goals, your financial needs and wants, and your expectations of each other as partners. While there will be loads to fight about—no family has more grist for the conflict mill than a blended family—you can choose to take a different path. Talk about everything: how you will use your money, how you will protect your children's future, and what you're prepared (or not prepared) to do as part of your blending.

BLENDING MONEY IN A BLENDED FAMILY

1. Pick a time when there is no additional stress (issues to be resolved, changes in circumstance, demands being made by ex-partners or children) to talk about how you will split the family budget. Be specific about how much of the child support being received will be kept for the child's individual use (school, extracurricular activities, clothes, travel, camp) versus how much will be incorporated into the family budget (shelter, food, transportation, family holidays). (See Appendix 1: Building a Budget.)

2. Acknowledge that you may be bringing very different money styles and expectations into the relationship. (Even if you've been married for a while, if you haven't had this conversation, it's time.) Will your policies on the kids' allowances jell? How do you see the splitting of expenses? Will you make budgets for the kids' expenses as a family or as individual parents? How will you teach your kids about money and the part it plays in their lives?

3. Look at both today's needs and tomorrow's. While the needs of the present will always shout louder, tomorrow's needs also must be addressed. That means protecting future income with life insurance and setting aside money that will likely be needed in the future (like educational savings) from current cash flow.

4. If you or your mate is paying child or spousal support, deduct those expenses from income first before allocating your budget proportionately. Like taxes, child/spousal support must be paid, so make that deduction before planning what to do with your money.

5. Set a regular date to talk about money at least once a month. As things change, you're going to have to decide how you will deal with them as individual parents and as a family.

6. Estate planning is very important and may be quite complicated in blended family situations. Seek expert help. No will kit will address this adequately!

7. Scorekeeping is a relationship killer. Avoid it like the plague.

10 • FIFTY-FIFTY ISN'T ALWAYS FAIR

Carrie and Justin had been living together for just over a year, splitting all the expenses equally. Justin had a good job, while Carrie was finishing her Ph.D. Justin had always made more, but Carrie had enough from her work at the university to live. Then she lost one of her incomes and had to turn to her savings to make ends meet. She and Justin were still splitting costs fifty-fifty but it wasn't working, and she was steadily growing resentful.

"When I told Justin that I was running out of money and needed him to pay more of the expenses, he didn't understand why," Carrie told her friend, Leo. "He said, 'You'd have to live somewhere and pay rent, right? At least here your share is just $450 a month.'"

"Did you explain that you're not making what you used to?" asked Leo.

"I did," said Carrie, "but he says that's my problem, that I have to find some other way of contributing my half. He makes ten times what I make." Carrie knew she sounded whiny but she was desperate and not sure what to do next.

"Do you have any other options for places to live?" asked Leo.

"I don't want to live anywhere else," she said, tears springing to her eyes. "I love Justin. I've just got to figure out how to get him to see that this isn't fair."

"Have you told him that?"

"I tried when I first found out my income was going down, but he didn't hear me. I told him the fifty-fifty split wasn't fair for all kinds of reasons. He eats way more than I do, so why do we split the groceries half and half? All he did was offer to lend me some money until I could get another job to replace the income that I'm losing."

"And that won't work for you because . . ." prompted Leo.

"I'd wind up feeling like a dependant rather than a partner. If we get married and have kids, will I owe him after my maternity leaves because he's picking up more of the expenses, or will he expect me to go into debt to keep up my 50% of the expenses?"

"So, what's his problem? Can't he see how frustrated and afraid you are?"

"He seems just as frustrated because he sees equality in a relationship as splitting things fifty-fifty. He wants me to use up all my savings before I ask him to 'subsidize' me."

"Wow, that's rough," said Leo, running his hands through his hair.

"I've totally stopped going out with him and his friends. I don't have the money to eat out."

"And he goes anyway?"

"Sure does. And last month he came home with a bonus from work and told me all the things he was planning to spend it on. I just ran from the room crying. He thinks I'm an idiot."

"Is it that he's stingy? I never really saw him that way."

"No, it's more like he's clueless about how this is affecting me. Whenever he's stressed he tends to just ignore the situation and hope it'll go away. He eventually offers to pay for some things if I go on and on about how I can't afford them. But that leaves me feeling like I'm begging, so most of the time I just take a pass on whatever it is I need."

While loads of people go into relationships thinking the fifty-fifty approach is the right one to take, it often isn't. It may be equal, but it isn't fair.

The most constructive way of handling family income and

expenses, particularly when one partner makes more than the other, is the "mine, yours, ours" approach.

This method of sharing incomes calculates what you'll each contribute to the family coffers, proportionate to your income. Add your incomes together to come up with the family income. Divide your income by the family income and multiply by 100.

If you make $24,000 a year after taxes and your partner makes $43,000 after taxes, your after-tax family income is $67,000. Your income divided by the family income looks like this:

$$24,000 \div 67,000 \text{ x } 100 = 35.82\%$$

You can round it down to 35% or up to 36%, but either way that's the percentage of joint expenses you should be paying to be "fair."

So, you would pay 36% of the family expenses while your mate pays 64%. Sounds like a big difference, doesn't it? Maybe it doesn't even sound fair. It is. In fact, it's the only way for you to contribute to the joint expenses and still have some money for individual savings, goals, and pleasures.

Let's say your family expenses total $3,200 a month. Your monthly income is $2,000, so your share is 36% and you contribute $1,152 to the joint account to cover all the things you've agreed are joint expenses: shelter, food, utilities, savings for the kids, kids' expenses. That leaves you with $848 from which you will do your own saving, work towards personal goals, and spend for pleasure.

Your partner's income is $3,583 a month so his or her share (64%) is $2,048, and he or she is left with $1,535 to spend on saving, personal goals, and spending for pleasure.

You've each contributed fairly to the family expenses and you each have enough of your own money to make choices and decisions without having to consult the other guy or feel like you are beholden.

Some people argue that the family money belongs to the whole family, that the full amount of income should be pooled and then divvied up as both partners see fit. Hey, if you want to do it that way, go ahead. Just keep in mind that both partners need

- an account in their own name;
- a credit card in their own name to build a credit history;
- individual savings (Registered Retirement Savings Plans and Tax-Free Savings Accounts can't be held jointly);
- involvement in all financial decision making; and
- thorough familiarity with how the family money is being managed on a day-to-day basis.

Ali and Fatima met when they were in high school. They married and had three children. Ali worked hard as a supervisor in a manufacturing plant and Fatima worked as an educational assistant at an elementary school. She took care of everything related to the kids, including child care in the summer when they were all out of school. Since Ali made 70% of the family income, he thought he should have 70% of the say. When Fatima's income fell in the summer, she had a hard time getting him to pick up more of the family's expenses even though she was saving the family a fortune in daycare costs. It got to the point where Fatima couldn't buy anything for herself or the children without Ali's permission. Meanwhile, he thought nothing of walking through the door with a new big-screen TV or the latest gaming device.

If one of the reasons your income is so much lower than your partner's is because you are doing the majority of the child care or home care, at some point you need your mate to acknowledge the service you are providing to the family.

As an educational assistant, Fatima's work schedule matched her children's school schedule, eliminating the need for child care. That saved the family $1,200 in child care costs each month, which worked out to be $14,400 a year in after-tax income.

And then there were all the other services she provided for the family, the things every family tends to take for granted because they just happen: the meals, the clean laundry, the tidy house, the taxi service, the grocery shopping . . . the list goes on and on.

The debate has long raged about the value of what has traditionally been seen as women's work in the home. From raising children to cooking and cleaning, people have argued that it is these "free" services that allow the economy to function. And yet these services are in no way included in our measures of the economy. So they get "lost."

If you feel like the services you provide your family for free in your home are being taken for granted, only you can do something about that. Primary breadwinners—be they male or female—should not discount the services they might have to pay for if their partner walked out the door. Nor do they have the right to control the family purse strings simply because they bring home more of the bacon. The guy who fries it up in the pan has as much right to an equal say. In giving up income to have more time for the family, primary caregivers may have to demand that their "financial contribution" be acknowledged. That means

- having their own credit identity;
- building independent savings for the future; and
- sharing equally in the family's disposable income once all the bills are paid.

ESTABLISHING A FAIR SYSTEM

1. A fair system means that each partner's contribution is proportionate to their income so that they can also work towards individual goals and have some fun too.
2. Fair also means that the unpaid work done within a home is recognized for the economic value it offers the family. Money not spent on daycare is as valuable as the earned income used to pay for daycare.
3. Individuals should always have independent financial identities. That means having credit in your name alone, and saving and investing for your own future.
4. If one partner cannot be convinced that fifty-fifty is less than fair, the intervention of a counsellor or a family friend may be required to open up the discussion.

5. Once the agreement has been made about how expenses will be shared, they are NOT cast in stone. Changes in circumstances will require that you revisit the percentages so that the system you're using remains fair.

11 • I CAN'T HEAR YOU

Stephanie and Wayne had been married for 17 years when Stephanie told Wayne that she'd had enough. If he couldn't get his act together, she was leaving him. She was sick of his drinking, his self-centredness, and his irresponsibility. Wayne laughed, popped the tab on a beer, and sat down in front of the TV to watch the game. He'd heard Stephanie rant before. Many times. Many, many times. Now he could tune her out. She blah-blah-blahed and he just focused on the puck.

Stephanie was at her wits' end. She had yelled. She had pleaded. It didn't seem to matter an iota to Wayne. Here he was, unemployed again, sitting in front of the TV. If Stephanie didn't find another part-time job to tide them over until Wayne decided to get back to work, they were going to lose their home.

As if that wasn't bad enough, even when Wayne was working Stephanie couldn't get him to talk about the money with her. She'd tried everything. Every time she raised the issue of a budget or getting their credit cards paid off, Wayne just seemed to zone out.

Stephanie turned off the TV. Wayne groaned. "Are we going to do this again?" he asked.

"Just one last time," said Stephanie. "If we can't find a common ground this time, I'm filing for separation. You'll have to find somewhere else to live."

"Yeah, right."

"Here's the first draft," said Stephanie, tossing him a stapled sheaf of papers.

"What?"

"You'll see that you'll have to find another place to live and the kids will be with you every Thursday and Friday night and every other week-end," said Stephanie matter-of-factly. "I'm told the courts will decide on child support if you don't like what's there."

Wayne flipped through the pages he was holding. "Hang on now, Steph. What the hell?"

"No, Wayne, I've hung on long enough. You don't hear me anymore. You just block me out. So I've had it. I'm done. If you want to talk, I'll be down at the coffee shop. But I'll only be there for an hour. You decide what you want to do next."

And with that, she left. She closed the door quietly behind her and walked away, leaving Wayne stunned.

You've nagged your partner (because you felt you had to) to the point where it's like they're wearing earplugs. Now that you no longer want the role of police officer or parent, how do you change the dynamic? Shifting roles often takes drastic measures.

There are steps most people can take to avoid the desperate measure of seeking a separation. Very often, reluctant partners choose to block their mate's conversations about money because they don't want to have to budget or plan how they'll spend their money. Plain and simple, they just don't wanna.

One way to make it easy for your partner to talk about the money is to create a very basic plan for review. Make a budget that outlines the most obvious bills you have to pay to meet your needs: shelter, transportation, food. Then show the discretionary income that's left over (or not) and talk about how you'll use that for your wants.

The Magic Jars that became so popular because of the

TV show *Til Debt Do Us Part* are one way of making concrete how much money you have in each category but also that the money will run out. If you've decided that you'll spend $50 a week on groceries and $65 a week on transportation, both eating and travelling stop when the money in the jars runs out. Sticking with a cash budget is a great way of visually showing in very real terms that the money does, in fact, come to an end.

If your partner feels picked on—he may have racked up debt, she may have had trouble holding a job, or he may simply be horrible at dealing with financial details—you won't get very far in any discussion. To be heard, you'll have to change your approach. Quit talking about the mistakes that have been made. Focus on the actions you'll take together to move from where you are now to where you next want to be: on budget and solvent.

Look at how you may have played into your mate's propensity to duck and hide. Sometimes mates feel nagged because they weren't included in the decision making and are just expected to follow the plan. They feel they're being dictated to. They bridle at being treated like a lesser citizen or, worse, a child. There's the spouse on a decreed allowance, the mate with no access to the bank account, the partner who is told— instead of consulted—about important financial decisions. No wonder she just stops listening. No wonder he wants to run screaming from the room every time he is being informed about something new.

It's time to signal a shift in your own behaviour. Begin with, "I was wrong. Wrong to leave you out of the process, wrong to dictate what you should do. I want to fix this." Suck it up and admit you're part of the problem and now want to find a solution together.

And then there's the mate who is so optimistic about life in general you want to lop off his arm and beat him over the head with the soggy end. Every warning you raise, every concern you have is met with, "Hey, it'll be fine. You'll see. It'll all work out." And it does, but usually because you take steps to fix the financial accident you see headed your way before the collision happens.

Clearly, the nagging isn't working. Switch to demonstrating consequences instead. And instead of making the conversation all about avoiding mash-ups, try to refocus it on ways to achieve the things you both want from life. If you can put a positive spin on your financial chats, you're much more likely to have a willing ear.

Wayne met Stephanie at the coffee shop. When he walked in, she looked up, tears streaming down her face. His heart wrenched. He loved Stephanie and his kids, he just couldn't stand all the nagging. It didn't matter whether he was working or not, following the budget or not, there was always something she was at him about. He'd just learned to ignore her rants and wait out her fury. It always passed. So what was different this time?

"Hi," he said as he sat down in front of her. "Before we talk about what you said, I need to know whether you still love me or if you've already left me."

"If I'd already left you, you'd have gotten the finished separation agreement in the mail," said Stephanie. "But I'm serious. This isn't a game."

"I get that," said Wayne. "I'm not going to ask you what the problem is because that seems so . . . I dunno . . . so . . ."

"Obtuse?" asked Stephanie. "Yeah, it would be pretty obtuse. So, let me ask YOU. What do YOU think the problem is?" She wiped her eyes with the back of her hands, then started to rifle through her purse.

"I think you're under a lot of stress because I'm not working right now," began Wayne. Stephanie pulled tissues from her purse and blew her nose. He waited for some acknowledgement but she wouldn't even look at him. "And I think you're pretty mad because you think I ignore you when you try to talk about money." Stephanie's sigh was a shudder, but she looked up at him. "And I think you're feeling pretty desperate."

"And how do you feel?" she asked quietly.

"I feel a little ashamed that I've made you so sad. But I also feel like you blame me when I'm not working. You know my work is seasonal and yet every time I'm off you seem to get so angry at me."

Stephanie sighed again. "Do you remember last summer when you were making so much money and I said we should take a third of it and stash it away for when you weren't working, but then you decided you needed a new car?"

"Yeah," said Wayne. "I did need a new car."

"But you didn't have to buy one that used up all the money we could be pulling on right now," said Stephanie. "You got a bright and shiny new car and I got a second job to hold things together."

Wayne leaned back in his chair and looked at Stephanie, his brows pulled together. So that was it? She resented his getting a new car. Okay, he could deal with that. But before he could begin, Stephanie said, "And if you think I'm upset about you getting a new car, you're missing the point."

How did she do that? he wondered. How did she know exactly what was going through his mind? She continued, "It was the fact that you totally ignored the future because all you could think about was the here and now. How come I'm the only one who has to worry about whether the kids will have a place to live or food to eat? How come all the worrying is my responsibility?"

At the heart of most nagging are crappy communication and bad habits. But nagging inevitably results in whoever is being nagged tuning out the nagger. Whether your mate consistently says he will do something and then doesn't, or must be reminded to follow the path to which you've both agreed, or procrastinates until you think you'll go mad, if you nag it's because you don't have the imagination to come up with a better way of communicating. Time to learn some new skills.

The next time you're tempted to say, "You always promise but you never follow through," try "If you say yes, mean it. Or say no. I get mad when I'm disappointed, so just tell me what you intend to really do."

The next time you're tempted to say, "You've got to deposit that cheque today," try "The cheque needs to go into the bank. Let me know when you're planning to put it in so I can set up the online bill payments for next week."

Try using non-verbal signals instead of constantly repeating requests. Instead of asking for your mate's receipts each day so you can update the spending journal, put out a small box, decorated with a big smiley face and the words FEED ME, for him to deposit his receipts into. He'll be reminded to stick his receipts into the box and you'll know you've got 'em.

HELPING YOUR MATE TUNE IN

1. Acknowledge that a tuned-out partner means your communication is not working.
2. Decide what the consequence will be for you, your mate, your relationship, and your family if something does not change.
3. If you are determined to make the relationship and the money work, look for other ways of getting your message through to your buddy.

    - Create a basic plan (a debt repayment plan, a budget, a plan for earning more money) to deal with whatever issue is at hand, and ask your mate to be involved in all of the decision making.
    - Stop revisiting the past. Set a goal for the future and work towards that.
    - Talk about the consequences if nothing changes. Ask for suggestions on how you can signal each other when things are going off-track.
    - Commit to eliminating nagging and the need for nagging. Both sides have to be willing to change.

12 • SOMETHING'S GOTTA GIVE!

Terry and Graham had been married for nine years. With two beautiful children, a nice home, and solid careers, they looked like they had it made. Graham travelled a lot for work so Terry took care of the day-to-day money decisions for the family. They had a joint account for their family expenses and separate accounts, credit cards, investments, and retirement plans. Things looked pretty good from the outside. On the inside, Terry was pulling her hair out.

Graham had a tendency to bounce cheques he wrote to Terry. He was horrible at managing his money and was successful financially in spite of himself. He'd get loads of parking tickets that he wouldn't pay until he had to renew his licence. By then, the ticket costs had tripled and Terry would want to hit something. "That's a family vacation," she told him one day after he wrote her a cheque to cover the cost of the tickets she'd put on her credit card. "You just wasted a family vacation on stupid parking-ticket fees."

"You live in the city, you get parking tickets," Graham said matter-of-factly.

"You pay them on time, you spend two-thirds less," Terry retorted, spittle jumping from her mouth as if to drown him. "This cheque isn't going to bounce, is it?"

He gave her a withering look.

Most of the time their lives were great. Every now and then things went to hell in a handbasket because Graham didn't much care about money and Terry did. As the details girl, she saw when the overdraft fees kicked in; when the balances on Graham's credit cards went unpaid for months, racking up interest; when he couldn't scrape together the money for an RRSP contribution so he got a loan.

"Why are you so determined to waste your money?" she said one day as she waved his unpaid credit card statement.

"What do you care?" he retorted. "I'm not asking you to pay my bills."

"Remember when you got turfed from your last job because the economy went into the dumper?" she replied. "I had to support us both for almost nine months. How would we manage with our mortgage, the kids, and your debt if either one of us lost all or part of our income?"

"It's never going to happen," said Graham, ever the optimist.

"Like it didn't happen last time?" asked Terry.

"Hey, I supported you while you were off on maternity leave with the kids."

"No," she said, "you only think you did. I had the money saved for my share of the family expenses. And while you were out drinking beer and eating wings, I didn't go anywhere except to the park for those two years."

The final straw came when the cheque Terry wrote to the piano teacher bounced because Graham's last cheque to the joint account had bounced. She'd had enough!

Sometimes people come to relationships with completely different attitudes towards money. One is buttoned-down, the other laissez-faire. One is a rabid spender, the other likes to save. One looks to the future, the other can see only today.

Even small differences can cause friction, like with the couple that agrees they want to buy a house, agrees they're going to save, and then disagrees on where they should keep their savings.

While we're all familiar with the saying "Opposites attract," the reality is that most couples don't stay opposites. They end up compromising on a bunch of really important issues in order to make their relationship work. But if one half of a couple thinks the wedding should happen in the backyard, while the other insists on blowing $60,000 on a party, how do they compromise? If one person believes that having some money saved is priority one, while the other is constantly whining about what they can't buy, how long can the relationship stay afloat?

I believe that couples who really love each other and are prepared to work together to make a plan can overcome the differences they bring to the relationship. And I think couples who truly want to succeed together can change and meet somewhere in the middle. But you know what else I think? I think it's a really, really hard thing to do.

If one person has to bully the other to keep the balance in the balance sheet, the relationship won't last. Nor will it if one person is doing all the heavy lifting. It truly does take a team effort to ensure that both peoples' needs—and the needs of the family—are met.

If, in trying to take care of the money, you absolve your partner of any responsibility for the management of the family's money, that's your mistake. By taking on the role of boss and battling your mate to do the right thing, you'll be going from partner to parent. It's time for your mate to share the job of money management and see what it's like to carefully balance the ins and outs.

Terry spent the next day balancing the family's books. She reconciled the bank statements and printed out a copy of the household budget. Having made a tidy bundle of printouts, she waited for Graham to get home from work. When he walked in the door she greeted him with a glass of his favourite wine and a nice dinner. The kids were at her parents' house for a sleepover, so she knew she had him to herself. They ate and chatted about their day. As she dished up a slice of peach pie she said, "Are you wondering what you did right to get all your faves tonight?"

No slouch, Graham responded, "I was sort of wondering what was up. Dinner was delicious, by the way."

"Thanks." Terry glowed. "I have something else for you." She walked over to the small alcove in the kitchen and retrieved the bundle of paper, now tied with a bow.

"What's this?" asked Graham.

"This," she said, holding out the bundle, "is yours. I've done the family books for the last nine years. Now it's your turn." She handed him the package. "Everything is balanced and I've printed out a list of our regular bills by date so you can see when things have to be paid to be on time. Here ya go, buddy."

"There's no way you're going to make me do this," he said. "I'm always on the road."

"That's why they invented online banking," she replied.

"You're way too much of a control freak to leave this to me," he said.

"That might have been true once," said Terry, "but since I actually can't control what you do and how it impacts on me, I've decided you might as well be in the driver's seat."

"You're not going to yell at me when I bounce cheques?" he asked.

"Hey, if you want to bounce cheques, that's your business," she said. "I've removed my name from the joint account, and I'll do an electronic transfer each month for my share of the bills, so if you do bounce cheques, it'll only be you who has to deal with the problem."

"Oh," he said, a little taken aback. "That's a pretty big step."

"Desperate times . . ." she said as she went to the kitchen to get more coffee.

One mate's indifference to money is often a source of frustration to the other. Since money is clearly an issue for you, it should be at least a little important to them. But in trying to engage an errant mate, sometimes people try to do too much at once.

A better option is to pick one thing you want your spouse to pay attention to and address only that.

"Sweetheart, I think we're spending too much on eating out. If I'm prepared to limit myself to just $25 a week on restaurants, would you also agree that's enough? Can we do it in cash so we aren't tempted to dip into the bank account beyond what we've agreed?"

Over time you can cover lots of territory, but you may need to take it one very small step at a time.

"Honey, we need to find a way to increase the payments on our credit cards so we get them gone for good. I'm going to do my damnedest to cut back on the grocery spending by $60 a month to come up with the money. Would you be willing to trim back our cable/cellphone package for the next few months to save an equal amount that we could apply to our cards?"

Or "I've heard if we raise the deductible on our car insurance we could save up to $100 a year. Would you call the insurance guy and see just how much we could save if we doubled our deductible?"

Makena and Khari both had terrific jobs with great benefits. They both also had student loans. They decided to buy a pretty expensive house in the city together and Khari worked hard at fixing up the house to make it a great place to live.

Makena took a full year off work when she had each of their two children. So, they had a nice home and were focused on their family. However, with Makena on maternity leave for the second time, their incomes had dropped off.

Despite the fact that they had agreed on every choice together, Makena was feeling denied. Her maternity benefits weren't topped up by her employer and without the extra money, they were scrimping to make ends meet. Khari hated debt but Makena felt it wasn't so bad because later, when she was back at work and making great money again, they'd be able to pay it off easily.

Makena was frustrated because she didn't get to take the same vacations her friends took. She hadn't bought new clothes in ages. Khari was happy to come home, be with his children, cook a meal, and clean up. Makena wanted to go out for dinner. The two kids were a handful and she needed a break.

When Khari discovered that Makena had just spent $3,500 on a credit card buying stuff for the house and some new clothes, he flipped out, grabbed her cards, and cut them up. She cried. She yelled. She'd had it with his stupid budget!

When people in a relationship have different needs and wants, and they can't find a way to compromise on those

differences, the inevitable result is fighting. The fights aren't really about the money. The fights are about the fact that both parties have different priorities. The money is the tug-of-war rope.

In the best of all worlds, we will have talked about our approaches to money BEFORE we launched into a committed relationship. Unfortunately, most of us find it far too easy to turn a blind eye to the financial shortcomings of someone with whom we've fallen in love. Later we wake up to the reality that we're not on the same page and it's causing problems.

It's tough when you love a person and your money personalities are very different. And it's tough dealing with the sense of betrayal if the person you love deceives you. If the problem is a serious one—your mate, for example, is a shopping addict or a compulsive gambler—you may need to seek help from a professional or group.

If your partner is suffering from "keeping up with the Joneses syndrome," it may be that he is insecure about himself and needs to find activities that give him a sense of accomplishment. Or maybe your mate is bored and she is shopping to fill a hole.

It's time to sit down together and talk about your differences with compassion and an open mind. Don't jump down your mate's throat, no matter what she says. Listen and acknowledge how hard talking about money is. But talk. And keep talking. Explain how worried you are because your mate's behaviour is having an impact on you. Explain, for example, that you think it is a big deal to run up debt you can't afford to repay. If you have children, explain how your partner's negative behaviour is putting the kids at risk.

How you say things will be the difference between being too hard and being loving and compassionate. Love your darling-heart to bits, hug him, and tell him how much you want to help. If she's upset because she thinks you're too tight with the money, then implement a system where you each get a specific, agreed-upon amount that you can blow any way you want. It may be $100 a month or more or less, depending on your financial situation. Even if it's just twenty bucks a month, it's yours to spend, no questions asked.

Ultimately, the point is to get on the same page when it comes to how you will deal with your money. **The way a couple deals with their money—handles it, copes with disappointments, negotiates disagreements—is a pretty strong predictor of the long-term success of their relationship.** Since disagreements about money tend to be intense, if you can manage those disagreements with civility and with a focus on solutions, just about everything else will be easier.

GETTING FINANCIAL CO-OPERATION

So, what if you're there, at that place where you aren't talking about money and no matter what you do you can't get your mate to pay attention?

1. First, remember that a committed relationship is about figuring out what's important to both people in the relationship.

2. Think of something that's really important to your mate, something that she requires your co-operation for: "You're counting on me to get that bathroom renovated because

you want the privacy of an ensuite." Then talk about how your mate would feel if you didn't co-operate. Tell her that the money thing is as important to you as that whatever is to her.

3. Ask your partner to commit to co-operating because this is so important to you. Tell him that you're not going to nag or bug. He's a big boy and perfectly capable of monitoring his own behaviour. However, if he does not meet you halfway on your need, you intend to back off on his. "I think saving for the future is just as important as getting a new car. You can count on me to keep cooking great meals if I can count on you to sock away just $100 a month for the future."

4. Do whatever you've said you'll do. If you don't follow through on the consequence you described, your mate will quickly figure out you're a pushover and just wait you out.

5. What if your mate won't even talk about money? If you've been trying to get your mate to sit down and talk with you about the bills and how you're going to pay them and he just won't, you may have to take drastic steps.

    • Imagine your husband arrives home, yelling your name as he comes tromping into the house. You're sitting in the living room buck naked. On your right breast is printed OVERDRAFT: $372.34, on your left breast is printed CREDIT CARD PAYMENT: $238. Do you think he'll laugh? Will he pay attention?

    • Use your imagination. You can see where I'm going with this. If it's the missus that's been acting like an ostrich, you can just go ahead and write on yourself wherever you think she'll pay the most attention.

- You may have to take your prodding public. This is hard, because people are so secretive about their money. But it may be necessary so your partner can see your frustration, your anger, your sense of desperation.
- Whatever outrageous step you take to get your partner's attention, know that he might get mad or she might throw a hissy fit. Warn them ahead of time that if they don't start bringing some positive attitude to the table, you're going to get desperate and do something crazy.

6. Once you do sit down to talk, it's crucial to talk not only about what's important, but why it is important. If your partner wants to take a vacation away from home every year, he may have the travel bug or he may have a desire to get you away from other distractions. Or he may simply want you all to himself for a while. Is there a less expensive way of achieving his goal?

7. Pick your discussion time carefully. Don't try to talk when you're mad. If you're angry about your mate's most recent financial misstep, you're ripe for a fight. Hold off until you're calm.

13 • PARENTAL PROTECTION SYNDROME

When Alice and Fred agreed to let their son, Derrick, move home after he finished university it was because Derrick said he wanted some time to get his student loans paid off. Initially, he had some trouble finding work and a year turned into two years. Fred was enjoying Derrick's company so much that when Derrick asked for another extension Fred agreed.

Alice wasn't a happy mommy. At first she'd been very happy to help Derrick but she was now growing tired of his unwillingness to grow up. Derrick worked full-time but lived like a teenager. Alice did his laundry, cooked his meals, and tried to collect the rent he'd agreed to pay when he'd found full-time work. Derrick always had a reason for why he wasn't able to pay what he'd said he would. First his car needed repairs. Then he needed a new car. Then he was planning to take his girlfriend, Celia, away for a vacation.

"Isn't Celia paying her own way?" asked Alice when Derrick presented her with his latest excuse.

"Come on, Mom," said Derrick. "Lighten up. It's my treat."

"Your treat?" asked Alice, "How is it your treat if you're doing it while you're eating our food?"

"Oh, relax, Alice," said Fred. "Don't get yourself all in a knot. The boy works hard and he's hardly ever here."

"Really, you don't see the grocery bills. For that matter, you don't see that Derrick isn't acting like a grown man."

"She's got herself all wound up because she thinks my room is a pigsty," laughed Derrick.

"It is a pigsty," replied his mother. "I had to do three loads of laundry to get all the clothes off the floor."

"I don't ask you to do my laundry. That's just something you seem to love to do," said Derrick.

Alice fumed. "Love to do? Are you crazy? I just can't stand the smell of your dirty clothes piled up in every corner of your room." Then she rounded on Fred. "Are you going to sit there and let him talk to me this way?"

"What way?" laughed Fred. "You two have been at each other since Derrick was a teenager. Nothin' ever changes."

Alice left the living room. As she went into her bedroom, she slammed the door. She could hear her two boys laughing in the living room. What was she going to do?

A generation of parents has been criticized for making life too easy for their offspring. In an effort to give their children the best opportunities, the most support, and the deepest love, some parents have shielded their kids from reality, leaving them unprepared to deal with adversity. Children have turned into young adults who expect that their parents will do whatever it takes to make them happy, without giving much thought to the impact this has on their parents. And when one parent sees the need for an adult child to take responsibility and the other thinks things are just fine the way they are, the result is conflict and resentment.

So, how do you get your mate to see that coddling your womb-fruit is a bad idea?

While you may have initially agreed to help your adult child, once you recognize that the help isn't helping, it's enabling, you will have to change the game. You might begin by asking how much help is enough. Most parents haven't given much thought to how long is long enough.

"Will it be okay for Derrick to live here when he's 30?" asked Alice.

"Don't be ridiculous," said Fred.

"Why is it ridiculous? How old were you when you moved out on your own?"

"I was 17."

"And Derrick is 25. So, how long is long enough?"

You might suggest that if the enabling parent wants the adult child to remain at home, he or she assume all responsibility for that child.

"I get that you love having Derrick at home," said Alice, "but I think this has gone on long enough."

"I'm not sure why you're making such a big deal of this," said Fred.

"Because I don't think it's good for him. He can't grow up as long as we're doing everything for him. So, as of this point, if you want to eat, you both will have to learn to cook. Ditto doing laundry and cleaning the house."

"You're going on strike?"

"I'm not going on strike. I'm letting you see that if Derrick is going to continue to live here, you both have some work to do."

If you contribute to the household financially, you might reduce that contribution.

"So, since you want Derrick to continue to live at home, I think it only fair that we reconsider our contributions to the budget. With three working adults, I'm planning to reduce my contribution for shelter and food to $560 a month."

"What?"

"We're all working. We're all living here, taking showers, and eating. We should all be sharing the costs. So, as of next month, all I'll be giving towards the household expenses is $560 a month."

"You can't do that!"

"Can't I?"

"We won't make the mortgage payment."

"Then you'd best reconsider whether Derrick is going to continue to live here rent free."

Once your mate sees the light—you may have to take pretty drastic steps to help them get over this first hurdle—you'll have to come up with a plan for helping your adult child come to terms with the new reality.

"So, Derrick, your dad and I have been talking about it, and we've decided we're fine with you living here as long as you follow some new rules."

"New rules? Like what?" asked Derrick, not really paying attention.

"Well, the first is you'll be giving us 35% of your take-home pay as rent."

"Not on your life," said Derrick.

"Then you'll have to find another place to live as of the end of this month," said Alice. "It's pay rent here or pay rent elsewhere, but the free ride is over."

Derrick went quiet for a moment. "Okay, what else?"

"You're also going to have to learn to . . ."

TALKING IT OUT WITH YOUR MATE

1. Explain to your partner that you're not trying to be punitive. You want your adult child to grow up and be a strong individual who can take care of him or herself.
2. Suggest ways in which you would like to see your adult child behave differently.
3. Explain what steps you will take if your mate does not co-operate in helping you disengage from supporting your adult child's life.

TALKING IT OUT WITH YOUR ADULT CHILD

1. Lay down the new rules for cohabiting in the same home. "You can live here for the next six months while you figure out where you're going and what you're doing. Your moving date is June 12."
2. Do not provide spending money to an adult child, working or not. It is enough that you are providing room and board for a specific period of time.
3. Insist that your adult child assume household responsibilities. "It's your turn to cook dinner on Tuesdays, Thursdays, and Sundays."
4. Learn to listen to your child's problems and concerns without offering suggestions. Ask questions but offer no solutions. You want your young adult to learn to find solutions and make decisions.
5. If you see your adult child headed towards a mistake, ask them to consider the consequences of whatever action they're taking, but don't try to save them. Consequences

are the best teachers. Mistakes are how we know to do it differently the next time.

6. If your adult child is working, he or she must contribute 35% of his or her net income to the household, no ifs, ands, or buts. You can decide if you will use this money for expenses or save it to gift it back to your child when he or she moves out. But you want your young adult to learn to live within his or her means.

· · ·

As a species our greatest gift is our ability to adapt. Our greatest curse is our belief that wherever we are now is where we're going to be forever. So, while we're skilled at learning and growing, we think things will never change. We are our own highest hurdles. We have to work at getting our heads wrapped around the fact that change is necessary and action is required.

The world is not static and neither is your life. It doesn't matter how much you wish things would stay the same. They won't. Hold tight to the way things were and you're going to end up very sad and, perhaps, broke.

As a child growing up in Jamaica, I had no idea that paradise would turn into a political nightmare and my family would be forced to leave home and start over. When I married for the first time, I was under the impression that marriage was forever. But that would have meant being miserable for the rest of my life. Despite the fact that change was necessary, it was hard. And divorce has, for my whole life, been cast as failure. That's what divorce is, right? But how could staying in the wrong relationship ever be cast as success?

I've moved countries, moved houses, changed husbands, had children, changed careers, said goodbye to friends too soon, and accepted having to do things I always swore I would never do. Each time I've been forced to change my game, dealing with change has gotten easier. Not less painful, just less surprising. And my barriers to change have come down as I've learned some very important lessons:

- Home is wherever you are.
- Love is wonderful until it isn't.
- Change is easier with some money in the bank.
- You gotta know when to fold 'em.
- I am strong.

As soon as you think things are set, along will come a force to push you in a direction you may never have imagined. You don't have to allow yourself to be pushed, but you do have to think about your diverging paths and choose the one you'll follow. And regardless of which one you choose, you will have to choose again and again and again, because there is no permanence.

Each time you experience a change—any change, good or bad—look at your life and how you're living it, and your money and how you're using it. If you lose your job and try to maintain your old lifestyle, things will eventually fall apart. Buy a house and try to keep up with your old friends' entertainment plans and you'll end up living in overdraft. Have a baby and keep getting manis and pedis twice a month on your maternity-leave benefits and you'll go broke.

Instead of worst-casing what will go wrong if you attempt to change, spend some time thinking about how much worse things will get if you don't change course. Imagine yourself down the road dealing with the implications of your current actions.

When you decide that you can no longer stay the course—that change is as inevitable as your next breath—it's important to accept that what comes next will take tenacity and gumption. Whether you're changing something in your own life, or trying to help someone else see that change is a must, making the change happen won't be a cakewalk.

Practise patience. Don't be judgmental. Keep your sense of humour. If you take two steps forward and one back, that's okay; you're making progress. Bit by bit you're moving towards a different future.

As long as you're doing your best, you're doing fine. We are all works in progress.

Part Three

BREAKING THROUGH DENIAL AND DELUSION

People have an amazing ability to believe with all their heart that the things they wish were true can become true. When that belief fosters hard work and creativity, it is a good thing. When it leads to denial of our limits or to delusions of grandeur, not so much.

It's one thing to believe in yourself. It's another thing entirely to be unwilling to do the hard work of making sure those dreams don't turn into mirages. And as for all the people who don't even want to know—who have buried themselves up to their eyeballs in self-deception—geez Louise!

Denial is one of the most well-documented psychological defence mechanisms. We readily accept that alcoholics deny they have a drinking problem. We understand why drug abusers are unwilling to acknowledge their dependency on their drug of choice. But what of the run-of-the-mill, day-to-day deniers?

Look in the mirror. You're one of them. Psychologists say we all partake in denial to a greater or lesser degree. In the extreme, regardless of overwhelming evidence, a body will continue to deny the existence of a problem because said body just doesn't want to have to deal with the truth. Ranging from flat-out rejection of reality—"I am not selling my home. There's no way the bank will make me. I'm a single mom with three kids! It would be a public relations disaster"—to an amazing ability to minimize the importance of the truth—"Sure, I've got a ton of debt, but everybody's got a ton of debt"—people seek to keep reality at bay.

While it can be very destructive, the ability to look the other way is one of those tricks we learn to help us deal with the disappointments that arise in our lives. Hubster isn't as attentive as he once was. Mom shows a decided preference for my baby brother. This job is only until I figure out how to launch my small business.

Sometimes people choose to remain ignorant—"I don't want to know how much this is costing me in interest!"— because being informed would mean accepting the need to do something differently. Denial is so much easier. Some people experience denial because the truth is too hard to bear— "How could I possibly lose my home?" Their minds shut down and refuse to process the new information because it is just too painful. And sometimes people embrace delusion because they've experienced success that makes them feel invincible, as in, "I am in complete control. I've got this!"

No one can get away with denial forever. Eventually reality, made worse by days, months, or years of being ignored, will bite you in the butt. And yet, it's almost impossible for a body to recognize when it is in denial. You better hope to hell someone loves you enough to step in and tell you to pull your head out of the sand.

If you're living with lovies who are in denial, opening their eyes will be the biggest gift you ever give them. If your lovies are delusional, they will beat you back with the forces of Wellington at Waterloo to hang on to their delusions. But if you really do love them, or if their denial and delusions are hurting you, arm yourself for battle.

14 • DELUSIONAL THINKERS

Geoff was a self-made man. He started his own landscaping business in his 20s and after 15 years had four greenhouses and a staff of 80 during peak periods. From the get-go he'd been determined to make the business work, so he took only the bare minimum as pay—just enough to live on. In about year 10 he won five really big landscaping contracts and the money just kept rolling in. Geoff had made it.

When his bookkeeper, Lanie, told him that he better slow down on the spending, he just laughed. "I'm making so much money I can't possibly be overspending," he replied. After years of going without, Geoff was making up for lost time. He bought himself a snappy new truck, bought his wife a new van, and took the whole family, his mom included, on a two-week vacation to Costa Rica.

Lanie had been keeping Geoff's books from the beginning. His mom's best friend, Lanie had watched as Geoff did everything right to make the business work. She was proud of his success. But she was a little concerned about the latest trend she was seeing. It was almost as if having gone without for so long, Geoff was determined to spend all the money he could.

When the family returned from Costa Rica, Lanie decided to have another word with Geoff to explain where the fabric of his business was fraying.

"You've spent a lot of money in a really short period of time," Lanie said.

"It's fine," Geoff replied. "Our cash flow is solid and we have money in the bank."

"We won't if you keep this up," Lanie replied. "You're spending the contract retainers at a wicked clip. How are you going to do the initial material buys without extending your line of credit?"

"So, we'll extend it," said Geoff matter-of-factly. "The bank won't have a problem with that. I've got signed contracts in hand."

"But you already have a line that's costing you almost $200 a month in interest."

"C'mon, Lanie," said Geoff. "That's the cost of doing business. That's nothing compared to the money we're bringing in."

Lanie chose her words carefully. "The bank is perfectly happy to extend you all the credit you need to hang yourself. You've worked hard to build this business up. But with the mortgage you've got on the greenhouse property, and $50,000 already on the line, you could find yourself overextended. And you know you need a new backhoe in the spring. That's more financing. I'm just saying that I think you should slow down a little."

Geoff was getting irritated with Lanie. Maybe she was getting too old to see that you needed to borrow to make a business work. Besides, she was only a bookkeeper. She couldn't see the big picture. As long as he was making his payments, everything would be fine. "Okay," he said to Lanie. "Maybe you're right." Then he decided he'd start looking for a younger, more progressive advisor.

Money delusions come in all shapes and sizes. There's the "We make so much we'll never spend it all" delusion that comes after you've achieved a certain level of financial success. Sadly, those people might spend it all, and sometimes even more, on credit.

Then there's the "As long as we're making our payments

we're fine" delusion. Having never calculated how much interest they'll end up paying, or how long it'll take to get out of debt, folks are quite happy to live in a bubble of ignorance.

And then there's the ever-popular "It's only $___. How can that be a problem?" delusion. Unwilling to add up their small indulgences, these people commit financial suicide by a thousand cuts.

Delusion is linked to denial, as in, "I don't have to track my spending. I make more than enough money." The denial: money is a finite resource. In choosing to deny reality, folks then set about creating a delusion to support their belief.

Gary and Edward had been together for more than 11 years. When they bought their first home, they were happy with a two-bedroom bungalow on a small lot in a quiet neighbourhood. As Gary's interior design business took off, he wanted a bigger canvas to work with at home. So he talked Edward into buying up. Since Gary was the major breadwinner, Edward agreed. "If you think we can afford it."

Over the years they renovated just about every room in the house, and the kitchen twice. When they had friends to dinner, as they oohed and aahed over Gary's latest installation, Edward would laugh and say that Gary could always find something to fix in their already perfect home. The third time Gary wanted to refinance the house, to pay for a backyard upgrade, Edward put his foot down. "This has got to stop, Gary," he said. "We're already mortgaged to the hilt. And I'm worried about how we'll get this paid off before we retire."

"Hey, with property values going up, we just add more value to the resale price every time we make an improvement."

There are people who repeatedly borrow against the equity in their homes to pay off vehicle purchases, pay down credit card balances, or finance renovations. They're operating under the delusion that real estate prices will always go up. There are people who continue to accept credit limit increases on their credit cards and lines of credit. They're operating under the delusion that lenders wouldn't give them access to credit they couldn't afford to pay back. And there are people who believe that because they work hard, they should also get to play hard, regardless of whether they have the money to pay for their pleasure. They're operating under the delusion that they can have whatever they want whenever they want it.

Delusions show up all over the place. If you're banking on winning the lottery as your retirement plan, you're delusional. You're more likely to be struck by lightning twice than to win the lottery. If you skip filing your tax returns, you're delusional. The Tax Man will just assess you at his whim and then go into your account and take whatever he wants. (Yes, he can do that.) If you're paying bills late, living in overdraft, or spending your future income when you go shopping, you're delusional. It's only a matter of time before you hit a wall.

Before you can help a person with his or her delusions, you must gather the facts that tell the real story. But you can't just take something (the delusion) away. You must find something with which to replace the delusion so there's less of a sense of loss, and more of a sense of changing direction.

Arush is married to a lovely woman named Chanda. Both are teachers. Chanda helped put Arush through school, earns more, and just had a baby. Arush thinks gambling online, playing golf, and having fun with the boys is the be-all of life. Arush and Chanda are living well beyond their means. Chanda knows it. She's distraught. Arush thinks Chanda is a tight-ass and wishes she'd loosen up.

Chanda decided to prove to Arush just what's been happening with the money. She got six months' worth of credit card and bank statements and tracked where every penny had gone. Then she put all the info on a spreadsheet. It clearly showed that, as a couple, they were overspending by almost 25%. It also showed that Arush was spending six times as much on entertainment as Chanda was, and that Chanda was spending nothing on interest while Arush was spending almost $475 a month making just his minimum payments.

When they sat down together, he spent a lot of time telling her this was exactly what he expected of her and that she was wasting her time with this. He wasn't giving up his golf. And he wasn't about to become all buttoned down about money, if that's what she was hoping for.

Chanda pulled one chart out of her stack and pointed to it. "At this rate, by the time you get your debt paid off, you'll have spent $63,762.97 in interest," she said.

It's very easy, when we think our mate, best friend, or parent is delusional, to let a money talk disintegrate into a war of words because "we know we are right." **Toxic talks come from a combat mentality.** While your mate may feel the need to win, if you join this battle you both will lose. Resist the temptation to cast what the other person is saying into "ridiculous" territory by reducing them to rubble with your witty words. The point is not to win the discussion; the point is to get your lovie to see things in a different light, to put reality where delusion has been living. For that, you need to have the facts at your fingertips, you must remain cool, and you should let the other person express their own feelings and thoughts so you can get to the bottom of the delusion.

"Tell me," said Chanda, "why you think it's okay to spend money on stuff we don't really need when we have all this debt."

"Everyone has debt," replied Arush, brushing aside Chanda's statement.

"Not everyone, my love, but we certainly do. And what else could we do with the $64,000 in interest we'll end up paying? You're always talking about wanting to travel. Wouldn't that money be better used on us than on paying interest to a bank?"

"If we put all our money towards paying off our debt, we'll be working our butts off and having no fun at all."

"Tell me one thing you want to make sure you can keep on doing."

"If I can't golf, my summer will be ruined."

Chanda ignored the drama. "So, how often do you think it's reasonable to golf?"

"I'd play every day if I could," replied Arush.

"I know you would; you love to golf. But you're going to have to get a job this summer if we're going to make any headway with the debt."

"What? You get to stay home and play with the baby while I have to work my whole summer?"

"No, that's not what I was thinking at all," said Chanda. "I thought you could work July and then you could take a month of parental leave and I'd work August. We'd put everything we can against the debt. And then next year you can get a part-time job on the weekends, or you can take over child care and I'll get a part-time job to keep the momentum going."

"All we'll be doing is working and taking care of the baby," whined Arush.

"Yes, it will feel that way for a while," said Chanda, "but working hard is how we get out of debt."

"Or we could just declare bankruptcy," said Arush.

"You may think that's easier," said Chanda, "but I've looked into it and we'll not only lose your car and the house because of the equity we have, but all the money we've put into Kanti's RESP will go too."

"Man, they get you whichever way you turn, don't they?"

"Actually, you did this, Arush, no one else. Nobody made you take out all that credit and turn it into debt. And now that you've had your fun, it's time to pay up. That's your reality."

"So, this is all my fault?"

"What do you think, Arush? Do you want to look at fault, or do you want to look at ways to solve the problem?"

DEALING WITH DELUSION

Since the only way to overcome delusion is with fact, you must gather information that you can present to bring your dear one into the here and now.

1. Insist on tracking every single penny spent during the month. Suggest it as a one-month exercise and then extend it to three, to get a good picture of where the money is going.

2. Use the information you've gathered to do a spending analysis. Alternatively, gather six months' worth of financial paperwork (assuming you can lay your hands on it)

and do a spending analysis. (A how-to for doing a spending analysis is described in *Debt-Free Forever*.)

3. Compare where the money has been going to where the money should be going (i.e., budget). (See Appendix 1: Building a Budget.)

4. If there is outstanding debt,

   a) calculate the monthly interest costs (for all the debt);

   b) calculate the total monthly interest by the time the debt is paid off; and

   c) calculate how long it will take to get the debt paid off.

5. Ask your dear one what his or her goals are in very concrete terms. How much will he need to go back to school? How much will her dream vacation cost? Talk about the money that could be used to achieve those goals if it were not being used to pay interest.

15 • I DON'T WANT TO KNOW

Victoria and Greg met in university, after which Victoria did a stint in China teaching English, while Greg moved to the West Coast to work for a start-up. The start-up blew up and 18 months later he was on the other side of the country working for an NGO. That's where Victoria connected with him again. She'd just returned home to hang out with her folks while she decided what she was going to do next, when she ran into Greg at a local bookstore.

It was a whirlwind romance. Six months in, Greg proposed and Victoria responded by asking to see his balance sheet. She'd worked hard to get her student debt paid off and she had the sense that Greg wasn't anywhere close to having his paid off.

Resistant at first, Greg pulled out all the old standbys: Don't you love me? Don't you trust me? Do you think I'm an idiot?

"Yes, yes, and I don't know," said Victoria. "That's what I'm trying to figure out. Because, while I love you, I'm not about to take two steps back financially. It's been a tough slog getting out of debt and I'm done with it."

Eventually Greg gave in to Victoria's insistence that they have the money talk. She asked him to gather up all his paperwork. He came with half of it stuffed into an old shoebox and she sent him away. "This is important to me," she said. "If that's not enough to make this important to you too, then I'm not sure we can get past this hurdle." A week later he showed up with his paperwork organized.

"Have you added up what you owe?" Victoria asked as she flipped through student loan statements, a vehicle lease, a couple of credit card statements, and an RRSP loan statement.

"Added it up?" asked Greg. Victoria shook her head. She loved this man but this looked like it would be more work than even she had anticipated.

"Don't you want to know how much you owe?" she asked.

"No," Greg said as he slowly shook his head from side to side. "I do NOT want to know how much I owe. I've got payments for everything and that's all I need to know."

Victoria opened her phone's calculator. She turned to Greg and said, "You owe $67,000."

"That's not possible," said Greg.

"It sure is," said Victoria. "You've got $18,000 left on your student loan, these credit card balances add up to $5,000, and who talked you into an RRSP loan for $8,000?"

"My advisor said it would be a good idea."

"Yeah, well, what did you do with your tax refund?"

"I used it buy a bed and a couch. I was tired of sleeping on a mattress on the floor and sitting on hand-me-downs. But that's still not $67,000."

"Your van is $36,000?"

"It's a lease."

"And your point?"

"In two years I just give it back."

Victoria started laughing.

"What?" asked Greg.

"Did you read your lease?" asked Victoria, trying to stifle her guffaws. "You've got a guaranteed buyout."

"What do you mean?" asked Greg, scrambling for the paper.

"Why didn't you read the lease?" asked Victoria.

"I dunno," said Greg, who was beginning to seriously dislike this exercise.

"You didn't want to know?" asked Victoria. But it was more of a statement than a question. "Well, you probably agreed to the guaranteed buyout because of all the kilometres you put on your van in a year. You'd have used up most of your lease allowance in the first 18 months."

"Yes," said Greg remembering the conversation he'd had with the salesman. "I could pay for the extra kilometres or buy out the van, which was the better deal."

"Okay," said Victoria, "but that means you're on the hook for the whole thing, so you have to add it to your debt."

They sat and talked about a debt repayment plan that would see him done with his debt in just 24 months. It would be a tough haul, but since Victoria refused to get married without having money in the bank to start their life together, he knew it was the only way.

People think that it's okay to just not know what's going on— everything will be fine. It won't. And when one partner wants the other to pay attention, and the mate won't, it's like a slap in the face. If money issues are important to one partner they must be important to both. **If a person insists on holding on to their ignorance, what they're really saying is that their own discomfort is more of an issue than their mate's priorities.** It's a selfish act and it should be seen as such.

Loads of people don't want to know about their debt. They refuse to add it up because keeping it in separate piles makes the debt feel smaller. Each time I've insisted that folks add up their debt—make it into one number—it's taken the wind out of their sails. "I don't want to know" is perhaps one of the most destructive financial attitudes. You know the old saying "Ignorance is bliss"? It's not. It's just ignorance.

Mary and Nathan had been married for six years when Nathan reached the end of his rope. "We have to make wills, Mary. Ignoring this issue isn't going to make it go away. We've got two beautiful kids and we have no plan."

"You're wrong," said Mary. "I plan on not dying any time soon."

"And do you think Trevor planned to die when he got knocked off his motorcycle last week?" Nathan had been stunned when his buddy was killed. At the funeral, he watched as Trevor's wife, Crystal, held their newborn baby and cried.

"I know Trev's funeral was hard on you," said Mary, "but you're over-reacting. Nothing bad is going to happen to us. Besides, where are we going to come up with the money right now to do something like make wills?"

"We have to find it," said Nathan. "I don't care how non-essential you think this is, I think it's a must-have and I'm moving it up on the list of things we're going to do this year."

Mary smiled. "Okay, okay," she said. She knew this would blow over as soon as Nathan had time to calm down about Trevor. "You come up with who you think would be better at raising our children than us and I'm there!"

Nathan didn't calm down. He made an appointment for Mary and himself to see an estate lawyer about wills and powers of attorney. Sitting in the waiting room before the appointment, Mary shook her head. "How did I let you talk me into this? You know what this is going to cost us?"

Sheilagh greeted Nathan and Mary warmly. As they sat on the large sofa in her office, she sat in an armchair to the side with a pad on her lap. "So, how can I help you today?" she asked.

Nathan looked at Mary and then said, "Mary and I don't have wills and I think it's time we did. She's not convinced they're important."

"I know they're important," said Mary. "I just think we still have things to think about and some time to do this. Nathan's got a bee in his bonnet right now."

"Do you have any children?" asked Sheilagh.

"We have two," said Nathan.

Sheilagh nodded and made a note. "And what do you think will happen if you die without a will?" she asked.

Mary and Nathan sat quietly for a moment. Neither actually knew what would happen. "It would be a big mess," Nathan finally said.

"It's not like we're going to die at the same time," said Mary. "The kids would still have one of us."

"Maybe," said Sheilagh. "But the pain of loss can be so deep that without a clear plan for how to cope, survivors often struggle with decisions that should have been made when there was no emotional stress."

Mary nodded. That made sense.

"Besides," said Sheilagh, "people have the weirdest ideas about what they can or can't do legally. For example, let's say Nathan was ill and unable to speak for himself. If you didn't have power of attorney in place, you wouldn't have the right to direct his medical care."

"But I'm his wife," said Mary.

"Means nothing without the right legal paperwork in place," said Sheilagh. "And if your mortgage came up for renewal and you're both on the title, you couldn't renew without his signature, even if both his arms were broken!"

"Huh," said Mary, the reality of the situation dawning.

"Have you thought about who will look after your kids if you should both die?" asked Sheilagh.

"No," said Mary. "I don't want to think about how my children would have to cope if I were to die."

"Not wanting to is natural," said Sheilagh. "Not doing it, well, that's kind of like sticking your head in the sand, isn't it?"

Some of the things you need to talk about are hard to address because the person to whom you must talk just doesn't want to know. Dealing with their own demise, imagining the sorrow or discomfort of others, making difficult choices that might tick someone else off can all be so insurmountable in people's minds that they duck and hide. But being a responsible adult means doing hard things when they are the right things to do.

When Matt and Caitlyn sat down to dinner, they were celebrating the promotion Caitlyn had just been given. "I am so looking forward to having enough money to not have to decide between a morning coffee and my next vacation," laughed Caitlyn.

Matt picked up a piece of garlic bread and popped it into his mouth. "I'm heading to San Diego next month for a week," he said.

"Aren't you the guy who told me yesterday that you're worried about the hours you've been losing at work? So you're going to San Diego?"

"Paul, Keith, and I made this plan months ago," replied Matt matter-of-factly.

"And you don't think you might have to change the plan because your circumstances have changed?"

"Nope," he said. He perused the menu. "I'm thinking grilled octopus and maybe the dolmades to start."

"You know what I'm having," replied Caitlyn.

"Quail!" they chorused. They raised their wine glasses, clinked, and sipped.

Caitlyn and Matt had been friends since high school. Every month they met for dinner. They'd dated once, briefly. Now they were the best of friends. They saw each other as much as they could, but when life got busy it was this monthly dinner date that kept them connected.

Caitlyn had always been detail oriented when it came to her money. Matt liked to fly by the seat of his pants. And it didn't much matter what Caitlyn said, Matt managed to change the subject so that they didn't talk about money.

"Ha," she laughed at him. "You are so determined to not talk about this stuff. Why is that?"

"I dunno," he said. "It wasn't something anyone talked about in my house."

"As opposed to my house," said Caitlyn, "where my mother shared the budget and put me in charge of cutting the hydro bill so we could go on vacation!"

People's family histories play a part in their willingness to talk about money openly. Come from a home where nobody talked about money—or worse, where money talks were drag 'em down fights—and it's not surprising folks are reluctant to put financial issues on the table.

Parents who feel they aren't good at managing their own money are hesitant to raise the issue with their children, continuing the cycle of not talking and not learning. But we are all exposed to so much temptation to consume, to easy credit, to the idea that what we own says something about us. Our reluctance to talk just leaves us unprepared to cope with the temptations and challenges.

The result is people who just don't want to know what's

going on in their financial lives. As long as they don't know, they won't have to address the situation they're actually in by talking about it or doing something differently. "I don't know" becomes the justification for not doing anything any differently. And "We don't talk about that" is the agreed-upon strategy for keeping "I don't know" in place.

GET 'EM TALKIN'

Getting people who don't want to know to deal with their reality will involve using strategies that get their attention and address the issues they are avoiding. You can

1. Be direct. "So, did you see the article in the paper today about the guy who died and left his wife with three kids and no insurance? How would the kids and I cope if you turned up your toes tomorrow?"

2. Use an expert. "I'm making the appointment for us. We're going together to talk about this issue with someone who knows more than we do."

3. Know the facts. If your mate, parent, best friend, or brother tries to obfuscate and you don't know the facts, they'll get away with it. Ask for the paperwork, gather the correct information, know the ins and outs of whatever it is you plan to discuss. "I know you think you only owe $18,743, but you're leaving out your overdraft and that buy-now-pay-later you signed up for. So add those in too."

4. Avoid blame, anger, or other negative emotions. "This is getting heated. I'm going to suggest we take a break and resume when cooler heads prevail. Let's make a date for coffee next Wednesday."

5. Insist that the truth be at the centre of the discussion. We are very good at colouring stories to make things look the way we want them to.

"Yes, I know I have that RRSP loan for $8,000 but that's good debt, right?"

"Dude, it's only good debt if you're using it to increase your net worth in some way. If you have an $8,000 RRSP and an $8,000 loan, you own nothing. So get that puppy paid off and then we'll talk."

6. Don't let it go. It may take several attempts to open up the Money Talk. And your attempts may be met with constant parries that leave you wondering how you're going to ever get through. Don't give up. Eventually you may have to set a date to at least begin the conversation. "Prepare yourself because next week we're sitting down to work through this."

16 • NOT ENOUGH MONEY TO BUDGET

It was a warm, sunny spring day when Gina and Scott met on the patio of their local coffee shop. After a hard winter being locked up in small apartments, it was good to get out and breathe. Just sitting in the sunshine made Gina happy. Scott, well, Scott was complaining about how much money he didn't have. But Scott was always complaining.

"Hydro bill almost killed me this winter," he said as he took a sip of his macchiato.

Gina looked at him over her skinny latte and grinned. "So, it wasn't the TGIF binges?"

"Don't even get me started. Do you have any idea how long it's been since I've done anything fun?"

"No money?" asked Gina, knowing that was exactly what was coming next.

"Exactly!" agreed Scott.

"Your problem isn't no money, it's no budget."

"What do I have to budget with?" asked Scott, his voice rising in objection.

"You make as much as I do, maybe even a little more," said Gina, "but you have no idea what you're doing with it."

"I pay rent, utilities, get my transit pass, bring in some food, and it's gone," moaned Scott. "Who needs a budget when there's nothing left to budget with?"

"Everyone needs a budget," said Gina. "Even if you're a Richie Rich, knowing where your money goes makes good sense."

"Like those guys bother with budgeting," scoffed Scott.

"That's how they got to be Richie Rich," replied Gina.

"Well, I don't think it'll make any difference," said Scott.

"It's usually the Poor Richards like you who think that having a budget isn't worthwhile," replied Gina. "But I can tell you from experience, keeping track of your monthly income and expenses lets you make sure your hard-earned money is being put to its best use. Knowledge is power, dude."

Convincing someone a budget is a good idea can be a tough job. People throw all kinds of excuses out for why they can't budget, with "not enough money to bother" at the top of the list. Having a single conversation is unlikely to make a difference, but over time you can demonstrate how having a budget puts you in the driver's seat.

Several weeks later when Scott and Gina met for lunch, the air smelled of lilacs. Gina took a deep breath as she pulled out her chair.

"This might be my favourite time of year," she said. "Next winter I have plans to run away for a week, maybe even two, so spring at least feels like it's coming faster."

"Run away where?" asked Scott.

"I'm not sure yet. Maybe Mexico, maybe Jamaica. Somewhere warm."

"Ha!" exclaimed Scott, "You've finally come to your senses. See, sometimes it's worth going into the hole."

"No, sir," said Gina, with a grin. "That's your answer, not mine. I'll have the money I need saved before I put that charge on my credit card. And the bill will be paid off before I go away."

"How the hell will you manage that?" asked Scott incredulously.

"You don't want to know," said Gina. "Every time we talk about money you stick your fingers in your ears and go, 'la la la la la' like I'm talking trash to you."

"Seriously, you have the money for a vacation next winter?"

"I will by the time winter rolls around," answered Gina. "I'll have the Cobb salad," Gina said to the waitress who had come to take their order. "Hold the blue cheese. And dressing on the side, 'kay?"

"Anything to drink?" asked the waitress.

"Water's fine," said Gina.

Scott ordered a turkey and sun-dried tomato panini, french fries, and a beer. "Okay," he said "you're going to go all budget on me again, aren't you?"

"Nope, I just wanted to tell you I'm going on vacation next year," said Gina in a tone that clearly implied she was winning.

"Fine," said Scott, "tell me how you did it."

"First off," said Gina, "a budget isn't like putting on a straitjacket. It's my choices for how I'll spend my money. And it lets me see if I'm living within my means." Gina pulled out a piece of paper from her handbag and unfolded it. She pointed to the top. "There's my income," she said, and as she ran her finger down the first column, she continued. "And there are my expenses. That's how I plan to spend my money."

"You just happened to have your budget with you?" asked Scott.

"Nope," said Gina. "I knew you'd be curious about how I was paying for the vacation you wish you could take, so I brought the budget along to show you how I'm doing it." Gina pointed to the row labelled "Vacation" and then pointed to the corresponding number: $160. "I'm setting aside $160 a month for my vacation fund."

A budget gives you control. Do you have dreams of things you'd like to have, places you'd like to go, experiences you'd like to, well, experience? With a budget, you set money aside for specific purposes, be it your children's education, that family holiday, or renovating the kitchen. With a budget, those dreams and aspirations don't have to go ignored because you keep getting to the end of the month only to find the money is all gone.

"Okay," said Scott, "I've tried that, but every time I get anything decent set aside, something unexpected comes along that I have to pay for and I'm back to zero."

"That's because you're doing it without a budget," said Gina. "A budget anticipates expenses. Without a budget, you think of most of your less regular expenses as unexpected. You've forgotten about some bill that comes less often than monthly so you're shocked and surprised when it arrives. With a budget, not only would you know when to expect that bill, you'd have set aside one-twelfth of the total each month, so paying it would be no problemo."

"So, you budgeted for this lunch today?" asked Scott skeptically.

"I actually did," said Gina, pointing to the Restaurants line. "I budget $125 a month for eating out, and when the money is gone I don't eat out any more. That's one reason I ordered water today. I make a choice to reduce what I spend each time so I don't blow through the amount too fast."

"Huh," said Scott, the light dawning. "So, your budget keeps you focused."

"Yeah," said Gina, "it's a lot harder to spend willy-nilly when you're on a budget because you've accounted for where the money is going down to the last penny."

"What do you do if you put some number in your budget and you miss?" asked Scott as he leaned back to let the waitress put his food in front of him.

"If you find a category isn't working because there's not enough money in it, you have to cut from another category to make the budget balance," said Gina. "So if something came up and I ended up spending $150 in restaurants, I'd have to trim the extra $25 from some other category."

"Like your vacation fund?"

"Exactly, and since I don't want to do that, I make damn sure I stay on track so I can have that vacation. With every cent accounted for, there are no surprises."

"Sounds like torture to me," said Scott, picking up a french fry, dipping it in ketchup, and popping it into his mouth.

"'Course it does," said Gina. She picked up her fork, dipped it in her dressing, and swirled the fork to gather up some salad. "You're one of the most undisciplined people I've ever met."

"Now, now, no need to go casting aspersions."

"Well, it's true. You're an in-the-moment kinda guy. Budgeting is about making a plan and sticking to it. Not everyone is prepared to be a grown-up and spend money consciously. You like the rush of spending on a whim."

Scott nodded, taking a bite out of his panini.

Gina continued. "People like you are most in need of a budget because you have no self-control."

"I like to do things on the spur of the moment, but I wouldn't go that far."

"Really?" asked Gina. "When Jay invited you to that concert last week, you didn't have the money to go, so why did you go?"

"That concert was great!" said Scott.

"You didn't have the money," repeated Gina.

"Yeah, I know. And I ended up shorting my cellphone payment so I'm going to have to find a way to catch that up."

"Damn, Scott, that's exactly what I'm talking about."

"So, if I called you for lunch today and your restaurant money was all gone, you'd have said no to meeting up with me?" asked Scott.

"I might have suggested you come to my place or I go to yours," said Gina. "Or I might have had lunch at home and then met you for a cup of coffee."

"Hmm," said Scott. "If I wanted to give this budget thing a try, you'd help me get started?"

"I sure would," said Gina, "and then maybe one winter we can take a vacation together."

"Maybe next winter?" said Scott.

"Maybe not," said Gina. "Don't expect too much too quickly. It takes time to get used to living on a budget. If you fall a little off-track in those early months, the trick is to correct your course and keep going."

"How often do you fall off?" asked Scott.

"Oh, I never fall off now," said Gina, "but I've been doing this for a while. Eventually it becomes second nature. But when you get started it's easy to underestimate how much you'll spend on categories like food."

"I have no idea what I spend on food. Do you just guess those amounts?"

"If you do, then you haven't really made a budget," said Gina, forking a piece of egg into her mouth. "For it to be a real budget it has to be based on your reality. And for that, you need to do a spending analysis."

"Which you're going to help me with," said Scott matter-of-factly.

"Yup," replied Gina.

"So, how often do you redo your budget?" asked Scott.

"About once a year, unless there's some big change like when I moved last year, or if I were to get a raise."

"And this is how you're going away next winter without coming back to a bigger credit card balance?" said Scott, waving his hand over

Gina's budget, which had been splashed with water and coffee and was looking a little worse for the outing.

"Yes, it is. It's not magic. It's discipline," said Gina.

"Where have I heard that before?" asked Scott, laughing.

I wish more people would help their families and friends like this. **Not everyone can deal with the concept of a budget in the abstract. Loads of people need concrete proof that money is an exhaustible resource to be convinced that a budget is an important tool.** And if those who already saw the benefit of budgeting spread the message more, we'd have a lot more people talking about planned spending and fewer bemoaning the amount of debt they have.

I know that people are reluctant to talk about money— except when they meet me at a store or in a parking lot; then it all comes pouring out. Ignorance is a huge barrier for so many people. We HAVE to start talking about money. We have to help each other figure out how money works and what tools we'll need to help us get—and stay—on track.

I'm tired of listening to the excuses for why people are bad with money. We're not all bad with money. Some of us do just fine. If people really want help, they need to start asking for it. And if people really want to help they must tell others, so everyone knows they're available.

Do you want to remain ignorant about money? To fall victim to whatever agenda bankers, lenders, and investment advisers have when dealing with you? Or do you want to get smarter about money and put yourself in the position of being able to make informed decisions?

Miriam has been helping her mom with her finances for about a year, starting just after her dad died. Her mom, Eleanor, lives alone with two cats. She still works part-time and receives 50% of her husband's pension.

Just five months before he died, Eleanor and Jack moved into a new seniors' apartment. It's a two-bedroom, which is too pricey for Eleanor's lower income. She's on a waiting list for a one-bedroom, but for now she's paying a higher rent than she would like.

Sitting at the kitchen table, Miriam reviewed Eleanor's latest credit card and bank statements. "Can you really afford to be spending $400 on clothes like this?" she asked her mom as she looked at the unpaid balance. "And you're paying to get the car washed? Mom, you can't afford that."

"Your dad always washed the car every Saturday," replied Eleanor. "He said it was important to keep it clean. I'm just doing what he said."

"Here, you ordered these candles online," said Miriam, pointing to a line on the credit card bill. "You're carrying a balance and you order candles?"

"I don't like it when the apartment gets that stale smell," said Eleanor. "The candles help keep the air fresh."

Miriam sighed. Her mother's cellphone bill was over $100, she was spending about $130 a month on groceries, and she went way overboard buying presents for her grandchildren's birthdays.

"Mom, you're living bigger than your budget. I have two kids to provide for and my own retirement to save for. I can't bail you out if you rack up any more debt."

"I'm not asking you to bail me out," said Eleanor indignantly. "I'm sorry I even asked you to help. It's just that your dad always did the money and I needed some help. But I don't need a lecture."

Miriam thought for a moment. Then she went over to her mom's change jar and brought it back to the table. She said, "Where's that big flip-chart paper dad used for his sales meetings?"

"In the second bedroom closet," said Eleanor.

Miriam found the pad and ripped off two pieces of paper. She grabbed a marker and got down on the kitchen floor with her supplies. "Okay," she said to her mom, "let's work through this together." Miriam wrote "Income" at the top of the page. "How much do you get a month to live on?" she asked.

"Well," said Eleanor, "I get about $750 from your dad's pension and another $550 from CPP [Canada Pension Plan] and $500 from OAS [Old Age Security]. So that's $1,800."

Miriam noted the amounts on the flip-chart paper. "And how much do you make from your part-time job?"

"Oh, anywhere from $400 to $600 a month," said Eleanor.

"So, we'll take an average of $500, which means you have a monthly income of $2,300," said Miriam, totalling her mother's income. "I want you to count out 460 coins. Every coin will represent $5, for a total of $2,300. Then we'll get busy balancing your budget."

"I really should roll these and take them to the bank," said Eleanor as she dumped the coins onto the table. She began to count. When she was finished, she scooped the remaining coins back into the jar. "Fine. I have 460 coins here."

"Great," said Miriam. "How much is your rent?"

"Fourteen hundred dollars a month," replied Eleanor, "and that includes my utilities." Miriam wrote down "Rent" and then wrote "$1,400" beside it. "That's 280 coins," she said to her mother. "So take 280 coins out of your pile and give them to me." Eleanor counted out 280 coins and handed them to Miriam, who placed them in a pile beside the word "rent."

"Okay, what's your next fixed expense?"

"Fixed expense?" asked her mother.

"You know, something with a regular amount that you have to pay every so often, like car insurance."

"Well, I don't pay my car insurance every month. I get a bill once a year," said Eleanor.

"Do you have the money set aside for the next bill?" asked Miriam.

"No," said Eleanor.

"Do you know how much it is?"

Eleanor got up and went into the second bedroom, returning with a folder. "This is where your dad put all the bills when he paid them," she said. She began to shuffle through the papers in the file. "Here it is. The last bill for car insurance was $1,450."

"Which works out to"—Miriam grabbed her phone and opened the calculator feature. She divided $1,450 by 12—"about $120 a month." She wrote "Car Insurance" on the paper and "$120" beside it. "That's another 24 coins," she said to her mother, who counted them out and handed them to her.

They continued listing expenses and the amount Eleanor was spending, counting out coins as they went.

Budget Item	Amount	Number of Coins
Rent	$1,400	280
Car insurance	$120	24
Cable/Internet	$120	24
Cellphone	$100	20
Apartment insurance	$60	12
Groceries/ Personal care	$130	26

(continued)

Gas	$140	28
Cats	$70	14
Medication	$95	19
Banking fees	$40	8

At this point Miriam said to Eleanor, "How many coins do you have left?"

"Five," said Eleanor.

"And there are a whole bunch of categories we still haven't covered, right?"

"Yes," said Eleanor, her brow furrowing.

"Okay, hang on to those five coins and just tell me what the expenses are and how much you're spending on them."

As Eleanor listed her remaining expenses and estimated costs, Miriam wrote them on the flip-chart paper.

Clothes	$200	40
Entertainment	$300	60
Gifts	$200	40
Travel	$170	34
Books and movies	$50	10

"So, that works out to another 184 coins and you only have five," said Miriam.

Eleanor sat, staring from the five coins in her hand to the flip-chart paper on the floor. "This can't be," she said. "It was fine when your father was alive."

"You had more income when Dad was still here," said Miriam. "If your income changes, you have to change your spending to match."

"So, what am I going to do?"

Miriam felt bad seeing her mother so distraught over her financial circumstances. "Don't worry, Mom, we're going to work it out together. But can you see why it's so important to have a budget? It's the only way you'll know if you're staying on track with your money."

Eleanor nodded her head slowly. "I see that now," she said. "When the coins started running low, I was almost ready to panic."

"No need to panic," said Miriam. "But you do need to plan."

SELLING THE BUDGET

1. Talk about budgeting as the solution to whatever issues the person you're helping is currently dealing with. Do they want to be able to take a vacation? Do they wish they had money to save for a home? Do they want to get their debt paid off, finally? Use a budget as the plan that gets them to the solution. Make the goal something that's important to the other person so that he or she is willing to entertain the discussion.

2. If you're dealing with someone who is very concrete, consider using a money substitute to create a physical budget. Get enough coins, bottle caps, toothpicks, or beans to represent the amount of money they have to work with each month. Get a large piece of poster board or open up an old cardboard box. Grab a black marker and get to work making categories and physically assigning the bottle caps or beans to each category.

3. Stress that budgets are flexible. Want to go on a vacation next year? Where will you take money (bottle caps or beans) from to add to the Vacation line on your budget?

Does the person you're helping have a bad spending habit or three? Give each habit a line on the budget, assign the appropriate number of toothpicks or coins, and then make the rest of the budget with what's left of the "money."

4. Insist that the person you're helping do the allocating of resources. If important categories are left off the budget, gently remind them about what's missing. "Oh, I just remembered, we have to set aside some money for maintenance on the car." Or "Hey, you know what we forgot? Declan's hockey fees."

17 • IT'S NOT MY FAULT

After three years in the same program at university, Emily decided to switch to one that suited her better. That meant she had seven years' worth of student debt when she finally got her undergrad degree. And then she fell in love with Graham. They moved in together and in just under a year she was pregnant. She still hadn't gotten a permanent position, but the two decided to buy a house. Graham had a pretty good income and, with a baby on they way, they both wanted to put down roots. Three years later, she was pregnant again, Graham had lost his job, and they'd fought over what he was or wasn't doing to fix the mess. The marriage disintegrated and now they were in a custody battle neither could afford.

As Emily broke linguini in two and dropped it into a pot of boiling water, she said to her mother, "I just don't know what to do. I'm two months behind on the mortgage, Graham isn't giving me anything for Brody until we work out the custody agreement, and I'm about to go on maternity leave with nothing saved."

Emily's mom, Brenda, saw the strain on her daughter's face. She was worried. Emily had lost weight and wasn't sleeping well. Brenda had offered to come and stay until the baby was born and help out as much as she could.

"Have you considered selling the house?" Brenda asked. She'd wanted to ask for weeks, but Emily was touchy on the subject.

"Mom, I've told you, that's not something I want do," Emily said, her voice rising. "Brody needs the stability of his home right now, what with his father leaving us high and dry. Can you imagine adding the stress of selling to my life right now? Can you?" Emily shifted away from watching the pasta boil to stirring the cream sauce. She couldn't make eye contact with her mother. She was so mad.

"Well, if you're behind on payments, doesn't it make sense to sell and get what you can rather than have the bank foreclose?"

"No," Emily said sharply, as she finally met her mother's eyes, "because whatever we get, Graham and I will have to split, and that'd leave me with not even enough to pay first and last months' rent on a crappy place. I'd rather just wait this out. Graham should have thought about the cost of leaving us before he bolted."

"He didn't bolt," said Brenda. "You threw him out."

"No, I didn't." Emily's voice rose to a screech. "He says that, but it isn't true. I told him he couldn't just sit on his ass waiting for a job. He had to do whatever he could because we had a baby coming and payments to make. It's not my fault he lost his job and wouldn't find another one."

"That's what you said when you told Graham you were pregnant again and he responded with less enthusiasm than you'd hoped."

"What?" Emily's voice was shrill and accusatory.

"You said it wasn't your fault you'd gotten pregnant, that it took two people to make a baby."

"Well, it does."

"Yes, but he didn't know you had gone off the pill."

"It was making me sick. I needed to take a break from it."

Brenda was used to Emily making excuses for everything that went wrong in her life. When Emily had talked Graham into buying a house that was bigger than they needed, Brenda tried to step in to tell them that they were rushing into home ownership before they were ready. But Emily responded angrily that she had hated moving from apartment to apartment when she was little. She wanted her kids to grow up in their own house.

"Okay, look, I'm not trying to make you angry," said Brenda. "I just think you keep saying that nothing is your fault, as if someone else is doing all this TO you. You have to take control of your life."

"I'm suffering! And you're blaming me?" shouted Emily. "I've tried to get steady work for almost three years and I'm still not permanent anywhere. I've busted my ass to make enough money to keep this roof over our heads while Graham has been looking for work. I can't help it if no one will hire me full-time."

There are people to whom bad things seem to happen time and again. From surprise pregnancies that complicate lives, to houses that decrease in value or become too expensive to carry, to illnesses that reduce their ability to work, to mates who disappoint or betray them, these people are always on the losing end. When someone or something else is always at fault for the bad things that happen to a person, you're looking at a classic case of sufferer mentality.

Sufferers typically see the responsibility for whatever befalls them as out of their hands. They think, "Bad things always happen to me." They feel powerless to change what's going wrong in their lives. And they look for someone to blame.

It is their attitude that's to blame.

In *Man's Search for Meaning*, Holocaust survivor Viktor E. Frankl wrote, "Everything can be taken from a man but one thing: the last of the human freedoms—to choose one's attitude in any given set of circumstances, to choose one's own way."

Instead of believing that the world owes them a better life, sufferers have to learn that a better life is theirs as soon as they accept responsibility for the life they have and decide to do things differently.

If you have a friend, mate, sister, or child who always seems to be followed by trouble, know that sufferers create their own reality.

When faced with an obstacle, people who are not sufferers do something to fix the problem, or cut their losses and move on. People who are sufferers don't seem able to shake the sense that everything is beyond their control. And they're wont to aggravate whatever mess they are in by adding more to their plate than they can handle.

"Em, you've created a lot of these problems yourself. And until you accept that and decide what you're going to do differently, you'll keep feeling as if life has it in for you."

"You're blaming me?" asked Emily incredulously. "This is not why you're here, Mom." She drew the last word out like an accusation.

"I'm not blaming anyone or anything," said Brenda calmly. "And this is exactly why I'm here with you. You need to get over this sense that it's all being done to you. It's been going on for too long."

"What are you talking about?" asked Emily. "When Dad left us I distinctly remember you crying for weeks."

"I was sad," said Brenda. "But I picked up the pieces of my life, raised you, went back to school, finished my degree, and made a life."

"And I had to come home from school to an empty apartment every day after school. I was lonely and afraid to be on my own."

"Oh, Em," said Brenda, "everyone is lonely and afraid to be on their own. Some people accept that and live with, and through, it. And some people, like you, refuse to live alone. I think that's why you rushed into living with Graham."

"He swore he'd take care of me," said Emily, tears welling in her eyes. "Then he just left."

Brenda sighed. Then slowly and carefully she said, "It's a big responsibility having to assume the job of making someone else's life work. You're a smart, capable woman, Em. Why do you need anyone to take care of you?"

Emily looked at her mother, taken aback by Brenda's words. Emily was smart. And she was capable. So why DID she need someone to take care of her?

Loads of people cast themselves in the role of sufferer, allowing others to take advantage of them or searching for someone who will alleviate their suffering. Is there someone in your life for whom everything seems to go wrong? "I tried to get a part-time job to pay off my debt, but the hours clashed with my schedule so it just won't work." Do you hear them say, "Poor me!"? Do you know people who think that everyone else has an easier life? "Marcie is so lucky. She's got a great husband and everything just seems to work out for her."

If you talk with a sufferer, inevitably the conversation will turn to their sad, pathetic existence: their unpaid bills, their inability to get out of the pay-advance cycle, their lack of money to take that vacation they should be able to take. They are the martyrs, the people who always expect the worst to happen. "I try and try, and it doesn't make any difference!" They focus on what's wrong in their lives—instead of on what's good—and seem to be addicted to sadness and chaos. "And I told her I'd pay her back, and I will. But what? Does she seriously think I'm not going to pay my rent so I can pay her back her lousy $200?" When you leave them, you feel tired, down in the dumps, worn out as their miasma rubs off on you.

In dealing with sufferers, it's important to remember that there's a BIG difference between saving them and helping them to help themselves. The goal is to show them that they can make a plan to change their outcomes, but first they have to change their attitude. They must move from suffering at the hand of fate to being in charge of their own destiny.

"Okay," said Brenda, "What can I do to help?" She was twirling the linguini onto her fork as she looked over at her beautiful, if messed-up, daughter.

"I don't know. I don't know anything. Tell me what to do," begged Emily.

"No," said Brenda, "I won't do that. This is your life; these are your problems to solve. And I have the utmost faith in your ability to deal with your life. So I'm happy to be your sounding board, but I'm not going to come up with solutions."

"I don't even know where to start."

"What's your biggest problem right now?"

"Getting Graham to drop the custody battle so I'm not wasting money on lawyers. Then buying the food I'll need for next week."

"Okay, so how do you think you can accomplish that?"

"I'll have to give him shared custody. But why should I after he abandoned us?"

"So, you'd rather punish him for making you feel abandoned than give your children's father the custody to which he's legally entitled? And you'd rather the kids have no relationship with their father—like you—than share them with Graham?"

"No. No, that's not what I'm saying," said Emily. But she got quiet as they ate their pasta. Maybe her mom was a little right.

Maybe you have a mate who believes debt is inevitable because, being so deeply in debt, he or she thinks there's no point in even trying to get out. You can ask, "So, how's that working for you?" Or, aware that your mother hasn't saved enough for retirement, you can ask, "Knowing you don't have enough saved, you're just going to live a miserably poor existence in your golden years?"

Bluntness is what it sometimes takes to help your sufferer see that it's time to put aside this theme of suffering. It may be easier to blame others, circumstances, or the fates for the crap they're dealing with, but blame won't get them to the other side of the river.

An important step for sufferers is to change the internal dialogue associated with suffering. Instead of "Poor me," sufferers have to teach themselves (and remind themselves) to say, "Okay, this is a challenge. How will I deal with it?" And instead of "It's not my fault," they have to say, "I may not have chosen these cards, but I'll decide how I play them."

"In terms of finding money for next week's groceries, what can you do about that?" asked Brenda.

"I just bought a couple of new things to cheer myself up." Emily looked at her mother's resigned face. "Yes, Mother, I know I shouldn't have, but I was blue and it helped. I'm going to take them back today and use that money to stock up the pantry."

"How can you make that money go as far as possible?"

"You used to manage on very little for groceries and we always ate well," said Emily. "How did you do it?"

"I created meal plans for the week and I made sure I got as much as I could for my money by buying on sale and using coupons."

"Will you teach me how you did that?"

"I sure will," said Brenda.

REDIRECTING THE SUFFERER

1. Recognize that most people hold on to their suffering because they are rewarded in some way for doing so: they get the attention they are seeking; they are admired for their martyrdom; they are listened to, stroked, and given positive feedback for all that has gone wrong in their lives. You must break this cycle first.

2. Ask sufferers if they genuinely like being in pain or feeling out of control, or if they're serious about taking control of their life. If they aren't ready, you can't help them. If they are ready, then . . .

3. Ask sufferers to reframe what they're thinking about in positive terms, or to substitute positive thoughts when they find themselves focusing on their suffering.

4. Help the sufferer set a very realistic goal and come up with the steps (make them small and very manageable) to achieve that goal. You want to move them from "Nothing works" to "I did it!"

IF YOU RECOGNIZE YOURSELF AS A SUFFERER

Do you find yourself saying, "It's not my fault"? Does it seem easier to blame your circumstances than deal with the problems you're facing? Does it feel like there's so much wrong with your life and there's nothing you can do about it?

You did that. You have made the choice to see yourself as not in control of your life. You have chosen to be miserable. You can hang on to your misery or you can choose to pick up the reins and turn your life in a different direction. But as long as you keep thinking about yourself as someone to whom life just happens, you will make that your reality.

Language is a funny thing. Our brains believe what our ears hear, and when our self-talk is negative, pathetic, sad, we come to believe it's true. I was having a chat one day with a young man when he referred to himself as "poor." I knew he didn't make a ton of money, but I was under the impression that he had enough. So I said, "Do you have enough money for your needs and some of your wants?"

"What?" He seemed surprised by my question.

"Can you keep a roof over your head and food in your belly, and still buy some of the extras?"

"Yes," he said.

"Then you're not poor. You're just a regular Joe. Stop calling yourself poor."

He laughed nervously. "Okay." He dragged out the word.

"Poor people don't have enough money to make ends meet. They can't choose to eat organic food, or decide to turn up the heat if they're cold. You're not poor, right?"

"No, I guess I'm not."

"But as long as you think of yourself as poor, you'll feel poor. And when you say it out loud you reinforce it to yourself. So quit the negative chatter and say thank you for what you do have."

Later he emailed me to thank me for helping him change his perspective.

18 · I'M RUNNING A BUSINESS HERE

Rosanne works hard. She's been working hard since she was 15 years old. When she turned 31 she decided she'd had enough of working for other people. If she was going to bust her ass it would be for herself. She opened a small retail store specializing in specialty and gourmet foods and started spreading the word. The store was popular and sales were good. But the rent was high and there were weeks, sometimes months, when Rosanne couldn't take an income from the business. The savings she'd accumulated to get her business going were almost gone, and she realized she must be doing something wrong. She called her cousin, an accountant, for a sit-down.

"So, you've been doing this for two years now?" asked Donna as she flipped through the store's latest balance sheet.

"Yes," said Rosanne. "I love running the store, interacting with the customers. I love finding new foods to share with my customers. But I've been using my personal savings to avoid taking money from the store until it's, you know, established, and I'm running low."

"How many months did you give yourself to get the store to a point where it could support you?" asked Donna.

"What?" asked Rosanne. "I don't understand what you mean."

"Well, you knew you'd need time for the store to take off, so you had some savings in place and that was really smart. But how long did you think it would take before the store was making enough money to support itself and you?"

"I didn't really think about that," said Rosanne. "How long should it have taken?"

"Hey, it's your business and your plan. You did have a business plan, right?"

"I had plans for merchandising and for getting the line of credit for the set-up and inventory."

"But no plan for ongoing cash flow management or how to grow the business?"

"Not really."

"Okay, how far off are you in terms of being able to take a regular income?

"Well . . ." Rosanne hesitated. "I'm not sure."

Donna sighed. "If the business can't support you, it's not a business." She smiled. "Like that woman on TV says, 'It's a hobby.'"

"I bust my ass running this store. I'm not playing around," Rosanne replied indignantly.

"I don't care how hard you work," said Donna. "A business that can't support you isn't a business. You might as well get a job working for someone else."

Rosanne looked like she was going to cry.

"I see it all the time," continued Donna. "People come to me, talking about being in business, but they can't find two red cents to support themselves or their families, never mind save for the future."

"Amazon still hasn't made a profit," said Rosanne.

"Ha, and you think Jeff Bezos doesn't take an income from Amazon? You're nuts. It may not make a profit, but believe me, that man lives just fine. You, on the other hand, have exhausted your savings and don't know when your store will be able to pay you regularly. Not the same thing."

"So, do I just close up shop after all this?"

"Is that what you want to do?"

"No, of course not." Rosanne threw her arms up and started to pace. "I just don't have a clue what to do next."

"Well, we have to decide if this business is viable and if you can hold out long enough to make it work. That's where you should have started. But let's look at the numbers and see what we come up with."

Some people go into business thinking that working for themselves will be easier than working for the Man. It's hardly ever so. While having their own gig can be extremely rewarding—and profitable if handled correctly—sometimes getting a job makes more sense. This is especially true if their business does not generate enough money to support them.

Sometimes people confuse being committed to growing a business with being overcommitted to self-employment. In the first instance, your lovie will have a specific plan for how she will manage cash flow and keep the business going, and a date by which the business will be supporting her. In the second instance, your dear one is flying by the seat of his pants, waiting to see if there is any money left at the end of the month to buy groceries or make rent.

Whether lovie is an artist, a plumber, a landscaper, a dressmaker, a restaurateur, a shopkeeper, a dentist, or a housekeeper, the business is only a business if it generates revenue sufficient to support itself and provide an income to the owner. Otherwise, lovie might as well get a job.

Some small business owners like to play math games when it comes to dealing with money issues. If, for example, they are taking a small income from the business at the expense of increasing the business's debt, the fall off the cliff at the end will be devastating.

One of the tests you can apply to see if a business has the legs it needs to stand on its own is called the three-of-five test.

It looks at how likely a business is to succeed. If the business has made a profit in any three of the past five consecutive years, it is said to have a profit motive, meaning it intends to make money. So, three-fifths of the time, the business must be making money or it's time to face the truth: the business is a hobby. (To apply this rule, owners must have planned to have enough cash flow to fund their business—and their personal expenses—for up to three years.)

If you get to the three-year mark and none of those years has been profitable, I'm sorry to say that you're not going to make it. Get a real job.

It's not uncommon for young (in experience, not age) entrepreneurs to overcommit to their business to their own (and their family's) detriment. In an attempt to be upbeat, to believe beyond a shadow of a doubt that they will be successful, to create the positive energy it takes to make a business fly, many entrepreneurs step over the line from passion to delusion.

Folks who have maxed out credit cards, driven lines of credit to the hilt, and hinted to spouses, parents, siblings, and friends that just $100 more will make all the difference have stepped over the line.

If after two years outlays continue to exceed intakes, it's time to wake up and smell the coffee.

Lester had always dreamed of having his own business. As a kid he cut lawns, walked dogs, and shovelled snow. After he graduated from high school, he did a business program at a community college and then went to work as a sales rep for a major manufacturer of office equipment. After five years of being on the road selling, selling, selling, he was promoted to area manager and then regional sales manager. By 35 he was ready to head out and start a business of his own. In his gut he knew he had a good idea. All he had to do was come up with the capital to make it happen.

Lester was a little surprised when 18 months later his wife, Trixie, turned to him and said, "Is the business going to start paying any time soon? Because I'm exhausted from working two jobs to support us while you play at being an entrepreneur."

A huge fight ensued. Trixie was tired and frustrated. Lester was tired and defensive. He hadn't expected the importation barriers, the amount of paperwork he would have to do, or the frustration of working 100 hours a week only to have the bank call him up and tell him he was late with his line of credit payment. The last time they called, he'd had to put together a package to prove to them the business was still viable. He'd spent hours gathering information, completing spreadsheets, and seeing his accountant (at $65 an hour) to get ready to defend his line of credit.

Intuit Canada, the financial and tax management software company, commissioned a survey of small business owners about their financial literacy. The survey found that 83% of owners operating for at least one year and employing up to 100 people had serious gaps in their knowledge. The survey asked 10 questions about basic business management like, "What is the role of the balance sheet?" and a whopping 44% of people averaged four or fewer correct answers.

If you are serious about your small business, you have to know EVERYTHING you'll need to do to keep the boat afloat, and that includes understanding all the logistical aspects of running a business, before you order business cards, borrow money, or start looking for write-offs! At the very least you should know

- how to write a business plan that includes your business and marketing strategies; an analysis of your strengths, weaknesses, opportunities, and potential threats; and financial forecasts;
- what the structure of your business will be: sole proprietorship, limited liability company, corporation, and the like;
- how to finance your business: government-backed loans, venture capital, grants, investors;
- how to set up your tax files and register with the Tax Man;
- which licences and permits you will need and which zoning and bylaw requirements will impact your business;
- your responsibilities as an employer if you have employees: payroll, labour laws, and workers' compensation board requirements; and
- who your resources will be: lawyer, accountant, bookkeeper, banker, insurer, et cetera.

It is easy to get excited about going into business for yourself. It's easy to do all the fun stuff you're good at. But being in business also means being prepared to do the crap. Nothing ticks me off more than having to sit down and calculate my HST return every quarter. I don't know why, I just hate doing it. And I would procrastinate forever if I weren't such a control freak. The government isn't to be messed with, and I don't want them dipping into my accounts to take money they think I owe, so I stay on the right side of the rules.

If you've considered going into business for yourself, having loads of support from family and friends is just the first step.

Dolores decided to turn her love of everything yarn related into a small business. She thought it was the perfect time to ride the resurgence in popularity of knitting and crocheting by opening her own yarn store. Her first investment: sending herself to a symposium for new entrepreneurs. It just happened to be in sunny California. Great. She paid for it with her credit card.

Dolores knew that one of the most important things in retail was location. She found a perfect little spot. It not only had enough space for storage, it had a lovely alcove she could use to hold knitting and crocheting classes. True, it was a bit more expensive than she had expected, but it was perfect. She signed the lease.

With a brother who was willing to build shelves and display racks, and a sister who was a whiz at website development, Dolores knew she was ahead of the game. She told her brother to spare no expense when it came to the building materials. And she let her sister have free rein on the website. She didn't know jack about technology so she stayed right out of it.

Six months in, sales still weren't covering the rent. She'd had to pay COD for her yarn deliveries and her line of credit was pretty much tapped out. She decided the business was just months away from taking off, so she asked her mom and dad for a small loan— just $10,000—to see her through. Not wanting to see Dolores's dream unravel, they agreed.

Things were getting better. Word was spreading about her classes and a group of four women decided to hold a Stitch 'n Bitch session in the alcove every Wednesday night. The group grew to six, then eight. They worked away, chatting happily as their needles clacked. Dolores loved the sound.

The $10,000 loan Dolores got from her parents was gone three months later. She was getting closer to covering costs herself. But with the store's one-year anniversary just around the corner, she still wasn't taking an income from the store. She wasn't sure she could make a go of it after all. But now, $30,000 in debt on credit cards and her line of credit, and owing her parents another $10,000, she wasn't sure what to do next.

Dolores thought she had a plan. What she had was a vision and a willingness to work hard. If it isn't written down with all the bases covered, it's not a business plan. A business plan should include

- a vision statement that clearly articulates what you're trying to accomplish;
- a thorough description of your company, product, or service;
- a description of how what you're offering is different from what's already out there;
- a market analysis that shows you know what your market is, who your competitors are, and where you fit in the marketplace;
- a description of your team, if you have one; if it's just you, a description of your skills and expertise;

- your marketing plan (how you will introduce your idea or product to customers);
- a one-year cash flow statement: where the money's coming from and where it's going; and
- revenue projections for one, three, and five years.

A business plan is, perhaps, the single most effective tool in creating a business that will fly. In completing one, you will not only have to look at the industry you're entering, you'll need to clarify your business ideas, identify opportunities, and create a plan for marketing, production (if applicable), and money management.

Starting a business without a business plan is like building a house without a blueprint. If you haven't tested the feasibility of your business idea, you're not giving your business the best possible chance of success. If you don't know who your customers are, how much money you'll need to see you through to sustainability, how you'll price your product or service compared to the competition, you're more about wishin' and hopin' than planning. Without a business plan, you won't be able to secure funding for your enterprise through either bank loans or investment.

Entrepreneurship is wonderful. Being self-employed can be very satisfying. Creating something from the ground up and watching it grow can make for a very happy life. Or a miserable one, if you haven't taken care of the details. So, are you in business or are you pursuing a hobby?

SMELLING THE COFFEE

1. Once a quarter, review your balance sheet and your cash flow. Taking stock of the financial facts is key to staying real. That means you're using a bookkeeping program or Excel spreadsheet to stay on top of the financial details.

2. Collect the money before you spend it. Accounts receivable cannot be spent until you turn them into cash.

3. Actively manage your expenses. Just because it's a write-off doesn't mean you should buy/lease/rent/do it. Money not spent is money you can use to support the business and yourself.

4. Not every month will be a profitable one; that's the reality for many small businesses. However, you should know what's going to happen next. If you're not going to be profitable for a specific amount of time, that should be a conscious, strategic decision because you're making an investment in the business. If the loss comes as a surprise, or it seems to have no end, it's time to retool your management processes.

5. Check in with family and friends. Ask for candid feedback when you review how you're doing. If your mate is helping to support your efforts, he or she should be a part of your decision-making process.

6. Consider an advisory board. Corporations have boards of directors; you can choose a couple of people with expertise in money, marketing, inventory management—whatever is applicable to your biz—and ask them to lend you their brains and experience twice a year.

7. Decide if stepping back a little—getting a job on the side to pay your personal bills and growing the business more slowly—makes sense as an alternative to being all in.

8. If being all in is the only way, decide what your limits are. How long will you carry the business? How much debt is enough debt? What will be your signal to bring the enterprise to a conclusion? Know your cut-off point.

19 · TOO BUSY TO BUDGET

Claudia is always in overdraft. For a few days each month, just after her paycheque has gone into the bank, she's in the black. Jeremy is no better. And the joint account, well, that's just a joke. When Claudia took an advance on her credit card to get her account into the black long enough to pay her son's rowing fees, Jeremy knew they had to do something about it. So they sought some help.

When Jeremy's sister, Allison, sat down with Claudia and Jeremy, one of the first questions she asked was, "Do you have a budget?"

"Ha," said Claudia, "like we have time for a budget."

"How much time do you suppose it takes to compare what you're spending to your budget?" asked Allison.

"It doesn't matter how much time," said Jeremy, "we haven't got it. Kendra does karate, Aaron rows, and Cathy volunteers with an animal rescue. We're constantly on the run. Who has time to manage money when there's so much else going on?"

"And where is that approach getting you?" asked Allison, looking directly at her brother.

Claudia jumped to Jeremy's defence. "It's actually my job to take care of the money, and I know I'm doing a crappy job of it."

"It's both of your jobs," said Allison. "You may do most of the day-to-day transactions, Claudia, but Jeremy can't claim he's too busy to look after his money."

"Listen, we both work hard, and the kids are in activities that take us out of the house five days a week."

"So you think Kendra's karate is more important than managing your money?" asked Allison.

"I didn't say that," said Jeremy.

"Actually, you did," said Allison.

"C'mon, guys, this isn't getting us anywhere," said Claudia. "Can you help us or not, Allison? I'm not going to sit here just to listen to what idiots we are."

"I'm sorry," said Allison slowly. "I'm not trying to make you feel like idiots. But I am trying to point out that money management should be a priority, and that if you keep making excuses for why you can't find the time, you won't ever make things better."

Claudia and Jeremy looked at each other. "Okay," said Jeremy, "no more excuses."

Claudia nodded in agreement. "No more excuses," she reiterated.

Some people are under the impression that money management takes loads of time. It doesn't have to. Sure, if you're always running to fix a problem, it may feel like you're spending a lot of time spinning your wheels. But that's more because you don't have a system than because the management itself is time-consuming.

I spend about one hour a month managing my money. One hour. A month. Sure, I've got it down to a science now. I post my receipts to my spending journal, which takes about 20 minutes a month. I pay my bills online and record those transactions in my spending journal too, which takes about five minutes a month. I enter my spending journal numbers into my budget at the end of the month and that takes about a half-hour. At first it took me a couple of hours a month to get it all in place, but now it's a breeze and I always know exactly how much money I have and how I'm doing with my spending plan.

Before you can get rid of the "too busy to budget" mindset, you must deal with it. If you don't, it will continue to crop up. It's such an easy excuse to use. But it isn't an issue of time, it's an issue of desire. **Most people who don't make the time to take care of their money don't want to have to be bothered with the details of money management.**

"Okay," said Allison, "describe the three things you wish were different when it comes to your money. You go first, Claudia."

"I wish we had more of it," laughed Claudia. "That would pretty well take care of most of the problems."

"I bet not," said Allison. "Between you, you make what?" She shuffled through the bank statements Claudia and Jeremy had brought with them. She waited. When she looked up Jeremy shrugged. Claudia looked down at her hands. "Are you telling me you don't know how much money you make?"

"Well, Jeremy and I just put enough money into the joint account to take care of the bills. We don't actually talk about how much we make. Do you and Ethan talk about your money?"

"All the time," said Allison. "That's how we know the money's going where we want it to go. Sometimes we fall off-track, but we use each other as a check and balance so that we can get back to business quickly."

Claudia caught Jeremy's eye and rolled her eyes.

Allison ignored her sister-in-law. "Hey," she said, "it looks to me that between you, you're bringing home about $7,100 a month. By the way, that's about a thousand a month more than Ethan and I make together."

Claudia said, "How can that be? You guys live in a nicer house and you took a vacation last year. I can't tell you the last time Jer and I took the kids anywhere."

"What are you talking about?" asked Allison, incredulously. "Didn't you all just get back from Ottawa?"

"That wasn't a vacation," said Jeremy, "that was for Aaron's playoffs."

"You travelled, stayed in a hotel, and ate food in restaurants, right?" asked Allison. "And how many times this year have you done that?"

Jeremy and Claudia looked at each other. The light was beginning to dawn.

When people claim they don't have the time to take care of their money details, it is sometimes because they don't want to have to face their reality. To fess up and face up means they might have to stop doing something they enjoy. Rather than come to terms with what's what, they choose ignorance so they can keep on keeping on, no matter how destructive that may be.

Folks often can't see clearly how their behaviour is actually getting in the way of their own success. For those trying to help them, drawing parallels can be an important way of getting the message home.

"Have you ever added up what you spend on the kids' activities?" asked Allison.

"Never," said Jeremy.

"Do you think we'd sacrifice the things the kids love to do?" asked Claudia incredulously. "Not for a moment would we consider telling Aaron he couldn't row or pulling Kendra out of karate."

"And the work Cathy does with her rescue is so important to her," said Jeremy.

"I'm not debating any of that," said Allison. "I simply asked you if you know what it costs."

Claudia and Jeremy looked at each other, seemingly confused by the question. "What does it matter? If we're going to do it anyway, what does it matter?" asked Claudia.

"It matters," said Allison patiently, "because you have a limited amount of money with which to work. You need to know how you're using it and what's going where, so you can plan properly. If the kids' activities are the most important, then you'll be willing to forgo other spending to have the money for those activities."

Allison pulled a spreadsheet from her handbag. "Here, I brought along a copy of our budget, so you can see how we plan to spend our money." She spread it out for Claudia and Jeremy to look at together.

If part of the money management problem is that whomever you're trying to help has never used a budget, introduce them to yours. Talk about how you use your budget to demonstrate why having one is so important.

"So," said Allison, as she pointed to the budget worksheet, "our budget is our plan for how we're going to spend the money we work so hard for. It helps us stay in control as we work towards our goals. And it helps us prepare for expenses that only crop up periodically." Allison pointed to the Property Taxes line on her budget. "Here," she said. "We only pay our property taxes four times a year. But we set aside money every month, which is way easier than having to come up with a bigger amount all at once when the bill comes in."

Claudia looked at Jeremy. "It was the property taxes that made me go into overdraft last month," she said. "I'd completely forgotten about them until I got the bill, and the first installment was due at the end of the month. So I had to transfer more money from my account to the joint account to cover them."

Jeremy nodded. He pointed to the Car Insurance line on Allison's budget. "Yeah, and the month before, the car insurance bill came in. I almost crapped myself when I saw the bill for $1,800."

"So much easier just to set aside $150 a month, don't you think?" asked Allison.

Without a budget, people think of most of their less regular expenses as unexpected. Having forgotten about the car insurance bill that comes once a year, they're shocked and surprised when the bill arrives. Having a budget means setting money aside for specific purposes, be it accumulating money for your children's education, saving for that family holiday, or building a stash of cash to pay the property taxes when they come due. (See Appendix 1: Building a Budget.)

"Okay, so can you see that having more money isn't necessarily the solution?" asked Allison. "The solution is using your money in smarter ways." Claudia and Jeremy nodded. "So, Jeremy," said Allison, "it's your turn. Tell me something you wish was different."

"I know this will sound selfish," said Jeremy, "but I wish we had the money to renovate the basement properly so I could have a workshop and a place to go when the kids have all their friends over. Living with three teenagers makes for a noisy house."

"I don't have any place special," said Claudia indignantly.

"Sure you do," said Jeremy. "The kids know to stay out of our bedroom. You go there to read. I go to the basement, but it's a mess. I just wish we had a little money to fix it up. I'd do the work, but there are supplies I need and there's never money for that kind of thing."

"There could be," said Allison. "It might not happen quickly, but you could start allocating a little each month to your basement fund. How much do you think you'd need?"

"About $4,000 should do it," said Jeremy.

"And by when would you like to have it finished?"

"By next October, maybe?"

"So, that's nine months," said Allison, whipping out a calculator, "which means you'd have to set aside about $445 a month."

"Yeah, that'll never happen," said Claudia.

"Well, you can aim for a little further down the road," said Allison. "If you wait until next summer to start, that would give you more time to save. You'd only have to set aside about $235 a month, then."

"Where are we going to find $235 a month?" asked Jeremy. "We're always in overdraft now."

Dreams and aspirations don't have to go ignored because you keep getting to the end of the month only to find the money is all gone. With a budget, instead of spending willy-nilly, you account for where the money, down to the last penny, is going. That means making choices. If you're working towards a particular goal, instead of buying coffee each day on the way to work, you allocate that money to achieving your goal.

"Hey, you guys eat out a lot, don't you?" asked Allison. "Do you know how much you're spending in restaurants a month?"

"Not a clue," said Claudia.

"Well, I bet if you figured it out, and changed how often you ate out, you guys could come up with the $235 a month Jeremy needs for this basement reno."

"We spend so much time on the road with the kids," said Claudia.

"Right," said Allison, "so it'll take some planning to prepare food for them so you don't have to eat out as often."

"That just means our grocery bill goes up," said Claudia.

Allison looked at her and started to laugh. "Good one," she said to Claudia. "Cooking from scratch will cost you a third of what you spend, and the kids will eat healthier meals."

"And I'm going to find the time for all this cooking where?" asked Claudia, bridling at Allison's laughter.

"Hey, you can spend money in restaurants if you want, but then you won't have money for the basement renovation."

"So, I'll help prepare the food for the road," said Jeremy.

"You!" said Claudia. "Like you ever cook!"

"I will," said Jeremy.

FINDING TIME TO BUDGET

1. The initial budget takes time to do properly, so set aside a day or two (or three) to do your spending analysis and create your budget. (See Appendix 1: Building a Budget.)

2. Track your spending in a spending journal. Bring home a receipt for every purchase you make. It takes about 10 minutes a week to record your spending.

3. Create a monthly bill summary by listing bills in the order they need to be paid by date. If some are auto-deductions, write an "A" beside these bills. Remember to enter these transactions into your spending journal.

4. Once a month, transfer the transactions from your spending journal to your budget to monitor your spending. This takes anywhere from 20 to 30 minutes, depending on the number of transactions you have.

5. Once a quarter, review the categories in your budget to make sure you're on track. This should take about 30 minutes every three months. If there are areas in which you are currently overspending,

   a) will you cut back spending to balance,

   b) will you spend less elsewhere to balance, or

   c) will you increase your income to balance?

20 • PARENTS WHO WON'T TALK ABOUT THEIR MONEY

Aubrey is very worried about her parents. Her mom is 62 and her dad is 63 and neither has much saved. While they've both worked hard, neither has ever cared much about the future. They always had lots of expenses, so getting to the end of the month in the black was an accomplishment.

Three years ago Aubrey watched as her parents bought a camper so they could go camping on weekends. A year later, they traded in the first camper for a bigger one. When Aubrey found out her parents had taken a holiday down south and were talked into buying a time-share, she knew she had sit down and talk to them about their plans for retirement.

Sitting with her husband over breakfast one Saturday morning, Aubrey started to get worked up. "Relax," said Miles. "They're making their bed and they'll have to lie in it."

"So, you think if my parents are destitute I'll be able to just stand by and watch?" asked Aubrey. "'Cause that's who I am?"

"No," said Miles. He was well aware of how responsible Aubrey felt for her family. It was one of the things he loved most about her. "Have you had any luck talking to them?"

"Not recently," said Aubrey, "but now I'm so upset and angry. They make jokes about parking in our driveway and living in their camper, which I don't find particularly funny."

"Okay," said Miles, "so, what are you most worried about?"

"You and I work hard to save what little bit of money we can. It ticks me off that they are not dealing with reality. I also get upset when I think Braden and I will probably have to take care of them at some point."

"Is your brother losing sleep over this too?" asked Miles, buttering another piece of toast.

"Not as much as I am," said Aubrey. "I feel if I don't do something now, it'll be worse when a crisis hits."

Sometimes children become parents to their parents. It's not a good role to take on. Parents who refuse to accept responsibility for their own future do not automatically have the right to turn to their children for help.

If you have parents who refuse to deal with the reality of their financial circumstances, no doubt you find that worrisome. You're probably wondering if they will become a financial strain. I know that it's easy for me to say, "This is not your problem to fix." But not stepping in is a hard strategy to implement. Saying no to parents who have taken care of you, put you through school, supported you through tough times seems selfish and unkind. And trying to talk to parents who will not share their financial information, but then ask for help, can feel like balancing on the edge of a razor blade.

"I know you lent your parents about $5,000 last year when they couldn't pay off their credit card," Miles said.

"I know I'll never see that money again, and that's fine. I just want them not to go into debt again."

"I'm curious," said Miles. "You're so sensible with our kids. Why are you such a sucker with your parents?"

"I dunno," said Aubrey, pulling her fork through her uneaten scrambled eggs. "I feel like I owe them. They're my parents."

"And if they ask to borrow more money?" asked Miles.

"I don't know," said Aubrey, her voice almost a whisper. "I just don't know."

Ultimately, if you have the resources and the desire to help, you will. But what if you don't? What if that last $5,000 you coughed up was the last $5,000 you could afford to give away? Or what if your parents or in-laws are asking you to draw on your credit to help them?

They may not be aware of the stress they are putting on you by asking for help. They may not be attempting to guilt you into giving them money. But the end result is the same. Even if guilt isn't the issue, and you want to help your parents because of a deep sense of responsibility to them, if that help is going to put you in jeopardy, if it's going to mess up your plans for a secure future, you must say no.

Saying no isn't going to be easy, but it is what you must do. Whatever money you've already given them, consider it a gift. But there will be NO MORE. You must deal with your own life and your parents must deal with theirs. If your parents can't see past Tuesday and it blows up in their faces, that's the way it is. Your parents have made their bed, now they must lie in it. If you continue to enable them, you have only yourself to blame for your anger and disquiet. Love them. Hug them. Don't give 'em another cent!

Unlike the parent-child relationship, in which parents are responsible for their children because they chose to bring them into the world, the child-parent relationship is different. Through their behaviour, your parents set the tone for that relationship. But at the same time, **your parents are adults and have to assume the responsibility of adults: to take care of themselves.** If you have a parent who is irresponsible with money, a parent who seems to have not one iota of common sense and no plan for the future, you need to recognize that this is not *your* problem. Above all, you cannot help anyone— not even your parents—if that help necessitates putting yourself at risk. All that does is create more problems.

How do you say no to a parent you love? It's tough. But it goes something like this:

> Mom and Dad, I know you're in a tough spot. I would be happy to help you figure out how to change what you're doing so things can get better. And if you want me to help you find a professional to help, I will. But I'm afraid I don't have the financial means to bail you out or offer you any support. I need to take care of my family and myself so I don't end up where you are right now. And I am determined to never be a burden on my children, so I must keep my financial house in order. Please let me help you figure out what you have to change. I love you and want to help, but not with money.

Some of the money conversations you may want to have with your parents may not be about financial support, but rather about knowing that they have taken the necessary steps to ensure their own financial stability.

"I can't believe how different you and your parents are when it comes to money," said Miles as he cleared the dishes from the table. "You're so detail-oriented and focused on the future, and they live for today."

"It's hard to watch," said Aubrey. "If we had the resources to take them in, you know I would. But the kids will be headed off to university in a couple of years and that's going to take a big chunk of cash."

"And you're still not sure we have enough saved for retirement?"

"No, I know we don't. We'll have to buckle down or we'll end up like my parents."

"That's not going to happen, Aubrey. You can relax about that. Have you tried coming at this from another angle?"

"Like what?"

"Well, your dad has always been the one in charge. Have you asked them how your mom will manage when he kicks the bucket?"

"I tried, but the conversation was a non-starter."

Talking to your folks about money may be tough. And it may not work the first time you try. But you should persist. You might want to use a story from someone else's life (fact or fiction) to broach the subject, as in, "Y'know what my co-worker Devi told me last week? Her mom and dad are just about to retire completely and they're very worried because they've got some debt and not a lot of money saved. Devi was so upset because she thinks her parents will need financial help and she's in no position to give them money. I felt awful for her."

See if the story creates an opening for you to talk about your parents' financial position. You could always add something like, "I hope that if you guys have any concerns, you talk to me early enough that we can do something about it, and not wait till the last minute like Devi's mom and dad."

It is amazing just how resistant parents can be when it comes to sharing their financial information with their adult children. But you'll do your parents a disservice if you stick you head in the sand. Here are five questions you'll want to ask your folks.

1. **Do you have a will and powers of attorney for both money and personal care?** This isn't about what's in the will, it's about making sure there's one in place. And if your folks haven't given any thought to how they'll pass on their assets in the most tax-friendly way, it's time to seek help from an estate expert. As for the power of attorney (POA), this document is critical, especially as parents get older. If they become incapable of managing their money or of making decisions about their health care, someone needs to be able to step in and do what is best for them. And you can't do that without their express permission: a POA.

2. **Where are all your financial documents?** That's the wills, the POAs, the insurance policies, the bank account statements, the investment statements. It's EVERYTHING. Suggest that your parents make a list of all their important account numbers and where they are located. If your folks are concerned about privacy, they can put the list in a sealed envelope and leave it with their lawyer or in their safety deposit box, provided someone knows where the document is kept and can access it.

3. **Have you made funeral arrangements?** We all have different wishes for how we'll be disposed of. Me, I just want to be baked and mixed in with the flowers. My daughter, Alex, knows. That info is not just in my will, because I may have to be planted before she ever gets to the will. So she knows. You should too.

4. **Have you got any long-term care insurance?** No matter how much you love your folks, having them move in because they need constant care can be a tough road to walk. Take it from me. I've been there. If your parents don't have any long-term care insurance, do they have enough money in their pot to pay for help when they need it?

5. **Do you need help with your money now?** This may be as much an observation as a question. If bills are laying around unpaid, you have your answer. If your parents keep buying stuff they don't need—if you see new stuff coming into the house every week, or there are five cartons of milk in the fridge, that can be a sign too. You can ask the question, but very often parents who need help will deny there's a problem. So you may have to do some Sherlocking to see if there are problems.

Parents reluctant to talk about their financial situation are also often unwilling to admit their failings to their kids. But not knowing, or the stress of having to deal with a situation for which no one is prepared, is worse than any pushback you may get. If your parents adamantly refuse to share, well, you've done your best.

Ultimately, if both your parents have to get part-time jobs to see them through retirement because they have been irresponsible with their money and unwilling to talk about it, so be it. Their life is their life and you're going to have to reconcile yourself to the fact that **your parents are responsible for their own decisions, just as you are responsible for yours.**

TALKING TO PARENTS ABOUT MONEY

1. Decide if you are prepared to work past the normal retirement age to support a mother and/or father who needs financial support. If not, are there other adjustments you're willing to make in your own life to help them out? If you expect your parents to be self-supporting, be prepared to say so. If you think you can help in even a small way, make sure you know your limits so you don't put your own future at risk.

2. Explain to your parents what you are doing in preparation for your own future. Talk about

   - creating your will and powers of attorney;
   - making your funeral arrangements;
   - how you plan to change your lifestyle: where you'll live, when you'll stop driving, who you'll count on for help;
   - long-term care options you've considered; and
   - how you'll cope when your mate dies: what will change, what your plan is for coping.

   Ask them what steps they've taken. Or use a friend's situation to introduce the topic.

3. Figure out who else may be affected by your decision to aid your parents financially (your mate, children, siblings, et cetera). Have a discussion with them. Everyone has to be on the same page or the inevitable resentment will ruin your best intentions.

4. What help are you able or willing to offer?
   - direct financial support: How much? How often?
   - time for care-related issues like doctors' appointments
   - monitoring parents' finances and helping with everyday tasks like cooking and cleaning

5. Who else can help care for you parents? Create a list of contacts/resources you'll be able to call on (family, friends, support workers, community resources).

6. What assets will your parents have? How will they use those assets?
   - How much is saved?
   - Where is it and how is it invested?
   - Do they have other retirement income streams?
   - Do they have insurance? What type and with whom?
   - Will they give permission for you to speak to their financial advisor/broker/planner?
   - Will they review their current budget with you?

7. Ask if there are any issues your parents are worried about. Again, you can use a story or an article from a magazine or newspaper to demonstrate the things other people are worried about to get the conversation started.

8.   Remain open, do not criticize, and treat your parents with respect. Even if they've bungled the whole deal, telling them so in a heated discussion won't help. They have to come up with a plan, and you're there to help. Help. Don't be a bossy-socks.

THE KIDS WANT TO TALK

If your kids are approaching you to talk about the tough topic of money, you better believe they love you. Take their interest as a genuine desire to be of assistance. Sure, sometimes they can be a little know-it-all-ish. Don't get distracted. Remember they are trying to assure themselves that you'll be okay.

1.   Keep calm and be open about your money. I know this goes against everything you were taught, but it's a new world and money's not a secret anymore. It certainly shouldn't be within your family. Gosh, if you can't trust the people who love you with the truth, who can you trust?

2.   Set clear boundaries. You're happy to share information, but you're not giving your children the right to make decisions on your behalf. If they want to help you, great. But that doesn't mean you're willing to let them take over. If you feel your child is better equipped to deal with your money than you are, make sure your child is clear that you want to know EVERYTHING that will be done BEFORE it's done. You can't abdicate responsibility or you shouldn't be surprised if you end up unhappy with the choices that were made.

3.   Remind your children (sometimes they forget) that you're not an idiot and that the tone they sometimes take with

you is offensive. If they insist on using that tone, end the conversation and walk away. "We'll have this conversation another day when your tone is better or I'm feeling more tolerant."

ASKING FOR HELP FROM THE KIDS

Oh, it can be so tough recognizing that you need help. It can be even harder asking for help from the people whose diapers you used to change. Get over it. If you need help with the management of your assets, if you find you are forgetting things, if you want someone to be a sounding board, your children should be natural choices.

1. Look objectively at your children and decide which among them are best suited to the job of helping you. One may have more experience. Another may have more time. Bring them together and ask for the help you need.

2. If what you need is financial support, you might be in for a shock, particularly if you've frittered away your money regardless of warnings from your young'uns. The world is a harsh place, and kids have it just as tough as you did . . . maybe even tougher if they're squeezed financially between two generations. Whatever you're requesting, you have to give your children the option to say no if helping you would compromise their own financial health.

3. Be prepared with ideas for how to solve your problem(s), and ask your children for their best ideas to add to yours. As a team you can figure out a lot more than you would individually.

4. If you've raised a money moron, buy professional help.

21 • IT'LL BE FINE

Gareth decided he wanted to buy a house. Approaching his 30s, he felt it was time to put down roots. He went to the bank, got preapproved for a $325,000 mortgage, and went shopping for a house. He knew he probably couldn't afford the mortgage his bank was willing to give him, so he set his sights on something in the $295,000 range. He'd be able to put 10% down and have a little money left to cover his closing costs.

When Gareth told his girlfriend, Roxanne, his plan, she had some questions. Did he know what it'd cost to carry the house? With his seasonal work—Gareth made good money, but there were times of the year when the work got thin—would he be able to keep up with the mortgage payments? "Earlier this year you had to borrow money from me twice to make your car payment," Roxanne reminded Gareth.

"I paid you back and took you on a holiday," said Gareth.

"Yes, you did. I'm just saying, there are times when you seem to run out of money."

"It'll be fine," said Gareth. "Having a mortgage is not a lot different than paying rent."

When Gareth found the house of his dreams, it cost $15,000 more than he had expected to pay. The real estate agent asked him what he was worried about. He'd been approved for a big enough mortgage, hadn't he? Yes, he had. And it was the perfect house. Besides, Roxanne would probably move in with him in a couple of months when it was time to take possession, and that would help him carry the difference.

Roxanne broke up with Gareth two months later, just as he was moving into his new place. She'd been offered a job with a significant pay raise and decided to take it even though it meant relocating to the west. Gareth moved into his new house on his own.

At first he didn't do things any differently. He played hockey with the boys on Wednesday nights and then went out for beer and pizza. On Saturdays he went clubbing with his sister and her girlfriends. They all felt sorry for him because of his breakup, and he was being treated well by some very pretty girls. Five months later, he was approached by a neighbour who wanted him to share the cost of building a fence. Gareth told him it wasn't a good time. Truth was, Gareth's credit cards were at the limit and he couldn't come up with even $100 to put towards building the fence. He felt trapped by home ownership.

Plenty of people make decisions without planning. From buying a home to having a baby to making a major purchase like a new vehicle, they jump into the dream without giving a second thought to what the implications will be. They seldom factor in what they will have to give up or what the change will cost long term. Their disposable incomes go DOWN, Down, down, but they don't cut back on their spending, so they end up turning to credit cards or a line of credit to supplement their budget. And so the digging of the debt hole begins.

Leena and Daljeet wanted a baby so badly. They had been trying for about three years with no luck. Each time Leena realized she wasn't pregnant, her heart felt like it was breaking. Daljeet watched, unable to console her. The one thing Leena wanted more than anything, and he couldn't give it to her. When their doctor suggested in vitro fertilization, Leena jumped at the idea. Daljeet hesitated. "What's this going to cost us?" he asked.

Leena couldn't believe he had asked that question. "You're putting a price on us having a baby?" she demanded more than asked.

"I'm trying to make sure that once the baby gets here we can still afford to raise him," said Daljeet pragmatically.

"We'll be fine," said Leena.

The first two attempts didn't work, by which point they'd exhausted their emergency fund. Daljeet was becoming anxious because further treatments meant they'd be taking on debt. Leena would not listen. She wanted a baby and that was that. "Three times lucky," she said with a big smile on her face as she insisted they use their line of credit to finance their next attempt to get pregnant. "It'll be fine, you'll see."

Daljeet wasn't so sure. If Leena did get pregnant now, they were going to face some tight times as they worked to rebuild their emergency fund, prepare for the baby, and deal with Leena's lower income on maternity leave.

Regardless of what you're planning to change in your life, if you want to do it without your dream turning into a nightmare, you'd best make a plan. If you're planning to finance something, your first step is to look at what that loan is going to cost you. Your second step is to live on a budget for four to six months that includes the loan repayment amount, to make sure you can manage the payment.

If you have friends, family members, or co-workers who are planning big changes, a few questions can help them clarify their goals and set some limits so they don't end up playing the "if only" game.

Can you afford it? There's an easy way to tell. Simply put yourself into the shoes you're thinking of buying. Let's use a home purchase as an example.

1. Figure out what the mortgage payments and other carrying costs (insurance, property taxes, utilities, and maintenance) will be. Don't skimp when you estimate. The numbers have to be realistic for the exercise to hold any water.
2. Subtract the amount you're currently paying in rent.
3. Save the difference. If you can't save the difference every single month, you can't afford that home.

What are you prepared to give up to get whatever it is you want? You can't have it all at the same time. If you're taking on new financial responsibilities, something's gotta give. Will it be eating out with friends? Will it be your annual vacation? Will it be your plans for a new vehicle? What are you willing to give up to make your dream come true?

What are the ongoing costs, how will they change over time, and do you have room in your budget for them? Take up scrapbooking and you'll always be buying the accoutrements. Take up babies and you'll be buying diapers, then books and toys and clothes, then cellphones and laptops, then residence and tuition. The costs may not look too big at first, so look down the road a bit. Buy a new house and in 12 years you'll need a new roof. It's a lot easier to budget $60 a month from the get-go than to come up with the price of a new roof in one fell swoop.

Are you ready for the responsibility? If you're financing your first vehicle, do you understand that your contract is binding? No, you can't get out of it if things in your life change or you decide buying a new car wasn't the right decision. If you're buying your first home, do you know that you're going to have to fix and repair, or pay someone to fix and repair, what will likely be your biggest financial investment? Skimping on maintenance is a no-go. If you're having children, are you ready for sleepless nights, a constant sense of being on duty, and the knowledge that your wee one is totally dependent on you? Screwing up isn't an option.

Have you demonstrated a financial commitment to taking the action you're planning? If you're buying a home, you'll have saved a down payment. If you're having a baby, you'll have saved an emergency fund and enough money to see you through maternity leave. If you're buying a big-ticket anything, you'll be using cash, not financing it and then paying through the nose because you couldn't delay your gratification long enough to pay in full on the day you bought.

Are you doing this for YOU? Some people buy homes because they feel pressure from their families to "stop paying someone else's mortgage." Some people have children because it's expected. And some people buy stuff to keep up with the Joneses. If you're contemplating any action that you're having second (or third) thoughts about, do not act until you are completely sure, beyond a shadow of a doubt, that it is what YOU want. If you let anyone talk you into taking such an action, you will live to regret it.

MAKING SURE IT WILL BE FINE

If there is someone in your life who you believe is making a big decision without thinking through all the implications, you can help them by asking the big questions. This doesn't mean bombarding them. It does mean asking them to think about the issues that relate to their decision.

1. Encourage them to slow down and take some time to think about their decision. So often, people get really excited about whatever it is they're planning, and they let that excitement carry them on a wave of activity without giving much thought to the decision.

2. Suggest using a pro and con list to help clarify the upsides and downsides of the decision.

3. Clarify their priorities. "So, you think this is a great time to have a baby. Didn't you tell me you wanted to get into a home of your own before starting a family?" Or "The house looks wonderful. Are you guys giving up on those travel plans you've been talking about forever?"

4. If the decision is inaction—as in, "I'll worry about that later"—remember that some decisions are so hard it's easier just to procrastinate. Telling people they *have* to do something only makes them defensive. Instead, ask them to think about the consequences of not making the decision. "So, if you put off saving for retirement for the next five years, how much more will you have to save each month to have what you want when you retire?"

5. Tell them the truth. Ah, the truth. Maybe the hardest thing to say . . . and to hear. This has been my hallmark, my trump card, when trying to get people to face up to their reality. It doesn't come easily to most people—telling the truth—but it can be a real eye-opener.

．．．

Everyone experiences denial. Many years ago I received an email informing me that my cousin had died: suicide by train. I didn't believe it. The woman I loved would never do that. She was strong and feisty and full of life. If she was hit by a train it HAD to have been an accident. Even when her mother told me her death was a suicide, I refused to believe it. It was some kind of mistake. That week I wrapped the side of my van around an underground parking column, cried my heart out, and ate a tub of rocky road ice cream. No, not one of those tubs you buy at the supermarket. The tub they use at Baskin Robbins to scoop out your cone! It was only several years later, when her son told me he had found a note in the pocket of his jeans, that I finally believed the truth. I was in total and complete denial.

Often, hanging on to a delusion is easier than coming to terms with reality. Living in denial is easier than facing up to the facts. If you're determined to take the easy path—if you don't have the gumption to get real—then you're banking on your delusion holding, and THAT almost never happens. Eventually, the dream will evaporate and you'll be left holding a bag of warm, soft, smelly stuff. If you don't want that pouch of poop for yourself or your lovie, you must toss those rose-coloured glasses away.

People who get jolted out of denial or delusion often spend the next stage of their life whining about how unfair life is.

Boo hoo.

No one is due all the good stuff just because he or she is a good person. Not a home of their own. Not a happy family. Not a fulfilling career. Success comes from busting your butt. No one can wish it into existence.

Successful people have to plan and work hard for what they want. So do you.

Part Four

DISMANTLING ENTITLEMENT

You might think entitlement is about stuff. Wanting stuff. Buying stuff. Measuring stuff. It's not. Entitlement is about being at the centre of the universe. Everyone's universe.

People who are entitled believe that everything and everyone exists for them. The tops of the asparagus spears: theirs. The biggest bedroom in the house: theirs. The money in your pocket: theirs.

Some people confuse entitlement with selfishness but they're different things. Entitled people don't just think of themselves as entitled, they think you're entitled too, as long as your entitlement doesn't get in their way.

Psychologists believe that some people's expectations of special treatment are due to an underlying sense of inferiority. Instead of having a high sense of self-esteem, the entitled act this way to mask a sense of inadequacy.

University of Texas at Dallas psychologist Robert Ackerman and Michigan State University personality psychologist Brent Donnellan joined forces to look at the subtleties of entitlement. They used the Psychological Entitlement Scale, which predicts people's tendency to feel they deserve a salary, to lack empathy in close relationships, to explode when they don't get their way, and even to take candy from children. They found that those who were exploitatively entitled had low self-esteem, lower empathy, and a greater tendency to admit to cheating. Hey, some people will do anything to get what they think should be theirs!

Living with someone who feels she deserves special treatment when she has done nothing special—or when her sense of entitlement is impacting on you—is tough. His demand for constant attention, need for admiration, preoccupation with his own attractiveness can be exhausting. Throw a little arrogance into the mix and you just want to shake the entitled until their heads fall off. Overcoming someone else's sense of entitlement and making it clear that you'll no longer be bowing to their every whim is also tough. Most entitled people will be unwilling to believe that you're done with their "specialness." They've gotten away with being "special" for so long that breaking their bad behavioral habits will require significant effort and the patience of Job.

Tact doesn't work. You have to be brutal to get across their moat and into their castle. These princes and princesses of entitlement won't give up easily. And the likelihood of them backsliding, even after some progress has been made, is strong.

As the person who is breaching the walls, you will have to be relentless.

As the person whose walls are being breached, you will be angry at having your specialness questioned. It's tough to give up the position at the top of the pile. But like Yertle the Turtle, if you insist on climbing to the peak on the backs of those who love you, you will end up in the mud.

22 • I WORK HARD, I DESERVE IT

Pammie and her best friend, Judy, have been planning a weekend away at a spa for the last six months. After Pammie got into a car accident, she used her spa money to fix her car. Judy was mad. "We've been planning this for months," she whined to Pammie.

"I know, hon, but I had no idea that I'd get into a car accident."

"Why didn't you put it through your insurance?"

"That would still have cost me $1,000 for the deductible, and the whole repair was just over $1,500. It wasn't worth the hit to my insurance rates."

"Well," said Judy, "I'm going anyway. Put it on your credit card and you can pay it off after we get back."

Pammie paused. She had been looking forward to this vacation with Judy for so long. Damn the car! Maybe if she . . . She shook her head. That was ridiculous. She knew what she had to do, but she was angry about having to rein in her impulse to go. Her response was sharp. "You mean my credit card that has a 19.9% interest rate? Do you have any idea how much that'll cost me in interest?"

"So, get a cheaper card," retorted Judy.

Some people are under the impression that because they work hard they deserve to have the nice things in life. Having slaved away in the mines all day, they feel entitled to a pint with the boys, that to-die-for jacket, or a well-earned vacation.

If you want to drop money on a vacation and you have the money in the bank, you can do as you please. It's your money and as long as you're living within your means and taking care of the future, you can spend your money any way you wish.

As for you dopes who are planning to put that vacation on credit and then carry the balance around, you've proven you don't deserve the vacation by dint of the fact that you didn't prioritize it enough to save for it.

Donovan is a hard-working man. As the owner of a small renovation company, he's on the job six days a week, often 12 hours a day. Sometimes even longer in the summer. So when winter rolls around, Donovan feels he's earned the right to take a couple of months off and do some travelling. He was having dinner with his sister and brother-in-law one night when he told them he was planning a three-week trip down south to soak up some sun and do some golfing.

"How the hell can you afford that?" asked his sister, Marg. "You bought that house this year, and you and Karyn are planning on getting married in a few months."

"Hey," said Donovan, "I work hard. I deserve some good stuff too."

Marg's husband, Owen, laughed. "We all work hard, buddy. And if you have the money to do it, more power to you."

"I have a line of credit," said Donovan. "That's like money in the bank."

Marg groaned. "Sometimes, Don, I just wanna shake you," she said, a serious edge cutting through her seemingly good-natured response.

"What?" said Donovan, shrugging his shoulders, a boyish grin on his face.

"I think your sister is objecting to the fact that you're using a line of credit to pay for your vacation."

"Isn't that why they gave me the line of credit?" asked Donovan. "I'll be making great money again in the summer. I'll pay it off then."

Marg shook her head. Where should she even start?

Some people are willing to exchange their future incomes for the things they think they deserve to have today. People say,

- "We work really hard. We deserve a vacation."
- "I have a great job. I deserve to drive a nice car."
- "I do twelve-hour shifts. I deserve dinner out."

The thing about the "I work hard so I deserve it" attitude is that you can trick yourself into pledging many years of future income to the pleasures you're seeking in the here and now.

People don't think about how much interest they'll have to pay or how much more expensive whatever it is they're buying will be after they tack on the interest. Folks don't think about how long it'll take to get out of debt. And almost no one considers how it will feel if their circumstances change and they find they can't pay for that holiday (snappy new outfit, awesome cellphone, sexy new car) they deserved.

Nothing is deserved unless you've prioritized what you want and saved the money to pay for it. If you can't afford to save the money, or you're unwilling to cut spending elsewhere so you can have whatever it is you want, you don't deserve a thing!

DO YOU REALLY DESERVE IT?

Convincing someone that they do not deserve something they feel entitled to is no cakewalk. So how can you help someone work through this sense of entitlement? Try these two questions:

1. Do you have money in the bank ready to pay for whatever

you're going to buy as soon as the bill comes in? If the answer is yes, then your buddy is on her way to getting what she wants. If the answer is no, ask her how she will pay for it.

If her plan is to put it on credit and pay it off over time, better grab the calculator to demonstrate just how much said purchase will cost when the interest is figured into the price.

2. Have you taken care of all your must-haves, including savings? If the answer is yes, your pal is in the clear and deserves whatever it is he wants. If the answer is no, it's time to talk about how he may be sacrificing his financial stability to have the "I deserve it" item/experience.

Talk about the potential what ifs that could arise. If dudette is spending next month's rent money, how will she make up the difference? If dude's hours were to be cut at work, does he have enough stashed away to see him through? If sweetie pie is tapping her planned spending and her car breaks down, will she still have enough to get it fixed? If darling heart needed to take some time off to be with the kids, would he be okay financially?

23 • PETER PAN SYNDROME

When Dahlia finished university she expected to get a job and build a life for herself. Doing so turned out to be harder than she thought. She had to piece together part-time jobs, working retail, waiting tables, and temping to keep a roof over her head.

She was sitting with her brother, who had just graduated from college, talking about how tough it had been to get her first job. "Mitchell," she said as she pulled a sofa cushion onto her lap and hugged it, "I never expected it would take almost a year and a half to find a job I was actually qualified to do. I hope you don't think this independence thing is going to be a cakewalk." She smiled to soften the harshness of her words.

"Jarrod doesn't seem to have had as tough a time," Mitchell replied, referring to their elder brother. "He left school, got a job, and seems to be having a great life."

"If he were paying for that life himself, I'd be fine with it," said Dahlia, a sharp edge to her tone. "But he's sponging off Mom and Dad, and they keep paying for him."

"It's so frustrating since I have to pay my own way through college. I know Mom and Dad can't afford my tuition, but they seem to find the money for Jarrod."

"I think it's because he still lives at home. It's ridiculous: a 27-year-old man whose mother does his laundry. And I don't think he pays a cent in rent."

"Nope, and he doesn't contribute for groceries either, although he eats like a horse and doesn't think twice about bringing Sienna over for supper."

"She'll be knocked up and moved in in no time," said Dahlia bitterly.

From her lips to God's ears. Two months later Dahlia's mother called, crying. "Sienna is pregnant and Jarrod has broken up with her. How can he do that?" she sobbed. "I didn't raise him to be so irresponsible. That's our grandchild," she said, her voice heaving on the line.

"Oh, Ma," said Dahlia. "Jarrod's no better than a teenager. And Sienna is just as bad. I'm so sorry you're upset. But I'm glad they're not both moving in with you."

"We offered, but Jarrod said he's not ready to be a father."

"Big surprise," said Dahlia, her tone prickly with disdain.

"Dahlia, he's your brother."

"I know, Ma, and blood is thicker than water. Except that when it comes to his offspring, there are different rules. I hope he knows he's still going to have to support that baby."

"He should, but he always seems to come up short. He's got that huge truck loan, and I think his credit cards are all maxed out."

"What the hell is he spending all his money on? He's living with you rent-free. Don't you think you have a right to ask?"

"He has expenses."

"He makes twice as much as I do," Dahlia said indignantly.

"Yes, but you have Craig. It's easier for two people."

"Well, what about Mitchell? He's on his own and he's in school. And he's still paying his own way. How can you treat Jarrod like a child? He's a man. And this is just more proof that he will not grow the hell up."

"So this is my fault?" Her mother was growing angry.

"Haven't you and Pops let Jarrod live at home for the last five years without charging him a penny in rent? Aren't you still washing his clothes? For Chrissake, Ma, you treat him like a child. It's no wonder he has a horrible case of Peter Pan Syndrome."

Her mother hung up on her. Dahlia sighed. It was probably just as well. The next thing she was going to say to her mother would have made Dahlia *persona non grata* for months. She went looking for Craig to tell him about Jarrod's latest escapades.

Men who suffer Peter Pan Syndrome don't want to grow up. They skirt all major responsibilities. While their friends and siblings take on jobs, families, and mortgages, they work hard to remain footloose and fancy-free. They spend their money in bars, indulge their personal desires, buy the brightest and shiniest toys. They have no savings, often have loads of debt—they'll worry about it tomorrow—and seldom give a second thought to how their behaviour is affecting the people they purport to love.

Often the syndrome runs deeper than the superficial signs displayed by a man who is fun-loving and carefree with no roots suggest. Men who suffer from the syndrome can be hugely manipulative. Craving love one minute, they're seeking pity for their screw-ups the next. Fearful of appearing vulnerable, they substitute bravado and pride. Bruise their pride and you'll watch their charm turn into dangerous anger. Like a tempestuous three-year-old, they are wilful and demanding when challenged.

The psychologist who identified Peter Pan Syndrome in the early 1980s—his name was Dan Kiley—also identified Wendy Syndrome. This applies to women who act like over-indulgent mothers and allow their Peters to continue pretending they don't have to grow up. If you have an irresponsible man-child in your life, you need to look and see if you've been encouraging his self-indulgent and immature behaviour by playing the role of Wendy to his Peter Pan.

How do you know if you have a Peter Pan on your hands? Does he

- get extremely angry when challenged?
- obsess about looking cool (as he gets older, he also wants to look younger)?
- have difficulty expressing feelings of love?
- collect electronic gadgets like children collect baseball cards (he always has to have the newest device first)?
- act in a manipulative way to get what he wants?
- spend a lot of time hanging out with a gang of his buddies, playing sports, clubbing, and pubbing?
- avoid making commitments?
- seem to be a heavy drinker, drug user, or gambler?
- not follow through when he says he will do something?
- have an overprotective mother (or wife)?
- have a problem with authority figures?
- seldom engage in serious discussions?
- display a macho attitude to hide his insecurities and fear of rejection?
- avoid planning for the future?
- become extremely jealous?
- change his interests (and sometimes his girlfriends) frequently?
- seem very happy one moment and then frustrated or even depressed the next?

Have you mated with Peter Pan or do you have a Peter in your family? Want to do something about how his behaviour is affecting you?

First, you can't help someone who doesn't acknowledge that there is a problem. This is perhaps the biggest barrier to helping a Peter Pan to grow up. You can, however, stop being his Wendy. Do not support, respond to, interact with, or give any other kind of reinforcement to the negative behaviour.

You cannot have a healthy relationship with a man-child unless you are willing to assume the role of indulgent mother, in which case, don't whine. The man-child must accept that there is something wrong and seek help to change both his behaviour and his perception of himself as a free-wheeling, fun-loving boy.

The bottom line: You change how you deal with your Peter Pan and he grows up—or not. If he chooses not to, the next move is yours.

If maintaining the illusion is more important to Peter Pan than maintaining a relationship with you—in other words, if he isn't prepared to do whatever it takes to change to a healthier dynamic—you can continue to live with him and his delusion, leave, or kick him to the curb.

You might think you can separate the man and his behaviour sufficiently to be able to maintain a relationship, but it's only a matter of time until he does something that is detrimental to your family or becomes the straw that breaks the camel's back. (Hey, you're the camel!)

YOU can't fix this. HE must fix this. And if he won't, you'll have some tough choices to make.

ESCHEW BEING A WENDY

1. Once you recognize that you have a Peter Pan on your hands you'll have to decide if you're just going to live with it (no, it won't get better), or if you're going to stop playing the role of Wendy.

2. To stop playing the role of Wendy, you will have to insist that your mate, son, brother, or best friend change his behaviour.

   - If he gets extremely angry when challenged, walk away and refuse to interact until he has control of his temper.

   - Compliment him on his achievements instead of on his stuff or his looks.

   - Tell him you love him and ask for genuine reciprocation. Insist that he do something to demonstrate his love.

   - Ask him to stop buying new toys unless you've both agreed to the purchase. If he continues to spend money impulsively, create a joint account—to which he must contribute—to cover family expenses, and insist he meet that commitment before spending money on himself. Do not acknowledge or "appreciate" his new toys.

   - If he tries to manipulate you to get what he wants, disengage from the interaction. Make it clear you will only rejoin the discussion when he acts like a grown-up.

   - Ask him to limit the amount of time he spends on sports, clubbing, and other guy activities. Family

time, alone time, time doing chores must come first.
- Ask him to specifically commit when you need him to do something. Restate the commitment in your own words and get his acknowledgement. Present a consequence for his not meeting the commitment. "So, you're going to take my car in on Tuesday to have the winter tires put on. And if you don't, I'm going to take your truck and you're going to drive my car until you get those winter tires on, right?"
- Express zero tolerance for drug use, gambling, and intoxication.
- Do not support or encourage his rants about authority figures.
- Engage in a serious discussion about something in the news or something of interest to you at least once a week.
- Disengage from interaction when he displays a macho attitude or becomes extremely jealous. "I see you've put on your machismo cape, so I'm off. I'll find my own way home."
- Work together at planning for the future. The plan might be for a vacation, it might be for savings for the children, or it might be for building a fence.

HELPING WENDY RECOGNIZE HER ROLE

If the relationship between a Peter and a Wendy you know is working for both of them, there's not much you'll be able to do to "help." Resolve to just stay out of it. However, if Wendy knows there's a problem, is frustrated by the way her Peter behaves, or is concerned about his impact on the family as a whole—financially or emotionally—then

1. Ask Wendy if she's okay with being the only adult in the family. How does she feel when there are tough decisions to make? How are her stress levels? What would she like to see change?
2. If she starts complaining—"I don't have two kids, I have three!"—point out her role in enabling Peter to remain a man-child.
3. If Wendy assumes the role of martyr, ask her how that approach is helping to alleviate her anxiety or frustration. Then ask her what she thinks might actually help.
4. If Wendy starts punishing Peter, point out how that looks to other people, including their children. Is that the way she wants to come across? If not, how else might she deal with Peter?
5. Once Wendy has clarified for herself that she no longer wants to play the role of Peter's enabler, suggest the ideas listed in "Eschew Being a Wendy."

Danielle was a beauty. From the day she was born, people said what a doll she was, like fine china. And look at those eyes. Wow! She grew up as the baby of four children, the only girl. Her daddy adored her. Her mommy adored her. Her brothers growled when boys came by to take her out. As Danielle grew from teenager to adult she not only became more beautiful, but she kept her charming sweetness. Everyone loved her. They loved her so much nobody thought anything of the fact that she barely worked.

Sure, she had a part-time job at a chic makeup counter, but her parents had poured gobs of money into her education. First she got an undergrad degree in English. Then she decided she wanted to be a registered massage therapist. Halfway through her training she changed her mind and switched to an aesthetician program. She wanted to run her own spa one day; that was the dream.

When Danielle got married, her parents threw her an elaborate wedding. It started out as a smallish affair but Danielle just kept adding extras and no one ever said no. She asked so sweetly. There was never a cross word. She simply made her request known and her parents made it part of the plan. They ended up getting a line of credit so they could spend an additional $15,000 to cover the extra costs for Danielle's dream wedding. She insisted on a two-week honeymoon in France and Italy. She and her fiancé, Tony, had agreed to save for the honeymoon together, but Danielle's share never seemed to make it to the bank.

Eighteen months after the wedding Danielle decided to go house hunting. She'd had enough of apartment living. When she and Tony tried to get preapproved for a mortgage they were told that based on their income—mostly Tony's income—they couldn't get the house

Danielle wanted. They'd have to either settle for less house or come up with a bigger down payment.

Danielle went to each of her three brothers and secured $15,000 "loans" to up the down payment. They knew she'd never pay them back, but she was their little sister. Besides, they didn't know she'd been to each of them separately! Then she hit her parents up for $25,000. Bam! She'd increased the down payment by $70,000. She insisted that Tony ask his parents for money—to round the total up to $100,000— so she could have her dream home. He did. His parents said they would help as long as Tony agreed to repay the money over five years.

When Danielle started talking about having a family as soon as possible, Tony had had enough. He sat her down and told her they'd have to wait a couple of years to have a baby because they just couldn't afford it, what with the mortgage payments, the loan repayments, and the fact that she was only working part-time. She burst into tears and ran home to her parents, who opened their arms and reassured her that everything would be fine. Danielle's eldest brother, Dominic, asked Tony to meet him for a drink. His sister was very upset and Dominic wanted to know why Tony was being such a hard-ass.

Tony said, "You know I love her like all get-out, buddy, but we just can't make ends meet anymore. She keeps buying stuff for the house, and every store she walks into is willing to give her a credit card. I can't slow her down. Has she told you how much she owes?"

"No," said Dom slowly, "but hey, guy, that's what you signed up for when you married her. It's your job to take care of her."

"I want to take care of her," said Tony, looking into his half-finished glass of beer. "I really do." He turned the glass around and around between his hands. "But her expectations are so high there's no way to meet them."

"So, how bad is it?" asked Dom as he leaned back in his chair.

"Well, I still owe my parents $30,000 from that loan they gave us for the down payment. Has Danielle started paying you back yet?"

"Ha, are you kidding? I knew that money was gone when I handed it over." He took a sip of his beer.

"And you're okay with that?"

"Hey, man, she's my baby sister."

"Okay, so she soaked you and your brothers for $15K each and your mom and dad for another $25K, and you all think that's fine?"

"She borrowed money from the folks too? I didn't know that. Jack told me she'd hit him up and so we figured Mikey was on the hook too, but I didn't think she'd go back to the folks so soon after the wedding. I wonder where they came up with the money."

"You'd have to ask them. You guys don't talk about this stuff much, and it's one of the reasons you have no idea how demanding Danielle can be. I know she's cute as a button. That's part of the problem. I just haven't been able to say no. But now I have to. I'm barely carrying the house because she refuses to work full-time. And she's got about six credit cards all run up to the max. I'm not sure what we're going to do."

"Damn."

"Yeah, damn is right," said Tony, his shoulders hunched and his chin dipped to his chest.

"Do you think it would help if we all sat her down together?"

Tony shrugged. "Do you?"

"Maybe. I'll talk to the folks and see what they think. Clearly, this can't go on."

"No, it can't. I'm about this far"—Tony raised his thumb and fore-finger to denote no space at all—"from declaring bankruptcy."

Two men who loved Danielle beyond words stared into their beers and sighed. "Okay," said Dom as he stood up. "I'll get this round since you're broke. Let's go see the folks."

When they arrived at Danielle's parents' home, Danielle wasn't there. "Kathryn took her shopping to cheer her up," said Danielle's mom, Marie.

"Christ on a mountaintop," said Tony.

They went to the kitchen, where Marie made coffee. Danielle's dad, Big Mike, came up from the basement to join them.

"What's up?" he asked as he sat at the table.

Tony let it all spill out: the expensive engagement ring Danielle had to have, the honeymoon she didn't help pay for, financially squeaking into the too-big house, Danielle's constant shopping, the fact that she wouldn't work more than 18 hours a week, and her desire to start a family now. Danielle's family listened, nodding and tsk-tsking as Tony detailed where the couple was financially. It wasn't pretty.

"How did you let it get so bad?" asked Big Mike.

"You're kidding me, right? When she insisted on all that extra stuff for the wedding, I didn't see you putting your foot down," Tony responded hotly.

"But it was her day," said Marie. "We promised her a beautiful wedding."

"With no limits?" asked Tony.

"Hey, that's between us and our daughter," growled Big Mike.

"Maybe so," said Dom, "but Tony has a point. When she came back and hit you up for money for the down payment, how did you come up with the $25K?"

"I just took more off the house line of credit," said Big Mike.

"She had her heart set on that house," said Marie.

"And she has her heart set on a family," said Tony. "But how will we pay for it? She won't want to work at all once the kid comes along, so

I'll get stuck paying back everything. I just can't do it. I'm broke now."

Damn. Nobody said the word but it hung in the air over their heads like the grey cloud over Eeyore.

An hour later Danielle called to say she and Kathryn were going out for dinner and she'd be home late. "Like she thinks this is just going to blow over," groaned Tony.

"We'd better get your brothers over here and figure something out," Marie said to Dom.

"I'll call Angela," said Dom. "Maybe she'll have some ideas." Angela was Dom's wife of seven years. She was a smart woman who managed a career and two kids, and Dom knew he was blessed.

The brothers arrived, followed by Angela. "My mom came over to stay with the kids," she said as she kissed Dom. "We're okay for a couple of hours." Marie made more coffee and pulled out the biscotti, which she put on the table in front of the team that had gathered to solve the problem that was Danielle.

As Angela listened to the rundown from Tony, she admonished Dom. "I told you we shouldn't have given your sister that money, but you were determined."

"I know, I know," said Dom. "I had no idea how bad it was."

"Well, this is a mess," said Angela. "Who's going to break it to Danielle that she has to get a full-time job and grow the hell up?"

"Now, Angela—" said Marie.

"No, Marie," interrupted Angela, "you guys have treated her like a doll her whole life. She's smart and more than capable of making a good life for herself. She needs to understand that marriage is a partnership and that she has to accept her share of the responsibility."

"Okay, let's not squabble," said Dom. "We don't have time for that. We need to come up with a plan."

"Actually," said Angela, "Danielle needs to come up with a plan. She made the mess, she needs to figure out how to fix it. If we tell her what to do, we'll be treating her like a child. She's old enough to be a mother, so she's old enough to figure out her own mess."

"She'll just cry and say she's sorry," said Tony. "That's what she did every time I tried to have a conversation with her about the shopping or the credit cards."

"Okay," said Angela, "so we can't let that be ALL that happens. We know she'll cry. Marie, brace yourself. Here's what I think we should do. We'll all meet, then Tony, you need to lay out what the problem is, how you got into this mess, and how helpless you feel now."

"Helpless?" asked Tony, his machismo bridling.

"Oh, get over yourself," laughed Angela. "You're screwed so you better be willing to say so. The rest of us will sit quietly, clearly sending the message that we support Tony and expect Danielle to come up with solutions for the problems he's laying out."

"Is this an intervention?" mocked Big Mike.

"Hey, Dad," said Dom, "if that's what it takes to wake Danielle up, then that's what this is."

The family agreed to dinner on Saturday night followed by Tony's presentation to Danielle, with the family supporting him. Big Mike shook his head as he, Tony, Dom, and Angela walked to the door. "I feel like we're ambushing my baby girl," he said as he opened the door.

"Can you see another way?" asked Tony. Big Mike shook his head.

Everyone went home. It was going to be a long week.

Saturday rolled around, bright and sunny. Danielle had come home on Wednesday after dinner with Kathryn, but she had barely spoken to Tony. She was sulking and he was too busy trying to figure out what he would say on Saturday to care much.

"I'm going to the gym," said Danielle after breakfast on Saturday morning.

"I've got some errands to run," said Tony, who planned to spend the day putting the polish on his presentation. "I'll meet you at your folks' at four."

Dinner was delicious, as always. Marie was a fabulous cook. The cheese oozed from the lasagna, the garlic bread was crisp and chewy, and her famous Caesar salad did not disappoint. After dinner she served coffee and tiramisu in the living room. Everyone settled in. After taking a few sips of his coffee, Tony stood up. He turned to Danielle.

"If I wasn't already married to you, Danielle," he said, "I'd ask you to marry me again. I love you with all my heart. And I want to take care of you forever." He paused as she beamed up at him. "But I need some help, darling," he said slowly. "I'm afraid we're in a jam and I need you to help me figure out how to get out of the mess."

Tony had made three charts and put them on poster board so everyone could see. He pulled the first from the stack and leaned it against the unlit fireplace. It showed all the debt Tony and Danielle had. She looked at it, surprised at the direction the conversation had taken. Then she looked at her family. They all seemed to know what was going on. She looked back at Tony.

"I don't think we need to talk about this in front of my whole family," she said as her colour deepened.

"I think we do," said Tony. "So please bear with me. Your family already knows the problems we're having, because I've told them."

"You told MY family we're having problems?" Danielle said, her voice rising.

Marie held Danielle's hand. "Yes, baby, he has. And he was right to. We are a family. Families don't keep secrets. This needs some air and that's what we're going to do tonight." Danielle looked over at her dad. Surely he wouldn't agree to this. Big Mike was a very private man. Her dad looked at her, smiled and nodded. He, too, was here for the show.

Danielle looked back at the poster board. It showed their mortgage of $575,000 and Tony's line of credit, which was up to $20,000, along with the loan of $23,000 from Tony's parents. It showed the money she'd borrowed from Dom, Jack, and Mikey that she hadn't started paying back—$15,000 each—and the money she'd borrowed from her parents: $25,000. It showed the outstanding balances of her six credit cards, which totalled $17,745. And it showed their car loan of $39,000.

"You went through my mail," she said to Tony, her expression dark.

"You don't think your debt has an impact on me?" asked Tony. "If you were to have a baby and stop working, who would have to repay this debt?"

Danielle had the decency to look chagrinned. Tony handed Danielle a calculator and said, "Add it up." She took the calculator and put in the numbers. Her eyes widened as she hit Total. "Oh my God," she said, "we owe $744,745." The room was quiet. "We owe three-quarters of a million dollars," she whispered.

"It gets worse," said Tony, pulling the next poster board from this stack. This one showed their monthly incomes and expenses, not including consumer debt repayment.

Tony's income	$6,600
Danielle's income	$768
Total income	**$7,368**

Mortgage	$3,186
Property taxes	$400

(continued)

Home insurance	$120
Home decor	$600
Utilities	$292
Car payment	$600
Insurance	$125
Gas/Maintenance	$425
Cable/Internet	$160
Cellphones	$210
Groceries/Personal care	$800
Beauty (hair, spa, nails, waxing, etc.)	$200
Restaurants	$600
Clothes	$400
Entertainment	$300
Gym/Hockey	$300
Banking fees	$60

"This is our income and what we've spent on average over the past six months," said Tony. "I want you to add up our expenses." Danielle's beautifully manicured nails tapped away at the calculator.

"It comes out to $8,778," she said when she was finished. Tony wrote the number underneath the expenses.

"Now look at our total income," he prompted. "Do you see the problem?"

She stared at the board. The room was so quiet that when Baxter the pug farted everyone jumped. They all laughed. While it wasn't joyful laughter, it did break the tension.

"We're overspending by $1,410 every month?" asked Danielle, as if she didn't understand how that was possible.

"Right," said Tony. "You're putting money on credit cards that we don't pay off in full. So we're getting deeper and deeper into debt every month, to the tune of $1,410 a month."

Danielle gasped. Her eyes widened. "I had no idea," she said, her voice trembling.

"And this budget I'm showing you does not include even the minimum payments on our credit cards or line of credit debt." He waited for that idea to sink in. "When I add the minimum payments in, it takes our overspending up by another $800 a month, up to $2,210."

Marie couldn't control herself. She'd promised not to say anything but was so stunned by the revelation that she blurted out, "Oh heavens, how in the name of sweet Mary are you ever going to get out of debt?" Danielle turned to her mother and burst into tears.

"Okay, let's take a short break," said Angela. "Dom, will you call home and make sure everything is fine with the kids? I'll help Marie make some more coffee. Danielle, darling, I know it's a lot to take in, but it's been a while coming and Tony is sick to death with worry, so you better give him a hug and tell him you love him." She took Marie's hand and pulled her up from the couch and nodded to Tony to take her place.

Twenty minutes later, fresh coffee had been served and Danielle was sitting in the armchair, her back ramrod straight, her fingers picking nervously at her nails. The meeting reconvened.

"Okay," said Danielle, her voice almost a whisper. "What are we going to do?"

"That's what I want you to tell me," said Tony quietly. "You're a smart woman who's perfectly capable of getting what you want. Do you want to fix this?"

"Of course I do," Danielle said with a withering glance. "Of course I do." She stared back at the numbers. "But where do we even start?"

"Where do you want to start?" asked Tony.

"Well, it would seem to me there are some things I could cut right out of the budget."

"Like?" asked Tony.

"Well, like the gym and hockey."

Tony laughed. "Danielle," he said patiently, "I bust my ass at work every week and bring home a really good income. You think my hockey should be the first thing to go?"

"Well, I'm willing to give up the gym," she whined.

"But not the beauty routine? Or how about all the home decor stuff you keep buying?"

"I want us to have a nice home," said Danielle petulantly.

"Okay," said Tony, "I get that. But remember, we're spending $2,210 a month more than we make, and that's just with minimum payments, which doesn't even include what we owe to family." He drew out his third poster board. "If you want to have children in the next three years, here's what we'll have to put towards our credit cards and line of credit to get them paid off." He showed her the debt repayment chart he had been working on all day.

"We'd have to put $1,200 against our consumer debt every month to get out of the hole in three years," he said. "If you want to start a family sooner, it'll mean more in debt repayment. Two years at $1,800 a month or one year at $3,600 a month, which we have no way in hell of doing."

"So, what are we going to do?" asked Danielle plaintively.

"That's the big question," replied Tony. "What are we going to do?"

"All right," said Danielle, "you're saying if I want to get pregnant within the next two years, we have to come up with $1,800 a month for debt repayment AND we have to cut our spending back by $1,400 a month to balance our budget."

"Actually, $1,410," corrected Tony.

"Listen, buddy," she said, "if I can chop my spending by $1,400, you can give up $10 worth of your lunches at work."

"Yes, I can." Tony smiled. "So, where do you want to start?"

They got to work trimming their spending. "Let's lose the cable," said Danielle. Tony sighed. There went his sports channels. He took a red marker and sliced trough the $160, leaving $45 for Internet. "And I'm sure we can get a better plan for our cellphones, let's say $120 for both." He trimmed again. "I'm sure I can do the groceries for less than $800 a month. Let's say $600 and we'll see how that goes."

Tony continued to make notes on the poster board and Danielle directed. "Chop the clothes by $200, the entertainment by $100, and the beauty by $100. But I'm not giving up my waxing!"

"You're doing great," said Tony, who was keeping a running total on the calculator. "You've only got $605 in cutting to go."

"Okay, cut $600 out of home decor and take the other $5 out of restaurants."

"Okay, that gets us to a balanced budget. Now all we have to do is come up with the money for the debt repayment. Have you decided on two years or three?"

Danielle groaned. She'd forgotten all about the debt repayment. She had thought that with everything she'd already given up, she was in the clear. She hated this.

Tony saw the look on her face. "Hey, babe," he said, "we're doing great. I know it's going to be hard for a while, but once we fix this we can have a pretty good life. And we can start a family. Isn't that worth it?"

Danielle's sigh was like a shudder. "Yes, it's worth it. Okay, so if we say two years we have to come up with another $1,800 a month, right?"

"Exactly," said Tony encouragingly.

"What about that pricey education we paid for?" said Big Mike.

"You can make more than $700 a month with what we paid for your schooling."

Danielle glared at her father. Her mother jumped in. "You know, honey, you've always wanted to open your own spa. Don't you think getting some real-life spa experience first would make some sense?"

"Actually," Danielle said as she mulled over her mother's words, "that would be a good idea. Kathryn clears about $2,300 a month working at her spa, so if I got a full-time job, at least until I had the baby, that would mean an extra $1,500 or so a month, right?"

"So we'd only have to cut another $300."

Jack pointed to the Restaurants line on the budget. "Looks like you have some room here," he said. Tony swiped through the $595 under Restaurants and replaced it with $295.

"There," he said. "We did it."

"And now we have to live with it," sighed Danielle.

Many of us have people in our lives who are charming, sweet, cute, and totally irresponsible. They want the best of the best—even if it means going broke. Or they want to coast and bank on the people who love them to pick up the tab. Or their eyes are bigger than their wallets so they cajole others to spring for their treats. And the people who love them enable them to live the dream.

If there is someone in your life who wants to follow their bliss on your dime, and you've been letting them, when will you stop? Will they understand what you mean the day you say no because they've finally used up all your goodwill or your money? Will they be able to deal with reality at that point? Or will they go looking for another host to feed off?

Sometimes, sadly, these people are our children. Princesses—male or female—aren't born, they are built. Our progeny may have the makings of a princess from the get-go, but it is with nurturing and care that we grow them to full strength. Some kids are born with personalities bigger than their parents'. If their personalities aren't managed, these kids can become tyrants. The wilfulness, the determination to have their way, and the sense of entitlement that allows them to believe their needs supersede anyone else's are all reinforced in how we react to their demands.

No one has the right to ask another person to be responsible for them. Our mates, our siblings, our parents, our adult children, our friends are all responsible for themselves. When you assume responsibility for someone else's care and happiness, you are robbing them of the joy and satisfaction of self-reliance. You are laming them, just as if you had broken their legs. Are you paying for everything they desire so that you have the sense of being needed and wanted? Are you giving in to every whim in a pathetic attempt to keep their love? Are you supporting them financially and emotionally in their dependence because you just do not believe they can do it for themselves?

They can. And they will if you let them. But if you consistently bail them out or let them cajole their way into your wallet, when will they learn the important lesson that they are perfectly capable of taking care of themselves? How will they know they are strong enough and smart enough to handle their own lives?

If there is someone in your life who has learned to be financially dependent on you for whatever reason, there comes a point when you must cut the purse strings. Unless you are prepared to leave a lot—and I mean A LOT—of money behind to take care of them when you croak, that person you love better learn to stand on their own two feet.

You are doing no favours for the person you love when you allow them to maintain the illusion that they can have or do things they can't afford.

Breaking the cycle won't be easy. The more support you have, the better. Most important, you cannot be the person who comes up with solutions to the problems your loved one has created for him or herself because of their sense that they can have whatever they want. For someone to be committed to following through with the actions that will change how they live their lives, they must come up with their own solutions.

HOW TO HOLD A MONEY INTERVENTION

1. Get as many people as possible involved in the money intervention you're holding. The more people support your efforts to bring your son, best friend, mate, or parent into reality, the better. Since you're initiating, you lead.

2. Tell everyone what the problem is, in detail. Keeping secrets is a sure way to allow the manipulation to continue. The truth has to be on the table so everyone knows what's going on.

3. Have an initial discussion without the person for whom you are holding the intervention. This discussion should include

   a) when and where you'll do the intervention;

   b) the roles of each person there (i.e., who the spokesperson will be and what part the others will play); and

c) the consequences if the intervention is dismissed or ignored. What action will the people who love darling one take if darling one won't co-operate? Remember, empty threats will do more harm than good and if you're not prepared to follow through, don't even bother starting.

4. Use whatever ploy necessary to get darling one into the room: plan a dinner together, use a regular gathering if you have them, throw a party if you must. Begin by saying how much you love the person but that things have reached an impasse and must change.

5. Present the facts. All of them. Do it slowly and in detail. Make sure they are absolutely correct. No guessing or you may be caught out and then you'll have missed your opportunity to make real change happen.

6. Deal with objections calmly but firmly. Do not blame or express displeasure. Do not use labels like "spendthrift" or "shopaholic" or "irresponsible" or "child." Labelling will only get darling one's back up. This is a time to remain neutral.

7. Use "I" and "we" instead of "you" so that you don't seem intimidating or accusatory. So instead of, "Your shopping is putting our family at risk," say, "I feel at risk because all the shopping is creating more debt for us."

8. If the person says they're not interested, won't listen, won't participate, outline the consequences if things do not change:

   • If we continue on this path, we'll end up losing the house in six months.

- If you don't find a way to support yourself, my heart will hurt as I watch, but I will not offer you any more financial help.
- We are prepared to support you emotionally, but we've agreed not to give you any more money.

9. If histrionics ensue, take a break from the "presentation" and let them run their course for up to 15 minutes. Hearing the truth is hard. You should expect some upset. If the person wants to storm away in a fury, the other participants have a role to play in convincing him or her to stay and hear the truth. Do not threaten. If you must postpone to another day—while not the best option—make it clear that you're starting again on a specific day at a specific time. Everyone in the room has to make it clear that there WILL be another meeting and the issues WILL be discussed.

10. Ask the person if they want to fix the problem. If they do not, as a family you will have to make some tough decisions, which may include cutting the person off financially. If even one of you continues to support your darling one's disconnection from reality, she or he may never realize that their behaviour cannot continue. Everyone must be in agreement that they will no longer support their cute, charming, delightful parasite.

11. The person who is at the root of the problem has to be the person who is at the root of the solution. Resist the urge to come to the meeting with a plan and the expectation that your honey will buy in. If darling one doesn't come up with options as solutions, there will be no real buy-in.

12. Give lots of encouragement as the person comes up with

options for solutions. Encouragement doesn't mean fawning all over them. And no stopping before a complete solution has been proposed. Stopping halfway because, "Oh, baby, you're doing such a GREAT job and this is SO hard and you're WONDERFUL in so many ways," is just more of the same stuff that got you where you are now.

13. It is important, as you work through this process, that you identify something the person really wants as a goal to offset what they may be giving up: the spending, the not working, whatever their particular issue might be. Having a goal gives them something positive on which to focus. No goal means they're just losing stuff for no particular reason. Find a goal.

14. Ask your darling one to make a commitment in front of the group to the next steps they will take. Explain the consequences of their not following through (see step 10). Ask him or her to choose a buddy from the group: someone they can call for support as they implement the plan, and who will check in on their progress. Identify the time and place of the first (and second, third, fourth) follow-up meeting to discuss progress, challenges, and strategies, and to celebrate successes.

15. Don't expect the path to recovery to be a straight line. Setting that high of an expectation can be self-defeating. Expect lapses and plan for them. Failure, after all, isn't tripping and falling. That happens to the best of us. Failure is staying down. There will be stumbles. Have a plan for how you'll refocus your darling one to get moving again.

25 • LAZY LUCY

Lucy was a lazy girl. She loved shopping. She loved sleeping in until eleven. She loved clubbing and having lunch with her posse. Working? Not so much. She took the occasional shift as a substitute teacher, which gave her just enough money to keep her in incidentals. Her boyfriend paid for all their entertainment. "He's the guy, and the guy's supposed to pay," she told her mom. Her mom let her live at home rent-free while Lucy figured out what she was going to do with her life. "My mom's supposed to take care of me," Lucy told her boyfriend.

When Lucy's mom asked her to empty the dishwasher, Lucy groaned. When Lucy's boyfriend suggested she make dinner and they stay in for an evening, she called him cheap. Lucy wanted to have all the good things in life, but she wanted them handed to her. Work was a pain. Besides, she had worked three days this month. What was the problem?

No one told Lucy she was lazy. Some people thought it, but no one said it out loud. Lucy's mother, Aaliyah, was sympathetic to Lucy not being able to find a full-time job. When Lucy said, "I didn't go to university for five years to work retail," Aaliyah nodded her head and said how sad it was that Lucy just couldn't get a break.

Lucy's sister, Mirah, was often tempted to tell her sister just how lazy she thought Lucy was, but then she thought about the hissy fit Lucy would throw and decided that if silence was the price of peace, keeping quiet was worth it.

I am constantly amazed at the number of Lazy Lucys there are in the world. Why the hell do we send the message to our children, friends, or mates that it's okay to mooch off us? We pick up their tabs, clean up their dirty dishes, and laugh about just how little they get away with doing. It's not funny. It's manipulative and destructive.

Parents who let their adult children live at home with no expectation for sharing in the household chores are sending a clear message that their children don't have to do any work to maintain their own lives. Friends who let a moocher always take a pass on paying their fair share of the bill aren't being friends, they're being saps as their buddy continues to take advantage.

No one should put up with a Lazy Lucy. And if you love your Lucy, you should be particularly committed to helping her learn to stand on her own two feet.

- Friends will stop lending money or paying for outings. If you cannot have a friendship without the financial responsibility of taking care of Lucy, you're in an unhealthy relationship. So stop.
- Parents will make clear their expectations for their live-at-home adult child. If the child is working only part-time, then they need to pick up more of the at-home responsibilities like cooking and cleaning.
- Mates will sit down with their Lazy Lucy and discuss how they will share responsibilities moving forward. From household chores to paying for the needs and wants of life, Lucy will have to stop cruising and take on her fair share of the workload.

And what if Lucy won't change her game? What if, no matter what you say, she continues to get up at eleven, have lunch with her friends, work 10 to 15 hours a week, and mooch?

That's where consequences must come into play. The natural consequence of being lazy is not having the things people who work have.

Lucy's friends will make it clear that they are not picking up the tab. If she doesn't bring her own money—and show them the money before they go out—then they'll leave her behind and go elsewhere for their meal.

Lucy's parents will make it clear that they are not putting up with Lucy's slug-like behaviour at home. She must get up at seven, like everyone else in the family who is going to work, get dressed, and leave the house. (Feel free to change the locks and not give Lucy a key until she fully participates in her own life. Yes, lock her out.) In the evenings and on weekends, she must be a full participant in the cooking, cleaning, and maintenance of the home she shares.

Lucy's mate will make it clear that he or she will not support Lucy's lifestyle without her active participation. The consequences of mooching will be, at the very least, a full withdrawal of financial support beyond the basics (so noodles and ground beef, but no dinners out and no shrimp or steak). If Lucy wants more, she'll have work for it. Ultimately, the biggest cost will be the relationship itself if Lucy doesn't get with the program. After all, why would you want to tie yourself to a mooch for the rest of your life? The sex can't possibly be THAT good!

KICKING LAZY LUCY INTO GEAR

1. Decide on the consequences for Lucy if things don't change. Be committed to those consequences or don't even bother to have the conversation.

2. Set a date to have the conversation in which you explain the behaviour that must change.

   - "You're not bringing in enough money to cover your share of the costs, so you must make more money."
   - "You're not pulling your fair share of the work at home, so you must take on more of the chores. Will you do the grocery shopping or will you do the laundry?"
   - "You always show up without enough money to pay your full share of the bill. I'm not paying for you any more."

3. Explain the consequences:

   - "If you don't start bringing in more money, we're going to find a cheaper place to live. It won't be as nice, but it'll be what we can afford."
   - "If you don't take on more chores to pull your weight, then you'll have to find another place to live. You have two months to find a place."
   - "If you show up without money to pay for your own meal, we'll find a far less expensive place to grab a bite or we can cook at home."

4. Stick to the plan. If Lazy Lucy doesn't come around, you'll have to follow through or Lucy will know you're all bark and no bite.

. . .

The thing I don't understand about people who feel and act entitled to the detriment of others is why family and friends allow themselves to be cast in the role of the less entitled.

When I'm oot and aboot, I'm often stopped by people who want to tell me about the princesses they have in their lives. They describe in detail how entitled their lovie is and just how angry or frustrated or sad it makes them feel.

I listen carefully and then I say, "You did that."

Most people stop for a moment to consider what I've said and then nod slowly, admitting to their role in the creation of the epically entitled. Others burst into laughter with, "Boy, you don't pull your punches, do you?" Still others shake their heads from side to side sadly. They know they've had a part to play but don't know what they can do about it now.

We are each responsible for the relationships we have. It takes at least two for any interaction. If the person who is entitled is getting away with it, you are letting them.

If your sister reaches into your closet to borrow your new dress before you've worn it yourself, and you let her, you did that. If your daughter tries to convince you that she should have the largest bedroom in the house because she has more stuff and needs the extra space, and you let her, you did that. If your son insists that the crappy car you're thinking about buying him isn't good enough for him to been seen in, and you upgrade to a snappier, more expensive version you can't really afford, you did that.

All of these are situations have been described to me more than once by folks bemoaning the entitled in their lives.

You can keep playing the game—it's your relationship—or you can decide enough is enough and you're entitled to the same level of consideration and support that's being demanded of you.

Part Five

FIGHTING FEAR

Fear is the most crippling of all emotions. People do all kinds of dumb things because they're afraid.

People who are afraid their lives will never be better commit financial suicide trying to spend their way out of the misery that is their present. People who are afraid the person they love will leave refuse to do anything that will upset the apple cart. People who are afraid of being alone will buy their way into social circles. And people who are afraid someone will find out their secrets will take extraordinary steps to protect those secrets.

People are afraid of being seen as unfair, so they compensate by being nicer than they probably should be. People are afraid of being perceived as mean, so they refuse to ever say no even when no is the right answer. People are afraid of seeming uncool, so they load up on the accoutrements of cool.

Fear causes people to put themselves at risk without really understanding what they're doing. When Stanford researchers Peter DeMarzo and Ilan Kremer looked at what investors fear the most, they found that investors' biggest fear was not the loss of their money but the likelihood that they would do worse than their peers. So investors are prepared to gobble up pie-in-the-sky investment options rather than missing out on the next big win.

If you find yourself spending money you can ill afford to spare to keep up with your social group, that's fear. If you find yourself unwilling to ever spend money you do have, forgoing pleasure because your money pile will never be big enough, that's fear. And if you spend money on others because you know if you don't you'll be dog poop on their shoes, that's fear.

Let fear rule your behaviour and your life will suck. If you're always worried about whether someone likes you enough, whether someone loves you enough, whether you have enough, or whether you're being perceived the way you want to be perceived, you'll wear yourself out from the inside. If you don't want your life to suck, you're going to have to dig down deep to find the courage to change how you think.

You may not think of yourself as particularly brave. Maybe you think of bravery as something that belongs to those people who charge into situations with no thought for their own safety. You're wrong. **Being brave means looking fear square in the face and doing whatever it is that scares the crap out of you.**

If there's someone in your life who is a big scaredy-cat, your love and support can help them find their own courage so they no longer have to live in fear. You can encourage them to figure out what they're afraid of—really afraid of—and find ways to work through that fear. Sometimes all a body needs to step into the breach is some encouragement and the knowledge that someone is there to hold their hand.

26 • HE'LL LEAVE ME

Francie loves Steven with all her heart. They have a sweet little house, two beautiful children, and what looks like a great life. But Francie's BFF, Nora, knows that everything is not as it seems.

Francie works full-time as a claims agent for an insurance company. She starts at eight thirty and works until four thirty, with a half-hour commute each way. She picks the kids up from daycare around five each evening and is in a panic if she gets caught in heavy traffic and thinks she'll be late.

Steven works locally as a project manager for a large grocery retailer. He doesn't start work until nine and doesn't roll out of bed until Francie and the kids have left the house. He often works until seven. When he comes home, he expects the kids to be bathed and ready for bed and Francie to have a nice meal ready. The weekends are his time to recuperate from a long week at work. He drinks beer and watches every game on television. If it snows, he shovels, and in the summer he cuts the grass. That's about it for what he does around the house. He'll roughhouse with the kids but he doesn't do any of day-to-day parenting chores. He leaves all that to Francie because "She's just better at it."

One Saturday morning Nora was watching Francie do the dance of balancing the kids and all the housework she had to get done. She took a sip of her tea and said, "So, what's Steven up to today?"

Francie glanced over suspiciously. She'd heard it all before from Nora: Steven is lazy; Steven should help with the kids, he's their father; Steven doesn't know how good he has it. "Please don't start, Nora. I just don't have time for this today."

"When do you have time for anything other than work and house-keeping?" Nora responded.

"Listen, I have a good life and I'm grateful for it. Steven works hard all week. You know he puts in more hours at work than I do."

"So the work at home isn't work?" Nora asked sarcastically. "When was the last time that man so much as threw in a load of laundry? Oh, I know," she said quickly. "NEVER."

"Nora, really, I don't want to get into it now."

"When's a good time, Francie? When will it be the right time to tell Steven to get off his fat ass and help with the kids and the house?"

Francie looked up, her eyes shining with the tears she was holding back. "The last time I took your advice and told Steven I needed help, he told me I had to pull my weight and if I wasn't up to it, he'd take the kids and leave so I could have all the time I wanted."

Nora gasped. "He did not! You know that's an empty threat, right? He can't take your kids and he wouldn't leave. Where would he find someone as easy to get along with as you are?"

"Nora, just shut up," said Francie in a whispered shout. "I don't know that. He makes the majority of the money. If he left, how would I even begin to support Tia and Misha? The mortgage on this house is over $1,700 a month. And there are car payments and the kids' day-care. I could never manage on my own."

Nora was taken aback by Francie's ferocity.

"Besides," continued Francie, "I love Steven with all my heart. I'd die if he left me."

Some people are so insecure in their relationship that they let their mate get away with murder to keep them happy and at home. Whether they allow their mate to spend every penny and then some, or let their mate abdicate responsibility for kid and home care, some folks let their partners treat them like second-class citizens. Inevitably, this behaviour is also reflected in how money is treated. One partner makes more of the decisions, spends more of the money on personal indulgences, or insists on more of the control in order to keep the "lesser" partner in line.

It's hard to watch friends or family members be treated like doormats. People who feel like they're not good enough won't demand to be treated fairly in a relationship. Their insecurities allow their mate to take the upper hand and demand more—and get more—than they give. And when it comes to money, the submissive partner won't hold their mate accountable for financial behaviour that has a negative impact on the family.

Good relationships are about sharing: sharing the work, sharing the joy, sharing the money, sharing ideas, sharing a life. If one mate treats the other with less respect, if one mate controls the money, if one mate acts like the other is dispensable, the relationship is doomed. It is only a matter of time before the tinderbox explodes. It may be an affair. It may be an unmanageable amount of debt. It may be an argument that ends in physical violence. The disintegration started through inequity will end badly.

If you are watching someone you love turn themselves inside out to keep their husband or wife, know that this dynamic relates to self-esteem. The only way for the dynamic to change is for your lovie to gain a sense of their own worth. You might suggest counselling or activities that are empowering. Anything that creates a sense of worth and raises the person's self-esteem will help.

Jumping on your friend for being a wuss, demanding that they take control of their lives, suggesting that they are doormats won't help. People who see themselves as at risk or as having less worth in their relationship simply can't ask for more. Before they can expect their mates to see them differently, they first need to change the way they see themselves.

HELPING WITH SELF-CONFIDENCE

1. Accomplish something. Nothing builds self-confidences as much as accomplishment does. Suggest your friend take up a new challenge: running a marathon, trying kick-boxing, taking up karate. As your friend grows stronger physically, their spirit will grow stronger.

2. Face the fear. Being afraid is normal. Letting fear get in the way of life is debilitating. Ask your friend to pick one thing they are afraid of and do it. With each fear they face and defeat, their overall sense of fear will lessen.

3. Encourage failure. People are desperately afraid to try and fail. But with each trial and failure comes knowledge that will make the next trial more successful. Failure isn't forever; failure is the stepping stone to the next success. So when your friend is beating herself up for being a failure, remind her of the progress she's making.

4. Suggest books or articles that inspire self-confidence. Focus on stories about overcoming adversity or that describe how to meet a particular challenge. When I was in my twenties, I read the book *Feel the Fear . . . and Do*

It Anyway by Susan Jeffers. That book had a profound impact on my life. Books can do that.

5. Talk about what your friend wants from his life. It's important that he focus on what's important to him so he can better get to know what he really, really wants. It will take time, but with repeated chats about life and what the future could be like, your friend will begin to learn more about himself and his needs.

6. Encourage positive self-talk. If you hear your friend repeating words that diminish her value, ask her why she thinks she isn't worthy of full status in her family. Point out the things she does well. Encourage her to want to be in charge of her own destiny. Help her identify her inner critic so she can learn to quiet it.

7. Look at it from the kids' perspective. If there are children in the relationship, suggest that your friend look at her life through her children's eyes. Is settling for second-class status the lesson she wants her daughters to learn? Her sons?

8. Ask your friend to track his self-esteem and his general sense of happiness. As self-esteem rises, people often report feeling their spirits lighten. They have more of a sense of stability as they become less needy; life doesn't seem like the roller coaster it was. And they are less likely to self-sabotage.

27 • NO WAY OUT

Nathalia lived with her mom and her grandmother: three generations of women who had always just gotten by. They lived in a two-bedroom apartment, so Nathalia slept on a pullout couch in the living room. Her grandmother smoked like a chimney and Nathalia hated that her own clothes always stank as a result. But she didn't make enough money to move out on her own. Besides, her mom and grandma needed her share of the rent to make ends met.

When Nathalia met Charlie and fell in love, she spent weekends at his place. It was small, just two rooms in a basement. But it felt good to be out of the smelly apartment. She missed her mom but, really, she hardly saw her anyway. Nathalia worked days as a receptionist at a car dealership. Her mother and grandmother both worked the night shift at a major retailer, stocking shelves. So they passed like ships in the night.

Charlie suggested that Nathalia move in with him and that they get a bigger place. She was all for that. But she didn't know how to tell her mom. Then she got pregnant and that made up her mind. There was no way she was bringing a baby into that smoke-filled apartment. So she delivered the good news about the baby, and she and Charlie found a new place for themselves and their wee one. Money was stretched and Nathalia found she often needed to use her credit cards to make ends meet. Charlie was doing his best, but his only credit card was already at the max and he had no more wiggle room.

After Monique was born Nathalia found out Charlie had gotten another credit card, and that it was already at the limit. "I had to," he said when she told him she was afraid of all the debt they were taking on. "You weren't getting much from your maternity-leave benefits and there was that last course I wanted to take so I could finish up my apprenticeship. Once I'm done, I'll be making better money. So, it was a good investment."

Nathalia agreed. It made sense that Charlie put his course on credit if that was the only way for him to finish school. She wanted to go back to school too. But now, with a baby, it looked like that would have to wait for a while. They'd have to get some of that debt paid off or she wouldn't have any way of managing her share of the expenses and school too. It seemed so hopeless. Every time she turned around it was something. The credit card balances never moved, despite what she paid against them each month.

Nathalia decided she needed help. At church that Sunday, she asked her pastor if he knew of anyone who was good with money and could help her figure out what to do next. She explained that she felt like she was in a box. He nodded. Yes, he knew someone, but she was pretty tough. Was Nathalia up for the cold, hard truth? Nathalia nodded, relieved that someone might be able to show her some tricks to deal with the ever-growing debt. "Oh, I don't think she has any tricks," said her pastor. "She's a little too serious for tricks. Her name is Denise Dodgeson and she manages our church's finances. Let me have a word with her and see if she's willing to help."

A few days later Nathalia's phone rang. It was Denise. "I hear you're in need of some guidance when it comes to your money," said Denise.

"Yes, I am," said Nathalia. "I'd be so grateful if you'd be willing to spend some time with me."

"I would," said Denise, "but only if you promise to do exactly as I say. I've done this before and people always say they want to make things better, but they don't want to do the hard things necessary to make it actually happen. Before I spend so much as an hour with you, you have to assure me that you're serious about this."

"We are very serious."

"We?"

"My boyfriend and I. We both need help."

"Well, dealing with one of you will be hard enough. Dealing with two people who have messed up their money may be more than I want to take on."

"I promise you we are both very serious," pleaded Nathalia. "Please, Ms. Dodgeson, we have a little one and we can't keep doing what we've been doing."

"A little one? How old?"

"Monique is seven months."

"Okay," said Denise slowly. "Bring your baby, your boyfriend, and all your financial papers to my house and we'll have a look. Would Wednesday evening work for you?"

"Yes, yes. Wednesday is fine."

Denise gave Nathalia her address. "See you at seven," she said. "Bring everything you have that has anything to do with your money."

"Well, we haven't been very good at keeping records," said Nathalia.

"We can't work by guessing. You can go online and print your statements, right? Banks usually keep three months' worth online. So bring at least three months of bank account and credit card statements along with paperwork for any loans you have."

"Okay, I can do that," said Nathalia, relieved. She hung up and got busy collecting what she'd need for the meeting.

Wednesday rolled around and Nathalia, Charlie, and Monique arrived at Denise's promptly at seven. "I'm glad you're on time," she said as she opened the door of her pretty house. "I hate it when people are late."

"Thank you so much for agreeing to help us," said Charlie.

"We'll see if I CAN help," said Denise. "I won't know until I look at your papers."

She had made tea and put out a basket of banana muffins.

"Do you mind if I spread out a mat on the floor for Monique and some of her toys?" asked Nathalia.

"Oh, no, go ahead," said Denise as she came over to take the baby from Nathalia. Charlie unpacked a small bag, pulling out a blanket for the floor and a play mat to go on top, along with several small toys. He sat on the blanket and watched as Denise smiled and gurgled at the baby. "She's just beautiful," said Denise. "I've got three grown daughters and seven grandbabies of my own."

"You're very blessed," said Charlie.

"Yes, I am." Denise smiled as she handed the baby down to him. "I take it you're going to go over these with me?" she asked as she took the paperwork from Nathalia.

"Yes ma'am. I've been kinda looking after the money. Charlie works such long hours that I'm doing most of the bill paying."

"Okay," Denise said as she pulled out a chair and sat. "But, young man, you better know what's going on with the money too."

"Oh, I do, Ms. Dodgeson. Nathalia and I talk about it all the time. It seems that, lately, it's all we talk about."

"All right, let's see if we can get a handle on this." Denise looked at the first statement on the pile. She began circling items on the statement, some with a red pen, some with a blue pen, some with a green pen. She picked up a yellow highlighter and stroked through several items.

Nathalia sat nervously nibbling on her fingernails.

"Don't fidget," said Denise without looking up. "Pour some tea and have a muffin. I made them fresh." She kept at her circling. "Do you two have a budget?" she asked when she finally looked up.

"Sort of," said Nathalia.

"There's no sort-of budget," said Denise, waving her arms dismissively.

"Well, I mean, we know what we spend for our rent. It's $900 a month. And that includes utilities but not cable. And we spend about $350 a month on groceries."

"Are you sure about that?" asked Denise.

"No, I guess it's what I aim for," said Nathalia.

"Aiming and missing," said Denise grimly. "I've highlighted all the grocery transactions on your bank statements and credit card statements in green. I want you to add them all up and then divide by three, since you brought me three months' worth of statements." She handed the pile back to Nathalia. She pushed a pad of paper forward, along with a pencil and a calculator. "Start by noting all the grocery transactions on the pad. Then add them up."

Denise got up from the table and went to sit on the couch near Charlie and the baby. Nathalia started writing. She was a little surprised at the number of transactions that were circled. Charlie and Denise chatted quietly while Nathalia did the math. When she finished, Nathalia looked up and said, "Okay, I'm done. I guess we're spending more than we thought, Charlie. It averages out to $497.37."

"And I bet there are other things we don't know how much we're spending on," said Charlie.

"I bet you're right," said Denise as she rose and walked back over to the table. "I circled your restaurants in blue and your bank charges in red. And those yellow highlights, that's just random shopping I couldn't assign to a particular category."

Denise pointed to a transaction on Nathalia's credit card statement. "What's this for?" she asked. "It shows up every couple of weeks."

"Oh, that's for getting my nails done," said Nathalia.

"You don't have money to pay off your debt but you have money to get your nails done?" asked Denise as she put a hand on her hip. Her tone was scathing.

"I work hard, and it's just a small thing. It only costs me about $20. That's no big deal."

"Every penny you spend is a big deal," said Ms. Denise. "How many no-big-deals do you think you've been spending on?" She looked over at Charlie. "You too, young man. I know Nathalia doesn't smoke!" Nathalia looked at Charlie with an "I told you so" glare.

"Hey, don't look at me that way," he said. "I'm not the one who spends money on stuff like getting my hair done."

"Every six weeks," said Nathalia, glaring at Charlie.

"Okay, you two, you can stop this nonsense right now," said Denise. "Every cent you spend on wants—any kind of wants—when you've got so little money has to be considered carefully. You can't spend on wants if you don't have your needs covered.

"Your job" she continued, not giving them any room to interrupt, "will be to take all this paperwork home and do for every category exactly what you did for the groceries. You have to know what you've been spending to see how you've been using your money. Then you can decide what you really want to do with it."

"Okay," said Nathalia. "Is that it?"

"Far from it," replied Denise dryly. "Here's something else you need to figure out," she said, pulling a credit card statement from the pile in front of Nathalia. "Do you have any idea how much of your payments is going to interest and how much is going to pay off the balance?"

"No," said Nathalia. "I make the minimum payment every month, and if we have a little extra I try to put some more on it."

"I'll bet you're pretty frustrated at how small a dent those payments are making."

"Yes, I am," said Nathalia. "I feel like we're doomed to always be in debt."

"That's the problem with using credit cards if you don't pay them off in full every month," said Denise. "In no time at all, you've dug a hole and getting out becomes yet another problem.

"See this credit card balance here?" She pointed. "I want you to multiply this balance of $2,347.45 by the interest rate here," she said, pointing to a box that showed the interest rate of 18.9%. "Then divide by 12 to see what you're paying monthly in interest."

Nathalia tapped at the calculator. She multiplied 2347.45 by 18.9, divided by 100, and then divided by 12. "It's $36.97," she said.

"And what's the minimum payment in that little box?" asked Denise, pointing to the minimum payment box on the statement.

"Forty-five dollars," answered Nathalia.

"So, how much of your payment is going to actually pay off the principal?"

Nathalia tapped "45.00" into the calculator and then subtracted "36.97." "Oh heavens," she said, "just $8.03."

"If you divide $8.03 into the amount you owe, that'll give you an estimate of how long it'll take to get that credit card paid off," said Denise.

Nathalia's fingers clicked the calculator buttons. Then she did the calculation again. "That can't be right," she said. "It keeps coming out to 292."

"Oh, it's right," said Denise. "It'll take 292 months, or 24 years. Is that how long you want to be in debt to that credit card company?"

"Oh mercy, no." Nathalia's eyes widened. Charlie had stood up with the baby and was standing behind Nathalia, shaking his head.

"I had no idea," he said.

"Most people don't," said Denise. "Most people won't do the math to figure out their own debt repayment plan. They just merrily keep making the minimum payment, throwing a little extra on the pile when they feel like they can."

"So, why is that minimum set so low?" asked Nathalia.

"Do you know how the credit card company makes money?" asked Denise.

"From the interest it charges us," said Charlie.

"And from the swipe fees it charges merchants," said Nathalia, who had heard one of her bosses complain about the fees she was paying.

"Exactly," said Denise. "The longer you carry a balance, the more money the credit card company makes. Want to see how much?" Both Charlie and Nathalia nodded. "Multiply that monthly interest cost by the number of months it'll take to pay it off to get an idea. It's not a perfect calculation, but it's good enough for our purposes."

Nathalia tapped in "36.97" and multiplied it by 292. When the total, 10,795.24, popped up on the calculator screen, both Nathalia and Charlie swore under their breath.

"You eat with that mouth?" asked Denise.

"Sorry, sorry," they chorused.

"You see why credit card companies want you to carry a balance and ask you only for a small payment every month?"

"No wonder I don't feel like I'm making any headway."

"No wonder," Charlie repeated.

"So, you two have some decisions to make," said Denise. "You can keep operating as you have been and be poor forever, or you can make up your minds to do something differently so you can have a different life."

"I don't know anyone who isn't struggling," said Charlie. "The guys at work are always bitchin' about not having any money."

"And my mother and grandmother never have any extra money, especially since I moved out," said Nathalia guiltily.

"Your friends' and your parents' lives don't have to be your life. You can make different choices," said Denise. "Do you want Monique to grow up with the same frustrations you've had, or do you want her life to be better?"

"Better, of course," said Nathalia.

"Well, then," said Denise, "it's time to take control of your money instead of letting the tail wag the dog. Here's what you're going to do over the next week." Denise pulled the pad towards her and made a list of activities for Nathalia and Charlie. "Once you've done this, we can talk again. Is two weeks enough time?"

Both Nathalia and Charlie nodded as they silently read the list. "Two weeks it is, then."

There are loads of people who can't imagine not being in debt or who feel perpetually poor because they can't see a way out of their current financial fix. Determined to enjoy life in whatever way possible, they spend money to compensate for a sense of doom.

People who have little disposable income look at people with lots of disposable income and think, "I want that too." It's natural. But it isn't productive. And if spending on wants turns into debt, it comes at too high a cost.

Being afraid that things will always be as they are now is a sure way to keep them that way. It's called a self-fulfilling prophesy. Too much debt? Not enough income? No way out? You're right. As long as you keep thinking that you're trapped, you are. But it is you who have set the trap and it is you who are keeping the trap in place.

Change your thinking and you can change your life. Face the worst as you imagine it and then make a plan to circumvent that outcome. If you have the ability to work, if you become conscious about what you're doing with your money, if you set a goal and make a plan to achieve that goal, you *can* change your life.

Not everyone has the strength and the tenacity to change their personal circumstances. Some people can't escape the fear that they will always be poor. Some people don't want to do the hard work it will take to make changes. Those are the ones who will remain where they are.

But it doesn't have to be like that.

Years ago, when my family emigrated from Jamaica, the woman who helped to raise me didn't want to stay in Jamaica either. Daphne, whom I loved with all my heart, wanted her own opportunity. My dad got her a visitor's visa to the U.S. and she stayed. Daphne had learned to read and write at my mother's elbow. With little education and no financial nest egg, Daphne got busy creating a life.

Daphne worked a full-time day job and a full-time night job, looking after an elderly woman who needed an overnight attendant. Daphne learned to drive, bought herself a car, bought herself a house, paid for her legalization in the U.S., brought her children to live with her, and put her daughter through college. My Lord, the woman had fortitude!

Our circumstances do not define us. We can achieve

anything we put our minds to. We have the power to make life whatever we want. Some of us want more.

Daphne wanted more. And she busted her butt to get it. She made hard choices and she achieved a lot, moving from poor to not so poor, to secure. She made a life.

So, how do you do what Daphne did?

Like Nathalia and Charlie you must decide you want things to be different. You may need to ask for help to figure it all out and that's okay. Once you make a plan, you must stick with it even when you feel like saying, "Screw it, I just want to go out for dinner tonight." You can't ever spend money without first asking, "Will this get me where I want to go?"

I know other people spend money without thought. Afraid that life will never be any different, they give into immediate desires because they don't trust their future potential. That's why so many are in a helluva mess when it comes to their money. Small indulgences add up. If you put wants before needs, if you have no goals, if you can't see the big picture and don't have the gumption to do the hard work to achieve what you want from your life, then you'll likely make your self-fulfilling prophesy come true. But that's up to you.

STEPPING IN TO HELP

1. If someone comes to you seeking help, the first rule is to be completely honest with them. Do not sugarcoat the mess they have made. It doesn't matter how much you love them, or how hard asking for help is for them, only honesty will get them to a place where action is inevitable.

2. Show them the specifics of how their actions are working against them. Until you use real numbers, the whole discussion is up for argument. Say, "You're spending $86 a month on banking fees right now. Is that working for you?" and you're much more likely to get a commitment from them to change their behaviour.

3. Do NOT do the work for them. While loads of well-meaning, financially savvy parents and friends are willing to build budgets and debt repayment plans for their wayward lovies, until lovies do it for themselves, it isn't theirs! You can show them how by calculating a line or two, or by using examples. But do not do the work of putting together the whole plan.

4. Break things down into small pieces. Don't ask for too much change at the same time, or too much work to be done all at once. People become overwhelmed, throw up their arms, and reconcile themselves to always being in a mess. Break the process down into small steps so they can see their progress. Celebrate their successes. Then give them the next steps.

5. Know that change takes time and comes with some slips. Be positive. Don't let the slips derail the whole plan. "Okay, so this wasn't a particularly good week. That happens. Do you want to get back on track or are you going to wuss out and give up?"

6. Whenever you can, inject some humour. If you can deliver your message with some humour, it'll add a softening effect to the hard edges of reality. If you're no good at the humour thing, don't force it.

FINDING YOUR WAY OUT

1. Decide that you want your life to be different. Be willing to do whatever it takes.
2. Ask for help. If you don't know where to start, ask your friends, family, pastor, co-workers, everyone for resources and support. Having someone to guide you often means the difference between following through and giving up.
3. Buy a notebook to keep a spending journal and start tracking how you spend your money.

   At the top of the first page, write the amount you have in the bank. As you go about your day, collect receipts for EVERYTHING you buy. Whether you use cash, debit, or credit card, ask for a receipt. When you get home, sit down and make your spending journal entries.

   Every time you spend a penny, you deduct it from the balance. Every time you get a penny, you add it to your balance. Your spending journal will look like this:

JUNE

	Credits ($)	Debits ($)	Balance ($)
Income	3,274.00		3,274.00
Mortgage payment		-1,543.00	1,731.00
Insurance		-122.36	1,608.64

(continued)

Emergency savings	-100.00	1,508.64
Car loan	-375.00	1,133.64
Debit: Groceries	-86.72	1,046.92
Credit: Car tune-up	-71.63	975.29
Credit: Dinner	-47.61	927.68
Hydro	-110.10	817.58
Retirement savings	-330.00	487.58

Not only will your spending journal keep you in the know about how much money you have left in the bank, it'll keep you conscious about what you're spending.

4. Get six months' (three at the very least) worth of your financial paperwork and do a spending analysis. You need to see where you've been spending your money if you want to take control. (The steps for doing a spending analysis are outlined in detail in *Debt-Free Forever*.)

5. Make a plan for how you will deal with your debt. (Again, *Debt-Free Forever* has all the steps to making a plan.) Just throwing money at your debt without a plan is inefficient and means you'll likely end up paying more in interest than you need to. Don't waste money on interest; make a plan.

6. Set a goal. Your goals should be so clear that any Tom, Dick, or Harriet can look at what you're trying to achieve and be able to measure your success. Do you want to live in a different place? Own a car? Establish an emergency fund? Do you dream of owning your own home, going back to school, or having children? If you want to make something happen, you have to be clear about what it is you want, when you want it, and what you'll do to get it.

7. Post your goal somewhere visible so that when you are tempted to spend money on rubbish, you can remember why you're working so hard at controlling your impulses.

28 • CAN'T SAY NO

Patrick and Marcia have been married for 16 years. Patrick deals with the daily stress of managing the finances. Sometimes he feels stuck between a rock and a hard place because he hates saying no to Marcia and the kids, but he just doesn't know how he's going to manage financially. All three kids are involved in sports. Carson, Camden, and Christopher play hockey in the winter and soccer in the summer, and these sports have become the basis for Patrick and Marcia's socializing. Having all their fun wrapped up in their family's sports is very expensive.

Patrick makes good money as the manager of a hardware store. He also gets great deals on sporting equipment, which comes in very handy. Marcia is a customer service rep. Between the two, they bring home about $110,000 a year after taxes. It sounds like a lot of money, so they should be fine.

Two years ago they decided to refinance their house, pulling $50,000 from their equity to pay off their credit cards and pay down their line of credit (LOC). Patrick thought it would be a good idea to keep the LOC in place, just in case. "You never know when an emergency might pop up," he said to Marcia, who wasn't very happy about watching her mortgage go up.

She reluctantly agreed. It did make sense to have an emergency fund in place.

Last year they found out that Carson would need braces. It was an expense they had not anticipated. And then Camden broke his ankle jumping off the top of a soccer net, so Marcia lost work hours taking him to the hospital. What was it with kids? They put Carson in braces and Camden in a cast and watched as Christopher played so well that winter season that his coach actually suggested he had what it took to go all the way. He recommended a special summer camp for Christopher that would help him hone his skills for the next season. The camp was expensive, but how could Patrick say no?

"If we're going to send Chris to hockey camp, shouldn't we do it for the other boys too?" asked Marcia. "I don't like the idea of playing favourites."

"The other boys play, but not at Chris's level. I don't think that camp would take them," replied Patrick.

"Well, if not *that* camp, *a* camp," said Marcia. So, it looked like between the three boys Patrick was going to have to come up with about $6,000 for a month of summer camp. He just didn't know where he was going to find the money. And he didn't know how to tell Marcia and the boys that things were tighter than they imagined.

Spending money is easy. If you're not keeping track of it, it disappears almost without a trace. Sure, you can sit and say, "We paid the mortgage," or "We made the car payments," but the majority of what you spend beyond your fixed costs seems nebulous in memory. Like a great grey cloud that doesn't take a shape you can quite describe, the money just gets, well, spent.

According to the 2011 Canadian census and related surveys, the average income in Canada was $38,700, while the median income for individuals was $27,600 (so, as many people made less than $27K as made more than $27K).

When we hear those figures, we think that people who make $50,000, $75,000, or $100,000 a year should be able to buy whatever they want whenever they want it.

The reality is very different.

The pressure to keep up is staggering. And higher incomes often come with higher expectations—a nice house, a new car, myriad social events. If you're hanging with a crowd that's significantly above your social status, if you're participating in a social life that is eating into your savings, or if you've gotten into the habit of spending on credit to afford the lifestyle you think you and your family deserve, it is only a matter of time before your financial life implodes.

Hey, it's not how much you make; it's how much you keep. Income is only the issue when people make so little that they can't keep body and soul together. In that case, they must make more money. But for many, it's a matter of knowing what's truly important and sticking to their guns. Income is, after all, only part of the equation. Inflated expenses can go through a big income faster than green grass through a goose.

My golden rule is "You can't spend more money than you make." If you've been doing so, it's time to put the kibosh on behaviour that leads to financial ruin. It'll be tough news to break to your friends, family, or mate. Saying, "We can't afford that," or "Sorry, but I just don't have the money this week," feels uncomfortable, even embarrassing. But you can break the news now while there is still time to fix the problem, or you can wait until you've dug a debt hole so deep the only way out is bankruptcy. What do you think will be easier in the long run?

SAYING NO

If you're the money manager in the family and must break the news that things will have to change

1. Make a budget to show how much you have available to spend every month and what your must-have expenses are. Those include things like shelter, transportation, food, medical costs, clothes (for growing children), debt repayment (if you have debt), and savings for both retirement and emergencies. (Yes, savings are a must-have.)

2. Subtract the must-have expenses from your income, and the remaining money can be spent on nice-to-haves. Ask your family to help in deciding what those nice-to-haves will be.

3. Are there things you've designated as must-haves that you can eliminate or reduce so that there's more money for other things? An obvious example is cable. People consider this a fixed expense and equate it with a must-have. It isn't. If karate is more important than cable, chop back on the cable costs so you can come up with the money for karate.

4. If anyone whines, "Well, we used to be able to do everything else before," tell the truth. "Yes, but we did it by using credit and we're not doing that anymore."

If you've been hanging out with people who have more money than you, or if you've been playing the "keeping-up" game and things must now change, you'll have to decide whether you're just going to keep making excuses like, "Oh, Bob has to work that weekend, so we can't come to the wedding," or "Martha's family is coming into town. Sorry, can't make it to the concert." Or whether you'll go with the truth: "Gosh, we just redid our financial plan and we've decided to focus our efforts on other priorities for now. Instead of dinner out, how about coming over to our place for tacos and a movie? You bring the movie and a six-pack of Corona, we'll take care of the food."

29 · TIGHTWAD TOM

Mallory and Tom have been married for 11 years. They have three children: Kaylee, aged seven, and twins Josh and Jacob, aged four. They bought a home seven years ago, and the $247,000 mortgage remaining is all the debt they have. Mallory and Tom each have a car, both of which are about six years old. They also have credit cards in their own names. And they have six months' worth of emergency funds in a high-interest account. Mallory and Tom also have a curveball account for those expenses that pop up unexpectedly when you have a dog, cat, fish, and three kids.

Tom is determined to save every penny he can so they can pay off the mortgage in record time. Mallory would like to enjoy life and some of the sweeter things it has to offer. She wants to take a vacation. Tom says that's frivolous and they must focus on the mortgage repayment.

Together, their monthly take-home income is about $7,600, which they make fifty-fifty. Their monthly expenses, including the money they're setting aside for retirement and the kids' educational savings, total $6,400.

Mallory sat down with Tom to try to convince him that it was okay to take a family holiday together. "I think we're doing well," she began. "This is probably the most expensive time of our lives, what with a young family and a mortgage. We should be proud of ourselves for the way we have handled our finances."

Tom nodded. They were doing well, but that was because he was vigilant. Left to her devices, Mallory would spend more money than necessary on non-essentials and they'd have a mortgage for 25 years.

"It seems to me," said Mallory, "that you are in a constant state of anxiety about our money."

"It's important to stay on top of things," said Tom.

"Yes, it is," said Mallory. "But your anxiety is becoming a major problem in our marriage. I can't spend anything without you flipping out. And then I feel guilty. Remember last week, when you accused me of buying the most expensive toilet paper? For heaven's sake, Tom. It's toilet paper."

"Well, it wasn't on sale or anything. Mallory, you can be less than focused on the goal," said Tom. He didn't want to incur her wrath by telling her she was frivolous, which is actually what he thought of her spending style. The last time he'd used that word, she'd flipped a kidney on him.

"I don't know how to convey to you how big a problem this is for me," said Mallory slowly. "I'm very concerned that we're headed for disaster because of your unrealistic fear that I will spend our family into the ground. I feel like you don't trust me. I feel like your single focus on the mortgage repayment is leaving us with no real life. We don't go out to eat. If I bring home something new, you grill me about what I paid for it. And I had to fight you last year to get the kids into camp because you thought it was too expensive. I'm sick of having to justify everything seven ways from sideways."

Some people become so focused on a goal that they suffer from tunnel vision: all they can see is the end. To divert left or right isn't even up for consideration. And if you have a different opinion about how the money should be handled, YOU are the problem.

While taking care of the money details is very important, it isn't everything. Yes, you need to have an emergency fund. Yes, you need to pay for all that spending you've already done if you've racked up consumer debt. And you should be setting aside money for the future. But if you are already doing those things, then it's okay to also use your money to have fun. If you're so afraid of spending a cent that you can't enjoy the money you work so hard to earn, then you're creating your own poverty.

Life is about responsibility and protection, but it's also about joy and pleasure. If you're living with someone who can't see beyond the goal they have set, you'll have to help them create a sense of balance.

DEALING WITH A TIGHTWAD

1. Look over how much you have been spending and on what. Talk about what your needs are and what your mate wants to accomplish. Is the goal that's been set realistic? If you both agree it's a workable goal, then negotiate the things you'll spend money on and the things you'll cut back on to make sure you can achieve that goal.

2. If you do not agree on the goal—he wants the mortgage paid off within five years, you think it's fine to have it paid off before you retire in 15 years—you'll have to find common ground. The obvious answer may be to split the diff and go with 10 years. But there may be a better way to balance each of your needs and expectations, so talk about it.

3. Know that some people actually feel a psychological (and sometimes a physical) pain when they spend money. These tightwads don't know how to relax their spending. The spendthrift doesn't feel any pain when parting with money, but the tightwad's experience is exactly the

opposite: spending hurts. They have to learn to stretch their spending muscles.

- Suggest that you include a category in your budget for something you both want, with a specific dollar amount identified. Maybe you want to take the kids to a movie once a month and you'll spend $75, or you want to eat out on date night every two weeks, for a total of $150 a month.

- Agree that this is a must-spend category and if, for whatever reason, you don't spend it one month, you get to spend the accumulated amount the next month on something else that brings you pleasure. Failure to spend two months in a row means the money goes to charity.

- Once your tightwad has grown used to this category of spending, add another.

4. If your objection is that you don't like everything you do to be scrutinized but your mate wants to know where every penny is going, you might choose to use an allowance system. Each of you will get a specific, agreed-upon amount that you can blow any way you want, no questions asked. It may be $100 a month or an amount that is higher or lower, depending on your financial situation. Then you'll have some money you can use to have a great time and he will know there's a limit on your "frivolous" spending.

IF YOU'RE THE TIGHTWAD

Were you born a tightwad or did your life's circumstances make you so unwilling to spend money on anything but the essentials? It could be a bit of both. In a research study, people were asked to make buying decisions while their brains were scanned. About 30% experienced activity in their insula—the part of the brain that gets all fired up when someone is unfair to us or we smell something disgusting. So, there are people who are predisposed to feeling awful about having to part with money. It's almost painful for them.

If it is history that's getting in the way of your spending, think about how different your circumstances are now relative to the history that's haunting you. Also think about what you end up regretting or missing out on when you're reluctant to spend money.

There's a danger in maximizing the future instead of enjoying the present. If your tightwad ways put your relationships at risk or leave you feeling unsatisfied with your life, they must be tempered. So, how do you tackle your tightwad tendencies? With something called a "functional alibi." That's when you create a justification for spending the money by creating categories in which you are prepared to splurge. You may not be prepared to "waste" money on clothes, but good food is a must-have if you want your family to be healthy.

TAMING TIGHTWAD TENDENCIES

1. Set a date. Give yourself some time to get used to the idea of spending money by deciding on the date for the spend. "We'll book that vacation in two weeks. We'll have a Disney Night dinner and then we'll book the vacation as a family."

2. Focus on the use. Keep the functional capacity of a product you intend to buy front and centre to focus on the benefit you'll derive instead of on the cost you'll pay.

3. Create categories in which spending provides a positive payoff. If you don't take your wife on a vacation, living with her is going to be hell for the next year because she needs a break from her very stressful job. Or if you don't send the kids to a good camp, you're robbing them of the friends they would meet, the experiences and learning they would enjoy.

4. Use plastic. Research shows that paying with plastic reduces activity in the insula, the part of the brain that makes you feel pain when you shop with cash. Bad for people who like to shop. Great for tightwads.

5. Bundle purchases. If you can tie purchases together, then you'll only feel the pain of paying once instead of each time you buy. Subscriptions are one example of a bundled buy. An all-inclusive resort holiday is another.

30 • CAN I BUY YOUR LOVE?

When Phyllis was raising her children, money was tight. After her husband died, she used every penny to make ends meet. There was no money for presents or vacations. When Phyllis was 49 she met Garth. A lovely man who had lost his wife to cancer seven years earlier, Garth treated Phyllis like a princess. At 54, he was semi-retired. He ran his own business but was grooming his son to step into his shoes, so he functioned more as a consultant and didn't have to spend as much time at the office. This gave Phyllis and Garth time to travel, which they did more often than not.

When Phyllis was home all she wanted to do was visit with her grandkids. Her son, Blake, had two boys and a girl. Her daughter, Dianne, had one daughter. Dianne was a single mom, as Phyllis had been, and accepted all the help she got from her mom. But Blake's wife, Rebecca, objected when Phyllis would arrive with armfuls of gifts for the children.

"It's my pleasure," Phyllis said, as Rebecca frowned at the bags of clothes and toys. "I couldn't do it for my own kids because there just wasn't enough money. Why can't I do it for my grandchildren?" Phyllis couldn't understand why Rebecca was being so difficult.

"Mom," said Rebecca in a patient if patronizing tone, "I don't think the kids should always associate your arrival with new toys. It's important that they learn 'enough,' and you give them far too much."

"Would you rather I didn't come as often?" asked Phyllis, her feelings hurt. She wanted to spoil her grandkids. Wasn't that her right as their grandma?

"No, we love it when you come," said Rebecca, "but we love it because you're here. You don't have to bring presents—and not so many at once—every time you visit. I'm not asking you to do anything different than my own mother. I've told her that I'd rather she limit the gift giving too."

"Your mother gets to see the kids every weekend," said Phyllis. "I see them less often because I'm away."

"You're welcome as often as you like. And if you want to spoil them a bit, spend time with them: take them to a movie, the art gallery, or the museum. Just not so much stuff, okay?"

"The art gallery!" said Phyllis under her breath. "I'd bet they'd much prefer that to a new iPad!"

There are people who believe that money, and the things that money can buy, are as important as experiences and real connections. They try to substitute stuff for the love they don't know how to give, or they expect to get stuff as a demonstration of love. When we don't have enough time, we substitute stuff. When we don't have enough patience, we substitute stuff. **Money becomes the means to purchase the healing balm that will cure all.**

If you have a rabid gift-giver in your life, it may take some work to convince them that their company, their time, their help is more important than anything they buy you. People who always show up, arms laden, are tough to say no to. But if you're determined to reduce the amount of stuff, then you'll have to be very clear and forceful in how you deliver your message.

"Mom, the kids love you for YOU. If you want to give them a few gifts on birthdays and holidays, that's fine. And if you want to help set aside some money for when they go to college or university, that's great too. But I'm going to have to insist that you not bring toys and clothes every time you see them. It's not good for them."

"I love them. I don't see what the problem is with a few gifts."

"I know you don't. But I insist. If you continue to bring loads of stuff every time you come, I'm going to have the kids donate those gifts to a children's hospital or a shelter, where someone who has far less will appreciate them."

Money—and the things it buys—is used not only as a replacement for the time people think they should be spending with those they love, but also to try to make up for everything from a small misstep to unforgivably bad behaviour.

When Silvie and Shane met they were both students, broke and making their way through university. Silvie knew the way to Shane's heart. She was a fabulous cook and would make his favourite dishes and experiment with new recipes to surprise him. They didn't have to go to Thailand because Silvie could cook superb Thai food, and they would cuddle up together, feeding each other small morsels and wrapping each other in their love.

Shane loved doing things for Silvie. When her watch broke, he found a guy who agreed to fix it in exchange for some help rewiring his shop. When Silvie wore out her favourite boots, Shane found a guy who agreed to resole them in exchange for Shane's help hooking up a new home-alarm system. Having little or no money made little or no difference.

Shane graduated and became an engineer, travelling the world and bringing Silvie back exotic presents from the countries he visited. Silvie finished her degree in history and political science and then went on to law school. They married and a few years later bought a home. They were very successful financially, but spent less and less time together. Between Silvie's 100-hour work weeks and Shane's travels, they actually had to make dates to see each other. When birthdays and anniversaries rolled around, they tried to outdo each other with the splendour of their gift giving. Silvie showed up at work after her 10th anniversary wearing a beautiful diamond ring. Her co-workers oohed and aahed, telling her how lucky she was to have such a great husband.

When Silvie started an affair with a lawyer at her firm, she did it because she was lonely. Tired of coming home to the perfect house and eating alone, she longed for the days when she and Shane would curl up eating veggie pad Thai. They had gotten everything they wanted but had lost something she valued even more.

In the early days of most relationships, the simplest of gifts are often enough to make us rejoice in the love we have found. As time passes, as our mates make mistakes and seek to be forgiven, expectations rise. Money can become a substitute for safety, for respect, for a sense of being a team. People who are extravagant gift-givers are often seeking acceptance and love through the gifts they give. People who accept those extravagant gifts are implicitly giving their permission for the substitution of money for love.

Money—and what it buys—can become a substitute for the love we think we should be getting. If you are so afraid of losing love that you must buy that love at any cost, you've already lost.

Ultimately, **money cannot replace whatever it is that is missing in a life.** Since money is only a tool—a means of buying the things we need and want—after the glow wears off, the stuff we have bought has very little significance for us. That's one reason why, no matter how much we longed for something, very soon after getting it, our attention turns to the next thing we want. And when we allow money to become a substitute for the real relationships we need in our lives, we end up buying lots of stuff and never being satisfied with any of it.

Arianna had been married to Dustin for only two years when he hit her the first time. He was an insecure man and she was a doll. After a party at a friend's house, Dustin accused Arianna of flirting with his old roommate. Arianna said they were having an innocent conversation. Dustin hit her. Then he hit her again. Arianna ran from the room and locked herself in the bathroom. Dustin sat outside the door, crying and pleading with Arianna to forgive him.

The next day Dustin acted as if nothing had happened. When he came home that night, he had a beautiful bracelet for Arianna. She was so touched by his clear sense of remorse that she forgave him.

Six months later, after a fight about her working late, Dustin hit Arianna again. This time he split her lip and blackened her eye. She called in sick for the rest of the week, and on the weekend Dustin took Arianna shopping for new kitchen appliances.

Eight years and two kids later the pattern continued to repeat itself. After each episode of abuse, Arianna would collect, and each time she did the price tag went up. Dustin learned to salve his conscience with his wallet. Arianna learned she could have all the stuff she wanted if she just put up with Dustin's temper.

Dustin and Arianna's dynamic continued through a long and very unhappy marriage. Oh, there were moments of joy, weeks when nothing bad happened. But when Dustin lost his temper, Arianna paid in bruises and, sometimes, broken bones. She continued to make excuses for Dustin because "she loved him" and "for the sake of the children." All the while, she collected a beautiful home, a new car every couple of years, clothes, jewellery, and trips wherever she wanted to go. Dustin couldn't live without Arianna's adoration and Arianna couldn't survive without Dustin's generosity.

If you are witness to a relationship in which money is a substitute for respect and caring, you should intervene. You may not be loved for doing so, but to stand by silently and watch, shaking your head, is almost as bad as participating in the abuse. Look for local facilities where the abused mate can seek help. Talk to him or her about how unhealthy their relationship dynamic is. Bring someone who has had a similar experience and can talk about potential outcomes into the conversation. If the abused person still refuses help, keep trying. At the very least, let them know that you know what's going on and that you'll be there for them the moment they come to their end of their rope.

"Arianna, I've watched you and Dustin do this horrible dance for years, and I want to say something to you," said Jane. "We've been friends for a long time, and I should have said something before."

"I don't know what you're talking about," said Arianna.

"You and Dustin seem to have this deal, this agreement, that he can smack you whenever he feels the whim and you'll forgive him if the present he's offering is good enough."

"Don't be ridiculous. I know Dustin loses his temper sometimes, but we don't have any deal. He just feels bad. You know I love him and I'd never do anything to hurt our family."

"You may not see it clearly, Arianna, but it's a deal. He hits. You hurt. He pays. You stay."

"I don't see how this is any of your business."

"It's my business because I have to watch my friend get beaten up. I have to watch your children watching their father hitting their mother. Without any help, they're going to think this is normal. It's not normal."

"Maybe not normal for you, but every family is different."

"I know you're deep in denial now, but there will come a time when you have had enough. I just want you to know that I love you, and when that time comes, I'll help you."

PUTTING THE RELATIONSHIP BEFORE THE MONEY

1. If you are uncomfortable that money is being substituted for—or used to manipulate—a relationship, you must address the issue. Choose a comfortable place and tell the person that this is an important talk, even if it isn't an easy one.

2. Start by explaining how you feel and why you feel that way:

   - "I'm uncomfortable when you give the kids too much stuff because I think it sends them the message that you're just a Santa. I want you to share your wisdom and joy with them, not just shower them in gifts."

   - "I know that he showers you in gifts every time you have a drag 'em out fight, but that means he's assuaging his guilt with stuff. He's buying you off. Are you happy taking the pain that comes with the stuff? Because when I look at you guys and where this might end, my heart breaks. I know you love him. But that means you either have to help him deal with this or take yourself out of harm's way."

- "I don't think we should keep escalating our gift giving. It's time for us to cut way back and focus, instead, on spending time with each other. I'm lonely, and beautiful things are no substitute for sharing ideas, talking about life, and just being together."

3. Ask the other person to explain how he or she feels and what he or she thinks you need to do to put the relationship first.

4. If things get heated, take a break. Set a date for the next discussion and leave the issue with a question you both have to answer next time, like:

   - Why are we so uncomfortable talking about this?
   - How can we focus on the things we really love about our relationship?
   - How can you show the children you love and support them without burying them in stuff?
   - What do YOU think we need to do differently?

5. Come up with alternatives that address the relationship/stuff substitution issue.

   - "You wish you could spend more time with the kids. I know that. Why don't we set up a twice-a-week Skype date so you can catch up with them when you're away? You won't feel like so much time has passed without your seeing them."
   - "Are you willing to stop accepting his gifts? Would you tell him that gifts are to celebrate your love, not to say sorry for hurting you?"

- "I think we should limit our gift budgets for each other to $___. We'll have to get really creative, but our relationship will be about the time we spend together, not the bright and shiny we buy. What do you think?"

. . .

A little fear can be a good thing. While we think life would be far better with no fear at all, fear serves a purpose: it makes us think twice. Thinking twice is a healthy response. But seizing up and not stepping forward is not.

I've spent most of my life afraid of things. I look brave, I know. And I am, because each time I come face to face with a fear, I refuse to let the fear win.

When I first started in sales, I puked every single day before work. It took a year for me to master the fear. When I first started doing presentations or appearing on television for interviews during book tours, I used to toss my cookies beforehand. My palms would sweat. My breath would grow shallow. I'd want to run and hide. I didn't.

I remember coming down with a wicked stomachache before I was due to fly out for a big presentation I had to make. I looked at myself in the bathroom mirror and said, "No way, baby. We're not missing it." Then I put myself in the car, drove to the airport, got on a plane, and did the deed. It was fine. Of course it was fine. It was just fear trying to get the better of me.

One of the reasons fear often wins is that we live too much either in the past or in the future. If you have a tendency to look at all the other things that have gone wrong in the past, that can freeze you in your shoes. And if you look forward with only a worst-case focus, it's no wonder you're paralyzed. Working at staying in the present, dealing with what's real in the here and now, can help make those small steps forward feel right. The next time you have to do something scary, spend a couple of minutes focusing on your breath and staying in the present. That should help.

Since you're likely to feel critical about decisions you make if things go south, you might as well do the thing you feel in your core is the right thing to do. If others are being critical of you or your decisions, remember, it's not their life to live; it's your life and you must live it in a way that makes you strong and happy. What's a life worth if it's lived walking a path others have set for you? What's a life worth if you're never challenged and never grow?

I've immigrated, left a physically abusive partner, gotten divorced three times, had two kids—both of whom scared the crap out of me with their shenanigans—and spoken in front of thousands of people. I've experienced fear in myriad iterations. I refuse to let fear win.

I've learned that every time you stare fear down, you grow more courageous, more confident, and more willing to try something you would previously have thought absolutely impossible.

I know it's hard to feel the fear and do it anyway. I know it is. But allowing fear to dominate your life isn't the way to live a life full of joy. How can you be happy if you're always letting fear get the better of you, hold you back, keep you down?

I've learned how to deal with my fear. You can too. I have a great life. You can too.

Part Six

CONTROLLING IMPULSES

Carrying a ton of debt? Impulse control may be your problem. Of all the people with whom I've worked, this is the single most common issue at play. Once upon a time people were limited in how impulsively they could spend, because their money would run out—what you had in the bank was all there was. When credit cards and lines of credit came along, the natural stop—having no money—was blurred by the ability to put purchases on credit.

To make matters worse, as people spent years edging closer and closer to their credit limits—the next stop sign—they learned that banks were willing to give them higher limits and more sources of credit, as long as their credit scores were shiny. To keep those scores shiny, all folks had to do was make sure they made their minimum payments on time.

An entire generation has grown up believing that they can have whatever they want whenever they want it. And that disease has spread to older generations too, as the use of credit has caught on. Now people are retiring with record levels of debt.

With no traffic signs to slow them down on the impulse-shopping highway, people have allowed their impulsiveness to run rampant. And each impulse purchase brings with it a reinforcing rush of brain chemicals that makes shoppers feel great.

There are loads of psychological studies showing that shopping activates areas in your brain that boost mood, at least for a little while. Those great feelings result from the brain chemical dopamine, which is released when we experience something challenging, exciting, or new. People have greater or lesser amounts of dopamine in their brains, which explains why some people can walk away from temptation while others behave impulsively in the face of it.

According to psychologists, shopping is an enormously rewarding activity because it turns on this happy chemical in our brain. Because we've accidentally turned it on over and over, shopping has become a tried-and-true way of feeling better, which is why so many people hit the mall when they're angry, bored, or sad. The impulse to react to shopping signals is so strong that you must be purposeful if you want to stop those signals from hijacking your behaviour.

Convincing people that impulse shopping can be detrimental to their health—and perhaps also to yours—is a tough sell because a) people hate change, and b) why would they want to give up something that makes them feel so good?

Impulsiveness can be a huge barrier to having the life you want. Drip by drip, each impulsive action drains the resources you would otherwise use to create that life. And little by little, what you really want takes a back seat to the high experienced with every purchase. Hit a new store and watch your dopamine levels skyrocket! You get to explore, experience textures and colours, and when you finally decide on that gorgeous jacket, a burst of dopamine seals the deal.

Impulsiveness takes all forms, but the end result is the same. Impulsive people give up their big wins in life for the sake of all those little feel-good moments.

31 • ACQUISITION ANNIE

Annie and her sister, Portia, had been close all their lives. So when Portia suggested they pool their resources and buy a house, Annie was in.

They bought a lovely four-bedroom, two-and-a-half–bath house with a finished basement that Portia turned into an in-home daycare so she could stay home with her three-year old daughter, Julianna. She had five kids signed up to come Monday through Friday, and two older siblings who would come after the elementary school bell rang.

Annie worked in fashion. She made great money as a buyer—more than double what Portia made—for a major retailer. Annie was an acquisition hound. She loved to shop and had found a way to do it for a living. She did it for pleasure too. She just couldn't pass up a deal.

With a bedroom for each sister and a beautiful bedroom for Julianna, Annie decided the fourth bedroom should be her walk-in closet. At first Portia objected because she thought the idea was ridiculous, but as she watched the boxes and boxes of clothes, shoes, handbags, and other stuff being unloaded from the moving van, she realized Annie was going to need that extra room. Portia didn't complain because Annie had heaps of stuff with the tags still on—and a habit of buying two of the things she really liked—so whenever Portia needed a new outfit she would just shop Annie's closet. Since Annie rotated her wardrobe seasonally, Portia had no idea just how much stuff Annie had until she saw it all coming into the house.

When the sisters had gone to be preapproved for the mortgage on the house, there was a small hiccup. It turned out that Annie was carrying quite a lot of credit card debt. She assured Portia it was no problem. "With my income, I can have this all paid off in a couple of months," she said. The banker looked at her income and nodded.

"Your individual expenses won't go up by much, because you're combining two households," said the banker. "Would you also like a line of credit on the house for emergencies, or in case you want to buy some new furniture?"

Portia said, "No," just as Annie said, "Yes." They both laughed. Annie prevailed. Since most of the down payment was coming from the sale of Annie's condo, Portia let her have her way.

Four years passed and Portia watched Annie bring more and more stuff into the house. She now had Julianna to shop for too, and Portia just couldn't get Annie to stop buying clothes, toys, books, anything that caught her fancy for her niece. It actually made Portia a little uncomfortable. But Annie was generous and Portia didn't argue too much.

It wasn't until the mortgage came up for renewal that Portia found out Annie had run the line of credit to its $30,000 limit. She was aghast.

"I thought we were doing this to build up some equity so we could each get a home of our own down the road," said Portia. "All the equity we should have built up has been more than gobbled by this line of credit."

Annie got angry. "I have to use my credit card for business travel," she said. "Doesn't it make more sense to pay it off with this lower-interest line than to keep it on my credit card?"

"Doesn't work reimburse you for your expenses?" asked Portia.

"Most of them, but not the stuff I buy for myself," said Annie, using a tone that intimated Portia's question was stupid.

"Well, what do you do with the money you get back for your expenses? Don't you use it to pay off your credit cards?"

"No, I just put that money into my account," Annie said.

"So, you're spending the money on travel and then you're spending the money again on stuff, and carrying the balance?"

"No," said Annie. "I told you, I pay off my credit cards."

"Using the line of credit for which we are both on the hook?" asked Portia. "Can't you see that makes me responsible for the debt too?"

"It's not like I'm going to stick you with it," said Annie, her chest puffed up and her eyes wide. "Geez, you think I'm trying to screw you or something?"

"I don't think you're trying to screw me," said Portia, lowering her voice to almost a whisper. "I think you've got a shopping problem and you're out of control. And I'm afraid for you, and for me and Julianna."

"I'd never let anything happen to Julianna," said Annie, bursting into tears.

"Maybe not on purpose," said Portia. "But suppose you lost your job. How could I carry this house and pay off that line by myself and take care of Jules? Maybe your shopping is a little out of control?"

Annie's tears stopped as she narrowed her eyes. "I don't have a problem."

"Really, Annie, cos you think normal people have 137 pairs of shoes? And why the hell do we need four TVs for a family of three? And as for the stuff you keep buying Julianna? I've told you, it's too much."

"Too much, too much," said Annie. "You didn't think it was too much when I made the down payment on this house."

Portia sighed. This wasn't going anywhere good. Afraid Annie was going to implode financially, Portia decided to make a plan get through to her.

In a society where everything is aplenty, *not* shopping takes effort. Not shopping requires conscious choice. And it means looking for the things—things that don't involve stuff and more stuff—that make life rich.

We're very good at fooling ourselves into thinking our stuff is important. We tie memories to our stuff. And even if we have something we don't really use, we hang on to it for sentimental reasons or because, well, we simply can't let it go. **Stuff is stuff. That's all. It is life that matters, not the amount of crap you have accumulated.** When you start putting the people you love and your experiences with them ahead of yet another inanimate object, you're on your way to being free of the acquisition affliction.

Sometimes when people shop, they're trying to use the emotional surge they get (yes, our brains reward us for hunting and gathering) as a salve for emotional gaps. If your need to buy things—to go shopping—has an emotional basis, you must find a way to deal with those underlying emotions rather than continue to use shopping as a balm. Experiencing life, getting active, and connecting with friends and family will all help.

Moving from an obsession with stuff to the things that bring true happiness often means finding a way to connect with others. Find a friend to go for a walk with in the great outdoors. Join a photography club and learn to appreciate the beauty of sunlight dappling on water. Get in on a game of pickup road hockey, take a swim in the lake, or go bike riding with a pal.

While there are some people who are true shopaholics and must seek professional help to curb their shopping addictions, most people who shop too much aren't sick. Psychologists estimate that about 6% of people are actually shopping addicts who need professional intervention. The rest may have an impulse control problem, or they may be so used to buying whatever they want whenever they want that they find it hard to walk on by. Happily, self-control is something that can be learned.

HELPING ACQUISITION ANNIE QUIT ACQUIRING

1. Suggest your Acquisition Annie limit shopping to one day of the week. That's all of their shopping: grocery store, drugstore, specialty retailers, everyone! If they can't get all the shopping done in one day, they can't do it that week.
2. Encourage them to shop with a list and only buy what's on the list. If they see something they want, they add it to the list for their next shopping adventure.
3. Challenge them to see how long they can go without buying the thing(s) they have a weakness for. So, if they already have lots of shoes, how long can they go without buying a new pair? If they do shop for their weakness, they have to start keeping track from zero again, and should always be trying to beat their best no-shopping streak.
4. Suggest they implement the "one in, one out" rule. If they really want the latest DVD, before they can bring it into the house, they have to figure out what they're going to get rid of. No cheating: they're not allowed to buy a new iPad and get rid of that horrible vase their mother-in-law gave them. They must choose a comparable thing to part with.
5. Offer to do things with them that don't involve shopping: go for a walk, join a gym and work out together, or take up a new hobby as long as it doesn't involve acquiring new stuff.

6. Ask the person to identify a goal towards which they want to work as they don't shop. It may be paying off a credit card. It may be saving up for a vacation so they don't have to put it on credit. Whatever it is, have them identify each time they did not shop when they wanted to. They can then transfer the money they would have spent to their goal. So, if they did not spend $137 on a new purse, they use that money to immediately pay down their credit card or move the money to their vacation savings account.

32 • INSTANT GRATIFICATION JUNKIES

Polly was a spur-of-the-moment girl. It was one of the things her friends liked most about her. She'd suggest heading off on a road trip or meeting at a party or grabbing dinner at the newest and snazziest restaurant. Everyone would pile into the fun. But Polly had a problem handling her money. Her roommate, Madison, was always having to cover Polly's share of the rent. Polly paid her back, mostly. And if Madison didn't have the money to go out, Polly would treat.

When the girls decided to move to a bigger apartment—sharing a bedroom was NOT working anymore—Polly hit a "buy now, pay later" sale for new furniture. "I've got 18 months to pay this off," she said triumphantly. "No problem. I'll just put $250 a month into my savings account and it'll be done. No interest. Pretty smart, eh?"

Her friends all nodded. Madison wasn't so sure. She'd seen Polly's plans go awry before and she wasn't convinced Polly had the discipline to see this plan through.

Polly came home one night and announced that she'd gotten a new job. She would be making more money and wanted to celebrate. She called up a half-dozen friends and made plans to go dancing. She sprang for bottle service at the club. And when her cash ran out, she blithely walked over to the cash machine and took out $60. An hour later she was back for another $60. And just before she left the club, she pulled out another $20 for the cab ride home. All in all, she'd taken $140 from her account and paid $15 in ATM fees.

When Polly came up short on the rent again, Madison had had enough.

"How is it even possible that you just got a raise and you can't make the rent?" she asked.

"I don't know," said Polly. "I guess I spent too much celebrating."

"Listen," said Madison, "I've got to pay my tuition this month. I don't have money to cover you. You need to find a way to come up with your share."

"From where?" Polly whined. "My bank account is already overdrawn by $250."

"What about that money you've been setting aside for the furniture? It's been four months. You should have about $1,000 by now. Can you use some of that?"

Polly looked stricken. "I haven't actually been doing that. I planned to but stuff just kept creeping up. Besides, I have plenty of time."

"Oh, Polly," said Madison, "how the hell are you going to come up with all that money if you can't live on what you're making now?"

"I'll get the money," said Polly angrily. "Never mind. I'll have it for you by the end of the week."

"The rent is due tomorrow, not the end of the week, and I don't have your share. If you can't come up with the money, I'm going to move home to my parents' for a few months until I can get a place on my own."

"Oh, Maddy, don't do that," Polly said, bursting into tears. "I would hate to live on my own. I need you. Please. I'll get the money today."

That's when Polly had the bright idea to hit a payday loan store.

When she showed up later with her share of the rent in cash, Madison asked her, "Where did you get it?"

"Does it matter?" asked Polly. "I said I'd get it and I did, right?"

Madison had a bad feeling. She waited a few days and then she said to Polly, "You know, Pol, I love you more than anything. But you're not good with money. Why don't you let me sit down with you and go over your stuff and see if we can sort something out so we don't have to keep fighting over the rent money?"

"No," said Polly. "Everything's fine."

Three weeks later Polly came home from work spitting fire. "What's wrong?" asked Madison.

"I'm going to throttle someone at the bank. You know that store I love on the way home from work? Well, I stopped and found a fantastic little dress to go out in this weekend. And"—Polly paused only long enough to take in a deep breath so she could bellow—"they rejected my credit card!"

"Oh, Polly," said Madison, "that must have been so embarrassing."

"I wasn't embarrassed," said Polly. "I just told the girl there must be a mistake, swore at my bank, and got her to hold the dress until tomorrow for me. But that bank has some explaining to do."

"Are you over your credit card limit?" asked Madison.

"That's never stopped me before," said Polly.

Damn, thought Madison. She's in even deeper than I thought. And rent is due in a week. Looks like I'm in for another fight.

Sure enough, rent week rolled around and Polly "forgot" again. Madison reminded Polly on her way out the door that morning. "Rent's due today." Polly mumbled and slammed the door behind her.

When Madison got home that night, she found Polly sitting in a puddle of tears with a half-finished bottle of wine. "Pol, what's wrong?" Madison asked.

"I've . . . I've . . . I've made such a mess of things," Polly stammered as she tried to catch her breath. "You're going to hate me."

"I can't hate you, Polly. You're my best friend."

"Well, you will, you'll see. I'm so stupid." Polly struck herself in the head with her small fist.

"Don't do that. Whatever this is, we can work it out. I've got your back, you know that." Madison pulled Polly into her arms and rocked her as Polly cried and cried. When her sobs quieted, Madison said, "Why don't you tell me what's wrong?"

It all came tumbling out. Polly was so overdrawn at the bank that there was no more wiggle room. Her credit card was completely tapped out. "How did that happen?" asked Madison. That's when Polly told her about the payday loan store and that she had borrowed $400 to make last month's rent.

"I had to pay them back $480 two weeks later, which left me short, so I skipped the minimum payment on my credit card. And now I'm short on rent again." She burst into tears once more.

There are people who have problems with impulse control. They see something. They want it. They buy it. Never mind if they're using money that should be going to pay the rent, buy the food, or keep the lights on. The immediate gratification of buying what they want outweighs the long-term consequences of spending that money.

If you have one of these people in your life, witnessing their self-destruction can be very, very hard. And if their behaviour is having a negative impact on you, emotions will run high. But an emotional response won't help them to see how their impulsiveness is hurting them, and by extension, their relationship with you. For that, calm heads must prevail.

It's easy to see these people as self-indulgent. They don't spend any time finding the best price. No planning goes into their buying decisions. I worked with one woman who went out for Chinese and came home with furniture. It is almost as if they can't help themselves. But they can. And they must. It may be up to you to show them how.

If you have friends or family who have missed a mortgage payment, are in overdraft every month, or have no idea where the money is going because of impulsive spending, you may decide to step into the breach to help them figure out what they're doing wrong so they can stop.

How? Start by helping the impulse shopper identify the triggers that cause them to make impulsive purchases. Do they shop when they're blue or bored? Will a fight with their mate trigger a spending spree? Keeping a shopping journal can help. Each time they have the desire to shop, they should write down what they wanted to buy, the price, and how they were feeling at the time. What happened to make them feel that way? Then they should look for patterns. Do they shop when they're sad? Are there days of the week or month when they're more prone to spend?

Controlling impulses takes a plan. And since the old rules— I like it, I buy it—aren't working, it's time to suggest some new rules.

Rule #1: Never carry more cash than you're prepared to spend that day. If you need $10 to get through the day, that's all you carry. No cheques, no debit card, no credit cards. You can't spend what you don't have.

Rule #2: Avoid places where you can spend money. Stay out of stores. Unsubscribe from retailer emails telling you about great deals. Stop the flyers and catalogues from coming.

Rule #3: Always shop with a list. Whether buying groceries, a birthday present for your BFF, or a new pair of shoes, never go into a store without a list. And never buy anything that isn't on your list. If, while out, you see something you think you want, write it on your list and GO HOME. If you still want it in 48 hours, you can go back for it, providing you have the cash to pay for it.

Rule #4: Use the "one in, one out" rule. Every time you want to buy something new, you must identify something old that you're prepared to get rid of. And it has to be a like-for-like exchange. So, if you're considering a new handbag, which old handbag will you give away? This rule helps impulsive people to prioritize. What are you prepared to give up to have that new whatever?

You must make it clear to the impulsive person how their behaviour is having a negative effect on you (or on someone else in their lives.) Don't pull any punches. Honesty is absolutely essential for you to have any hope of making the impulsive person WANT to change. They usually love their own spontaneity and will resist buttoning down. If you do not make clear what's at stake, they will appease you in the moment and then go right back to their impulsive ways.

In a quiet and very controlled voice Madison said, "Polly, I love you, but your impulsiveness is messing with your money and now it's messing with mine." As Polly sobbed, Madison continued. "I'm not prepared to live like this anymore. You have to tell me now whether you're willing to change how you deal with your money or whether you want to find a new roommate."

Polly cried harder.

"I'm going to give you a few minutes to compose yourself and then you're going to have to answer that question for me. I'll make some tea." Madison gave Polly a kiss and stood up. She watched Polly's heaving shoulders for a moment and then went to the kitchen. She busied herself making tea. She took some time to wipe down the counters and rearrange the spices on the shelf. When Polly's sobbing stopped, she brought the teapot and two mugs into the living room and placed them on the coffee table.

"Want me to pour?"

Polly nodded.

Madison handed her two fresh tissues. "Maybe you should go toss some water on your face." Polly shook her head and blew her nose. Her eyes were swollen and strands of hair stuck to her cheek. Madison brushed the hair off Polly's face. "Do you feel like you can talk about this now?"

"Not really."

"When, then?" asked Madison, impatience leaking into her tone. She had been pushed too far.

"I suppose we'd better do it now," said Polly.

The girls sat quietly for a long time, sipping tea but not saying anything. Then Polly said, "I don't know what I'm doing wrong or what I have to do differently. I don't want to turn into one of those girls who can't go out because she doesn't have any money for fun."

"Like me, you mean?" asked Madison.

"Well, you aren't exactly the life of the party." Polly smiled through her watery eyes. "Isn't that why we get on so well? Because we're so completely different?"

"That's partly true," said Madison. "But tell me, Polly, how great do you feel about the party we're at right now?"

"Yeah, not so great."

"Okay, so what's wrong with taking care of what you have to take care of and then having fun with the rest of your money?"

"It's so boring."

"Boring is better than the hot mess you're in right now! Let's make it simple: If it's a choice between getting a new roommate and cleaning up your financial mess, which will you choose?

"I don't want to live with anyone else."

"So, are you choosing me and a better financial plan?"

"Yeah, I guess I am."

"Okay," said Madison, "I'm relieved. I did NOT want to have to move back in with my parents."

"But you would have?"

Madison nodded. "I can't live with your irresponsibility anymore. I love you, but you're messing up my life."

"So, where do I start?"

"I have some ideas," said Madison. "It won't be easy. Are you ready for that?"

"Yeah, I guess."

DEALING WITH AN IMPULSIVE PERSON

1. Impulsive people often have no idea how their behaviour is negatively impacting others. You have to tell them.

2. Use specific examples of how their impulsiveness is a problem for you. "Polly, remember when we were going for a bite and you decided it would be great to try that new, very expensive restaurant? I wasn't prepared to spend that much money. That's why I only had soup and coffee. I went home afterwards and made a sandwich."

3. If you are out shopping with an impulsive spender (or listening to them talk about what they're going to buy), consider asking questions to help them see their impulsiveness.
   - Did you plan to buy this, or are you buying it because
     - it's on sale?
     - it's new and looks great?
     - it makes you feel good?
   - Would you make the trip back here tomorrow to buy this?
   - Do you have the money to pay for it right now without affecting anything else in your budget?
   - Are you buying this because you're too lazy to fix the one you have at home?
4. If you live with an impulsive spender and they prove to you that they cannot moderate their behaviour and keep their commitments, you have two choices:
   - Dump and run. Decide you've had enough and you're not putting yourself at financial risk any longer because of buddy's bad behaviour.
   - Prepay program. Buddy agrees to a prepay program so you always have his or her share of the money for the expenses in hand before they can spend it. So, if you share the rent and it's due on the 30th of June, your impulsive roomie must give you their share of the rent money on June first. Coming up with the money may take some finagling: selling something, getting a part-time job, cutting out all wants until this money is piled up.

If you live together and share family expenses, your impulsive mate must set up an automatic debit from their account to the family-expense account. After each paycheque goes into their personal account, the agreed-upon amount is automatically moved to where it needs to be to cover costs. And, no, they do not have access—a debit card or joint access—to that family account.

5. Being accountable to someone for a period of time often helps impulsive spenders get things under control. Whether it is a mate, parent, sibling, or BFF, having an accountability buddy can help the impulsive spender adjust their thinking. Together you can determine the spending plan your impulsive friend will follow. Yes, it's a budget. And only those things agreed upon by both of you will be added to the week's or month's shopping list.

Each time the impulse to spend off-list arises, the impulsive person must describe what they're feeling, why they want to spend, and where they will find the money in their budget. Needs come before wants, so the money can only be taken from other wants categories. If that new iPad is a must-have, will the money come from entertainment, clothing, or some other wants section of the budget? The accountability buddy has the final say on whether the purchase can be made.

The impulsive person cannot feel as though the accountability buddy is controlling them, or the plan won't work. Instead of, "No, Jack, you can't buy those shoes," the accountability buddy should say, "Hey, Jack, I know you love those shoes, so why don't you tell me what you're not going to spend money on so you can have them?"

"Well, I don't really need to spend $400 a month on groceries."

"Sorry, hon, that's a needs category, so you can't touch that."

"Entertainment?"

"Okay, so you're going to give up $200 of your entertainment money so you can have those shoes?"

"Yes."

"And you're prepared to stay home and watch movies in for the month to do that? What about Karen's birthday party? Are you going to take a pass on that?"

"No. Don't be ridiculous."

"Well, where are you going to get the money?"

"Fine, I won't get the shoes."

"Hey, if Karen's party is more important than the shoes, that's a choice you're making."

"I was going to wear the shoes to Karen's party."

"I guess you'll just have to make do with the other black shoes you've got."

"I guess."

33 • LIFE'S TOO SHORT TO WORRY

Gabriella and Beatrice had been dating for about eight months when Gabby suggested Bea move in. "I have so much more space at my place," Gabby said, "and you're always here anyway. I'd love it if we could be together all the time."

Beatrice wasn't so sure. While she was crazy about Gabby, she had seen signs that Gabby was a good-time girl. She loved to eat out. Vacations were must-haves. And she had a $400 a month Grey Goose habit that made Bea shake her head.

"I'm not sure," said Bea.

"Don't you love me?" asked Gabrielle, hurt that Beatrice was rejecting her suggestion that they move in together.

"I do love you," said Beatrice. "But we are very different when it comes to how we handle our money, and I'm not sure how things will work if we're living together."

"Hey, whatever you want is fine with me," said Gabrielle. "You handle the money. You're way better at it than I am."

Beatrice fell for the line. A year after she moved in, she realized that there was a big difference between what Gabby said and what Gabby did. And it was eroding their relationship.

When Gabby came home with a big bonus, she suggested they take the cruise they'd been talking about for months. Beatrice had been diligently squirrelling away $250 a month into their vacation account, but they were still about $3,500 away from their goal.

"Come on, this is found money," said Gabby. "Let's go on the trip."

"You still have $21,000 worth of student loans to get paid off," replied Beatrice.

"Don't be such a killjoy. I'm making my payments. This is for us. We both want to do this."

"You have been making payments, but you're on the 10-year plan. Do you realize you'll have paid for your education twice by the time you're done?"

"But I'll have gone on a cruise too," laughed Gabby. "Life's too short to always worry about doing the right thing." Gabby said the last three words in a deep, ponderous voice. "Let's have some fun too."

Beatrice thought about giving in. They did have a plan for Gabby's student loans, and Beatrice was throwing extra money at them whenever she could. Maybe Gabby was right.

"Okay, okay," said Beatrice. "You win. Let's go on a cruise." Gabby danced around, laughing and clapping her hands. She grabbed Beatrice by the waist and spun her around. As she did, the mail flew out of her hands. Laughing, they both bent down to pick up the envelopes.

"What's this?" asked Beatrice, turning a credit card envelope over in her hands. It was addressed to Gabby.

"Oh, must be one of those offers we're always getting." It was true that Gabby was often offered new credit cards and lines of credit. Beatrice assumed it was because Gabby made more than she did.

"I wonder what great offer they have for you today," Beatrice said as she started to slit the envelope open.

"Don't open my mail!" Gabby grabbed for the envelope.

"Your mail?" said Beatrice a little confused by the fierceness of Gabby's response. "I thought it was just some credit card offer." She held the envelope out of Gabby's reach. "Is there something I should know?"

"No," said Gabby, "just give me my mail."

Beatrice handed the envelope to Gabby. "Why don't you open it up so we can both see your great offer?" she said slowly, challenging

Gabby to walk away. Gabby threw the envelope at her.

"If you have to know everything, Ms. Killjoy," she said as she stomped away. Beatrice picked up the envelope and opened it. It wasn't an offer. It was a credit card statement for an account Beatrice knew nothing about. The balance was $5,678.24. Beatrice gasped. As she ran her fingers down the current charges, she saw the cable package Gabby told her she'd negotiated for a third of what showed up on the bill, multiple transactions for restaurants, and a dozen retail purchases, including several at the liquor store. She followed Gabby into the bedroom.

"How could you do this?" she asked, feeling betrayed by Gabby's deceit.

"How could I have some fun?" responded Gabby. "With the allowance you have us on, how could I ever have any fun? I had to get that card."

"So, you just nodded and agreed when we talked and then went out and ran up a credit card?" asked Beatrice, folding her arms over her chest.

"Don't get all high and mighty with me," barked Gabby. "If you weren't such a tightwad we could have more fun and I wouldn't have had to use credit."

"Didn't you say you wanted to save for the cruise? Didn't you say you wanted to save to do renovations on the bathroom? You told me those things were important to you too."

"Why can't we do them and then just pay them off like everyone else?" said Gabby. "Why are you so obsessed with not having any debt? Why are you so dead set against having some fun?"

Beatrice started to answer and then stopped, turned on her heel, and headed for the door. Grabbing her jacket, she called over her shoulder, "I'm going for a walk. I need some time to think."

There are people for whom spending comes first because, as they like to point out, "You could be dead tomorrow." Having fun in the now is the name of the game, damn the consequences. They are the grasshoppers in our lives, more concerned with chirping and singing than with laying up food for the winter.

Never imagining that things can go wrong—have you ever noticed how often they actually do?—the "life's too short to worry" type ignores the need to stash away some cold hard cash just in case. They say things like, "Bad things don't happen to good people." And they love their toys. Boy, do they love their toys.

Living with a grasshopper can be very difficult if you're an ant: you like to plan, you consider potential downsides, and you take precautions. Grasshoppers' live-for-today attitude can be very appealing because their spontaneity is attractive. But their don't-give-a-damn can be wearing when it means you feel like you're the only grown-up in the room.

So, can grasshoppers and ants coexist? Sure they can, if they make allowances for each other's strengths and weaknesses, and if they respect what's important to the other person.

Grasshoppers need to have fun. They want to play. Ants want to plan for the future, working hard in the present so they can afford to eat when winter comes. Those things are not mutually exclusive. Some fun now, some planning for the future gives life balance. Grasshoppers may not be able to imagine thirty years into the future and retirement, but ants don't have to sock away all the money for a date to be determined later. There has to be some focus on fun along with some focus on the future.

Enjoying the now does not mean compromising the future. So it's important that your grasshopper agree that if you are going to spend, you'll spend money, not credit.

Beatrice waited a day for tempers to cool before she asked Gabby to sit down with her to talk about how different their money styles were. Gabby was willing to talk because Beatrice had been gone for three hours the day before and Gabby figured this was as serious as she'd ever seen Bea.

Beatrice made coffee, pulled out a calculator and some bank statements, and told Gabby it was time to have that talk they should have had before she moved in. Gabby nodded. Beatrice made it clear that carrying a credit card balance was out of the question. "But, Bea," Gabby said, "the payments are fine because you know I have a good job, and I'll keep making more money."

Beatrice shook her head. This was non-negotiable. "What makes you think that if you can't save the cash to buy it, you should have it?" she said. "Clearly, if you aren't willing to save the money to buy what you want, you're really not that committed to having it."

"Sure I am," said Gabby. "Look at that cruise we've been saving for. It's still months away. My way, we could go this winter and then pay it off over the summer."

"So, you think it's okay to rack up interest so you can go right now?" said Beatrice. "Right NOW!" she repeated, with a big emphasis on "now."

"Well, yeah," said Gabby, knowing that what she was saying wouldn't win her any points, but determined to convince Beatrice that her way was fine.

"Okay," said Beatrice. "So we put the $7,500 cruise on your 19.9% credit card and pay it off over time. How much time?"

"What?" asked Gabby.

"How much time will it take to pay off the cruise?"

"A few months."

"A few as in three or a few as in seven?"

"Let's say five months."

"So, you're going to come up with $1,624 a month to get it paid off?"

"What?" asked Gabby. "Where did you come up with that number?"

"If you take $7,500 and divide it by five, you get $1,500. Then, take the $7,500 and multiply it by the interest rate and divide by 12 to come up with the monthly interest of $124. Add the $124 in interest to the $1,500 principal repayment and that's where I got $1,624."

"Okay, okay," said Gabby, "maybe it'll take longer than five months."

"How much longer?"

"Let's say a year."

Beatrice's fingers flew over the calculator buttons. She turned the calculator display so Gabby could see it. "You think you can come up with $645 a month?"

"It would still be that much?"

"It would," said Beatrice.

"Two years?" asked Gabby.

"Two years would be $430 a month."

"Crap."

"And you couldn't take another vacation during all that time because you'd still be paying off the last one you took."

"Damn."

"And you'll have paid about $2,200 in interest. So instead of putting that $2,200 towards your next trip, you'll have spent it paying for the trip we already took."

"That seems pretty dumb."

"Ya think?" asked Beatrice, but she was smiling, so Gabby smiled back.

Cold hard facts, that's what you need to reach the person who never thinks of the consequences, particularly when it comes to accumulating debt. So very often they can't see that they're doing anything wrong, so you have to spell it out for them.

"I know you think we put too much money into our retirement savings and should be spending more on fun," said Beatrice. Gabby didn't answer. "C'mon, tell the truth. That's why you're always bucking me on other stuff."

"Well, yes. I could be dead before I get to spend a penny of that money. What's the point?"

"How much do we spend right now, having the life we have?" asked Beatrice.

"I dunno. You do the money."

"Aren't you embarrassed not to know where the money is going?" asked Beatrice.

"We've had this conversation a thousand times. I don't care. You manage the money."

"Which is why you don't understand our priorities. You can't abdicate anymore." Beatrice pulled out a copy of their budget. "Here," she said, pointing to the last number in the expenses section. "This is what we spend a month."

Gabby looked at the number: $6,750. "That seems like a lot," she said.

"Look at our expenses," said Beatrice. "There's the mortgage, your car payment, our insurance, food, entertainment, clothes. It all adds up."

"Do we really spend $200 a month on the dogs?" asked Gabby.

"Not every month," said Beatrice. "But I like to put some away each month just in case we have an unexpected vet bill or something."

"Just in case. That's you," said Gabby.

"Yes, it is," said Beatrice. "I like to be prepared." She smiled, showing she was not in the least embarrassed by Gabby's jab. "So, if we don't save any money for the future, we can expect to get about $1,200 a month each from CPP and OAS combined. Between us, we'd have an income of $2,400. Do you think we can live on $2,400 a month?" asked Beatrice, pointing to the $6,750 they were currently spending.

"Well, our house would be paid off," said Gabby.

"Yes, if we do it right. But it still costs about $1,300 a month to carry this house without the mortgage. That's more than half our income gone."

To change your mate's (best friend's, sibling's, whomever's) mind about how she's handling her money, you need to have a conversation that is civil and fact-based. It's important that as you talk, you acknowledge the things that are important to the other person. But you must also help her step out of her shoes to see things from your perspective. And, when it comes to money, that usually means doing the math. So, sharpen your pencil, grab a calculator, and get ready to show her the money.

CONVINCING GRASSHOPPERS

1. If the conversation turns into a fight, your mate won't be able to hear you. Keep it civil and stick to the facts.

2. Be prepared with your calculations ahead of time so you're not fumbling your way through as you're trying to make your points.

3. Ask your in-the-now friend to imagine a different "now," the now of the future when he can't take that vacation because he's too busy paying for the last one, or he can't afford to do anything fun because he hasn't saved enough money.

4. If your mate questions your calculations, have him do the math for himself as you stand by to assist if necessary.

34 • DEAL LOVERS

Mimi was a deal hound. When something was on sale, she'd buy it. She walked into a store with her sister, Magna, and found camisoles on sale, three for $25. She picked up six. "It's such a good price," she said as her sister raised her eyebrows.

"Do you need six new camis?" Magna asked, already knowing the answer.

"They don't spoil," said Mimi. "I'll use them eventually." Magna had heard it all before. Mimi had a great reason to buy everything she bought on sale. An avid collector of coupons and daily deals, Mimi was always bragging about how much money she'd saved with her smart shopping.

"Show me the money," said Magna one day when Mimi was going on again about her smart shopping and how Magna should follow in her footsteps.

"What?" asked Mimi, tilting her head like a puppy.

"If you're saving so much money, how much of it do you still have?"

"Don't be silly," said Mimi. "If I save $5 buying something, I've saved $5. If I spend it somewhere else, that just means I get more for my money."

"Yeah," said Magna, "which means you haven't saved anything. I, on the other hand, actually put money into my retirement savings this year. You just have loads of crap."

"It's not crap."

"It's crap, Mimi. You have things you never even wear. You end up giving them away or donating them to charity to make room so you can keep shopping."

The world celebrates the deal lover—a breed of shopper who doesn't really care how much they're spending as long as they're getting a deal. Oy! Trying to get through to these people can sometimes feel like banging your head against a wall. So convinced they're doing something good because they're getting a deal, they can't see the bigger picture.

I've met people with cupboards, basements, garages full of stuff. I've met people who look only at the money they have saved, not at the money they have spent. And I've met people who buy daily deal coupons—spend money to get the coupon—but then never redeem it to get the savings.

We all know people who love to shop. But when that shopping turns into a compulsion to buy, and the shopper uses the savings they're realizing as the rationale for buying, smart shopping has turned into something not so smart. And when the shopping turns into debt, it's downright dumb.

If there is someone in your life who has been shopping up a storm to their own financial detriment, it may take several conversations—and demonstrations—to get the message through to them.

A great place to start is with a spending analysis. Most deal shoppers have no idea how much money is going through their fingers. So focused are they on what they're saving, they don't actually know how much they're spending.

Suggest they do a spending analysis or, better yet, do one with them. Take six months' worth of bank and credit card statements and add up all they money they've spent acquiring daily deal coupons, shopping in retail stores, eating in restaurants, and anything else that would fall into the category of wants. Divide the amount you come up with by six: that's how much they are spending each month on stuff they don't really need. Can they see why they're carrying a balance on their credit cards or going into overdraft? How could this spent money be better used to help them achieve a goal? Did they even know this much money was slipping through their fingers?

Doing an inventory of what they already own—with prices attached—can also be very useful in demonstrating the level to which their shopping has gone nutz. Add up all the shoes, scarves, handbags, jewellery, shirts, pants, dresses, jackets, bras, and panties. Assign prices and total them up. BTW, this isn't strictly a girl problem. Boys love their toys too. If you have a brother, father, son, or nephew who is a deal hound, total up what they've spent on wants so they can take a long, hard look at their reality.

Help your deal demon identify something he or she has long wanted to accomplish. Ask how the money spent on all those deals could have helped him or her achieve that goal. What better use could that money have been put to?

Mimi handed the spending analysis she'd done to Magna.

"So," Magna said, "it looks like you spent about $1,600 on things we'd classify as wants in October. Do you realize that if you had put that money against your mortgage, you'd have saved almost $2,800 in interest over the life of your mortgage?"

"What?" Mimi looked stunned.

"You could have turned that $1,600 into $2,800 in savings on your mortgage. And if you found a way to put an extra $1,600 against your mortgage every year, you'd knock $33,000 off your total interest costs.

"How do you know that? You're making that up!"

Magna turned her laptop so Mimi could see. She was on a mortgage calculator site. She put in the details of Mimi's mortgage while Mimi watched. Then she added one annual prepayment of $1,600 and hit Enter. Sure enough, there was the savings. She clicked the button that said "annually" instead of the one that said "one time," and Mimi watched the savings amount come up. She was astounded at the result.

People think it's hard to figure out savings and how they can accumulate if they're put to good use instead of simply incorporated back into cash flow and spent somewhere else. Finding a retirement savings calculator or a mortgage calculator on the Internet is easy. Make sure the site is Canadian, since ones geared to other jurisdictions use different formulas for their calculations.

Choosing to prioritize mortgage repayment or saving for the future over consumption of something new, sparkly, or luscious can feel like settling for salad when you're in a gourmet restaurant. But being disciplined enough to put financial security above the need to scratch your consumption itch is what responsibility is all about. And that's the message we need to deliver to our deal-focused friends and family.

Sure, new stuff is sexy. And the idea of a deal is sexy. Mortgage paydown or retirement savings won't be sexy unless we make them sexy. If you help your deal lover focus on tracking how much they're saving in interest costs and time by getting to mortgage-free faster, you can turn a mortgage-free home into a very sexy reality. And if you show your deal lover how to watch their net worth grow by focusing on how much more they own than they owe, you'll make preparing for a future without debt sexy.

Start bragging about the right things: not how much your new kitchen cost (or how much you saved when you put it in), but how smart you are to have a big fat emergency fund, no debt, and enough money going towards your retirement that you feel secure. Bright and shiny may be sexy in the short term. But having enough money to feel safe is long-term sexy.

REFOCUSING THE DEAL HOUND

1. Help your deal hound do a spending analysis to see where their money has been going.
2. Suggest your deal hound also do an inventory to see how much stuff they already have, and the value of that stuff.
3. Help the deal hound identify a goal they would like to accomplish to help them shift their focus from "shopping savings" to actual savings.
4. Show them real examples of how money they've spent could have been used to achieve real savings.
5. Talk to the deal hound about savings and financial security in a way that makes both sound appealing.

35 • KEEPING-UP KELLY

Kelly and her husband, Drew, have a great life. They live well, manage their money carefully, and have built up quite a nice nest egg. Their home is paid for, mostly because Kelly and Drew have always driven older-model cars, shopped carefully for their clothes, and made do with not-quite-the-latest cellphones, televisions, and appliances.

Kelly recently got a new job. After working hard to prove herself, she bagged the job of her dreams. The downside is that now she's working with a group of people who love to spend. Lunchtime is spent seeking out some new acquisition or having a meal in a swanky spot. Kelly is feeling some pressure to keep up. While she's been content to brown bag lunch for most of her working life, her new peers have raised the bar.

Drew was posting their spending journal to their cash flow budget and made note of how much Kelly was spending. "You took this job because it was a good pay raise," he said, "but now you're spending far more on lunches and other stuff. I thought we were going to put that extra money towards the kitchen reno."

Kelly shrugged. "I know," she said, "it's just that the girls at work eat out a lot."

"Well, just because they're stupid with their money doesn't mean we have to be dumb with ours, right?" said Drew.

Kelly replied, "I tried eating out just a couple of times a week, using my workload as an excuse for eating lunch at my desk the rest of the time."

"So, what's the problem with that?"

"When my team comes back from lunch having discussed a work issue, and they have a plan into which I've had no input, I feel out of the loop."

"Well, that's not right," said Drew. "If it's a working lunch that's one thing, but they shouldn't leave you out if you're back at the office working." He was getting upset. "That's ridiculous!"

"I'm the new guy," said Kelly. "I'm in no position to tell them they can't do what they've always done."

"You need to speak to your manager," said Drew emphatically.

"Yeah," said Kelly, but she knew she wouldn't.

Keeping up with the Joneses has never been riskier. Now that John Jones and his wife, Jenny, are using credit to supplement their income, keeping up with them often means sacrificing savings or, worse, going into debt.

Ever gone out for supper with friends, taken a look at the prices on the menu, and wished you could run away? Did you order a glass of water, graze on the free bread, have a bowl of soup, and pray no one would suggest you split the bill evenly? Or did you reach into your wallet, pay with your credit card, and promise yourself that next time you'd check the restaurant out before you agreed to meet your friends someplace new?

It's hard to say, "Sorry, I just can't afford that." We feel cheap. We feel like we might be left out of the fun. We are concerned about what others will think of us. So many people just do whatever they have to in order to keep up.

But if keeping up is putting you at risk financially, you have to draw a line and make it clear that you're not playing that game. Kelly could say to her co-workers, "I know I'm the new guy and you have your rhythms established. You all love to eat out. But Drew and I are saving for a kitchen reno and every meal I eat out with you puts us one step further away from our goal. But when you go out for lunch and come back with plans for work, and I've not had any input into them, I feel like an outsider and I'm not really committed to the plans. Is there any way we can have those conversations at work so I don't feel like I have to choose between staying connected with you and working with Drew on our new-kitchen goal?"

You may feel uncomfortable broaching the subject of not wanting to keep up with whomever is trying to drag you along, but you've got to tell the truth. Explain how you feel. Offer an alternative. Stick to your guns.

Caroline has been hanging out with the same bunch of girls since high school. Two of them married well and the third has been extremely successful in business. When the girls head off on vacation together, which they like to do a couple of times a year, Caroline has to put her trip on her credit card, which she knows she can't afford to pay off.

After her last trip with the girls, her husband, Connor, put his foot down. "I know you think you have to keep up with your girlfriends to stay friends," he said, "but this is getting ridiculous. Damn, Caro, you charged $467 for dinner one night. Are you crazy?"

"It was my turn to treat."

"You can't keep this up. You're carrying a balance on your cards. What would happen if either of us got sick? We've talked about this before. It's like you're running after these women as if your friendship with them is the be-all and end-all."

"I'm not running after them. We've been friends forever. You could never understand how close we are."

"Close enough to tell them how much debt you've taken on trying to keep up?" asked Connor. He looked at Caroline as she flushed a deep red. "I didn't think so."

While peer pressure is often seen as a teenage issue, more than a few adults are willing to blow a whack of cash to keep up with their workmates and playmates. And some people are prepared to blow money they have yet to earn by putting their keep-up shopping on credit cards or lines of credit.

We expect a lot from our lives. We want to live in a nice house, drive a nice car, and wear nice clothes. And we're deeply resentful when we see the things other people have that we can't afford. We're so determined to keep pace with our peers that we're willing to sacrifice our peace of mind, our family's security, and our futures just to show everyone we are doing as well as they are.

If you're hanging with a crowd whose social status is significantly above yours, you may always feel like the poor cousin. Or you may feel pressure to spend money you should be saving or using to achieve your family's goals. The drive to keep up is one reason why people making solid incomes often default to credit to buy the things and have the experiences they think they should be able to afford.

If you have a mate, sibling, or friend for whom keeping up is the primary objective, you need to help them see the damage they are doing to themselves and, potentially, their relationships.

People often forget what's truly important, choosing to focus on appearances and impressions rather than on security and balance. Regardless of how much someone earns, a life built around keeping up means a constant struggle between spending versus saving.

Imagine a world in which each of us walked around with a

sign on our back: a neon sign in a simple font showing our net worth. Those who look good but are "wearing" a pile of debt wouldn't be able to hide their financial indiscretions behind a shiny new car or snappy outfit. We'd all know they were living beyond their means and that their display of affluence was just that: a display. It isn't real. It's "peacocking."

Do you know anyone who had a wedding they had to pay for with credit? Peacocking.

Do you know anyone who bought a vehicle that was beyond their budget and lived to regret it? Peacocking.

Do you know anyone who claims they have no money to save but always has the newest toy to show off? Peacocking.

Do you know a brand hound who carries a balance on their credit card? Peacocking.

Do you know anyone who dresses, gives gifts, or picks up the tab to impress? Peacocking.

So, how do you deal with the desire to show off or the pressure to stay abreast of your peer group?

Sometimes the people we watch turning themselves inside out to keep up have no way to deal with the pressure they feel or the time it takes to accomplish a goal without going into debt. And sometimes they don't even realize the implications of what they're doing. I can't tell you how many times I've said something like the following to a princess—

> While John and Jenny Jones may seem to have it all, seldom is that really the case. You're only seeing the surface of their lives; you have no idea how solid or rotten their financial foundations may be. And since

> only the very, very rich have unlimited funds to make
> all their dreams come true at the same time, the rest of
> us have to choose carefully how we will use our money.

—only to have them respond with, "I never thought of that." This was usually a turning point. Once I helped them see that their keeping up was actually detrimental to their long-term financial health—and that the people they were keeping up with were likely in a big financial mess themselves—their barriers came down and I could give them strategies to overcome the pressure to keep up.

After you get the idea through to your lovie that the "keeping-up" game is unsustainable, here's a three-step process you can suggest that will help them quit playing once and for all.

Step one is to **acknowledge that you're feeling some pressure** and that it's making you think about doing things that are detrimental to your financial health. This is your "uh-oh" moment. Give it a name—say "uh-oh" and talk about it out loud. "Uh-oh. When Caren and Donna both showed up in those fabulous new outfits, I felt like the ugly duckling in my three-year-old little black dress. I know I looked fine, but I felt frumpy." Or "Uh-oh, I'm feeling a little jealous. I don't understand how my sister and her family can keep taking such fabulous vacations when Bobby and I haven't had a holiday in a couple of years. I feel like we're not having anywhere near as much fun as we should be."

Step two is to **refocus your attention** on something that is important to you. This is your "oh shucks" moment. "Oh shucks, I guess I could get a new outfit for the party, but I don't want to give up on my plan to build my emergency fund. And I don't want to give up going to Martha's wedding, and I'll need to have the money for that by July." Or "Oh shucks, I don't want to give up getting our car paid off in exchange for a vacation right now. The car loan will be gone in another six months, so after that we can start using the car-payment money to plan for a fabulous vacation in another year or so."

Step three is to **create a visual reminder** of the goal you're working towards to help you let go of the emotional reaction that could drive you to do something dumb with your money. This is your "okay" moment. "Okay, so I'm going to put a little card in my wallet. Every time I'm tempted to spend and don't, I'll add that money to my emergency fund and colour in another box on my card to represent a step towards my goal." Or "Okay, I'm going to start talking to Bobby about planning our trip so we can anticipate the holiday even though we're still paying off the car loan."

Ultimately, you're in charge of who influences you. **If you are influenced by people who put bright and shiny before solid and secure, that's a choice you make.** If you spend time with people who insist you pay up to keep up, you've made that choice. And if you let the things you see in magazines or on television diminish what you already have because what others have seems so much nicer, remember that you can choose not to buy the magazine or tune into the house porn.

Make sure you choose what works for YOU. When self-doubt creeps in—you are human, after all—go through steps one to three: acknowledge, refocus, and remind yourself of what's important to you, so that you can stay true to yourself.

NOT KEEPING UP IS OKAY

1. Every life has good and bad in it. Some people have more money. Some people have better health. Some people have closer family. Some people have care-giving challenges. Comparisons on just one vector don't work.

2. Remember that there is no way to really know what's what in someone else's life. A glittering castle may be what you see, but a crumbling foundation may be beneath all that glitter.

3. Goals are personal things. Working to achieve someone else's goals brings little or no satisfaction. Set goals that mean something to YOU. Then focus on achieving what YOU want.

4. Decide what's most important in YOUR life and work towards that. If travel is important, are you willing to prioritize travel savings over a new car every three years? If being with family is important, are you willing to work less to have more family time? Once you establish what's important, create a vision board that keeps your priorities visible so you don't get distracted by other people's priorities.

    To create a vision board:

    a) Get a large piece of poster board, magazines of all sorts that you can cut up, and glue.

    b) Cut out images that represent what it is you want to achieve. If you are planning to travel, you might choose pictures of locations you want to visit. If you'd love to learn to play guitar, surround yourself with images of guitars and people playing, along with the names of songs you want to learn to play. If you're not exactly sure what you want, look for pictures that appeal to you and cut them out for your vision board. Once a pattern emerges, you can refocus on finding pictures and quotes that better support your emerging goal.

c) Place a beautiful photo of yourself at the centre of your vision board and paste the cut-out images around the photo.

d) Use markers or paint to write your favourite quotes on your vision board. Or you can cut words or phrases from magazines to paste on.

e) Keep your vision board somewhere you will see it every day. You may want to occasionally add more images or quotes to keep the board fresh and yourself focused.

5. Acknowledge, refocus, and remind yourself of what's most important to you so that you can stay true to yourself and your goals.

36 • THE FAMILY SHOPPER

Bridget was a wonderful mom to two beautiful girls. She kept a lovely house. She had a career in which she made good money. She and Dixon had been married for almost 22 years. Everything was great. Well, almost everything.

Bridget had a bit of a credit card problem. Actually, the credit card balances were the result of her shopping issue. You see, as the acquisitions officer of her household, it was her job to keep the family stocked up on food, undies, sheets and towels, cups and plates and bowls, mats, dishcloths, hairbrushes, and shoes. Bridget was the family shopper.

Cast in the role of providing all the good stuff for the family, Bridget was constantly shopping. There was always a list for everything from clothes to new shoes to school supplies. Bridget turned her job as family shopper into an avocation.

She was a great shopper too. Focused on getting what she needed at the best price, each day at lunch she'd head on over to the local discount store and wander the aisles. Whenever she found something on her list, she felt like she'd hit a home run. She found towels at 70% off and cute clothes for her girls at less than half the regular price, and because Dixon fancied himself somewhat of a gourmet cook, she always bought him the latest kitchen tools. When she spotted a pair of designer shoes at a fraction of their original cost, she'd treat herself too.

Since Bridget was responsible for keeping her house beautiful, keeping her children beautiful, keeping her husband beautiful, she was always shopping. She hardly ever went into a store without buying something. New hand towels, a shirt for her husband, a set of glasses, yet one more candle. Her family had made her responsible for getting them what they needed and she took her role as buyer very seriously. So seriously, in fact, that her common sense went out the window when she went into buyer mode. The result: almost $7,000 in outstanding credit card balances.

Dixon didn't know how to get Bridget to put the brakes on. He loved her and thought she did a great job of balancing a busy career with caring for their family. He knew how much satisfaction she got from bringing home new stuff for the girls, for him, for the house. But he was watching those credit card balances rise. When Bridget's credit card company upped her credit limit, he knew he had to do something.

Most people who have taken on the role of the family shopper take their jobs very seriously. The hunting and gathering instinct is so powerful that they often shop unconsciously. They aren't aware if they are buying things they need or even want; it is the shopping itself that gives them a huge amount of pleasure.

Step one with the family shopper is to demonstrate just how much stuff they've bought and what that means in terms of money spent. Until they see the quantity of their purchases, they will continue to view their shopping as a little here and a little there. You could gather up all the unnecessary things with which they fill their family's life and ask the family shopper to estimate how much they spent on those things. Or you could ask them to go from room to room and collect ten items that are non-essential to their lives from each room. Then inventory and price those items.

Step two with the family shopper is to offset their pleasure in acquiring new stuff. That involves understanding the two parts of the brain that come into play when you go shopping.

The nucleus accumbens, which is your pleasure centre, is full of dopamine receptors; it lights up when you see something you desire. It's like the ignition of the fire of want. Your insula, which is associated with pain, is activated by the idea of having to part with your cold, hard cash. So, it's like a sprinkler system putting out the fire. There is, it turns out, a trade-off between really wanting something and having to pay for it.

Shopping with plastic can thwart your insula, bypassing it so the sprinkler doesn't come on. Credit cards are like an umbrella over your insula since you don't feel the pain of actually having to part with cash. When you swipe, your insula won't douse the heat of acquisition. Since you're not parting with real money, your insula won't rain on your parade and stop you from spending.

To remove the umbrella and bring the insula back into play, shoppers must make their brains feel the usual pain associated with parting with money.

Suggest your lovie shop with cash. Using cash is one way to engage the insula. Another is to keep a spending journal. That'll tell the insula that every credit card or debit charge will be deducted from the bank balance, and the insula will feel the pain of the money going away.

Step three with the family shopper is for her to break the shopping habit. Yes, shopping can become a habit and it can be a tough one to break, particularly for people who use plastic.

Shop on only one day of the week. Infrequency reduces the temptation to impulse buy.

Shop with a list and buy only what's on the list. If your lovie sees something they want, they must add it to next week's shopping list and buy it then.

If your honey has tons of stuff and just as much debt, suggest they declare a moratorium on shopping except for absolute essentials. Alternatively, make a game of it, challenging your honey to see how long they can go without buying anything other than the most basic needs. If they do shop, they have to start their no-shop count all over again. The game is for them to always be trying to beat their last best no-shopping streak.

BREAKING THE SHOPPING HABIT

1. Help the family shopper see that the acquisition of new stuff has replaced the goal of taking care of the family.
2. Suggest that the family shopper track their spending so they can see every penny they're spending and become accountable to the budget for purchases they are making.
3. Offer them suggestions for breaking the shopping habit, including:
   - shopping only one day a week;
   - shopping with a list; and
   - eliminating shopping completely for a period of time.

. . .

We all know people who have a tendency to go off half-cocked. As soon as something occurs to them, they react. These people can be the life of the party. Their spontaneity can be charming. But when urges get the better of common sense—when an impulsive reaction leads to regret—then it's time to rein in the impulsiveness.

Almost everyone has impulsive moments . . . you know, that sense that we just should, to hell with the consequences. While I don't consider myself a particularly impulsive person—I have always considered carefully what might happen next—even I have given into the "Sure, why not?" feeling that surrounds an impulsive action. Emotions play a huge role in our desire to be impulsive. If we're angry, stressed, guilty, or bored, we're much more likely to do something to shake ourselves out of our mood. Our brains want to be filled with happy chemicals, and if we have to buy something we don't really need to get to that good feeling, the better mood is worth it. Well, at least until the bill comes in.

But each time we give in to that impulse, the reinforcement we get from the feel-good chemicals makes us want to keep on keeping on. Just look at all the people who consolidate their debt with the intention of becoming debt-free only to find themselves back in hock up to their eyeballs two or three years later.

Most people don't want to change. They know they should. They talk about doing things differently. But when it comes to the nitty-gritty, most people are loath to pick a new path, clear the brambles, and walk on. The going gets tough and they revert to old ways. It takes a monumental effort and a lot of gumption to do things differently. It also takes a goal.

Whatever is driving the impulsive behaviour that's sapping your resources, you won't stop that behaviour if you don't replace it with consciously working towards something that is really important to you. If you're trying to help your lovie, finding that goal—that thing they can focus on—is the key.

Perhaps they want to go back to school. Maybe they'd love to own their own home. Their goal could be a family vacation, starting a family, or replacing their almost-dead vehicle. Whatever it is, only by choosing to focus consciously on something of real importance will they thwart the impulse to shop.

Warn them that the self-control required to limit impulsiveness is a limited resource. They can use it up. Trying to control too many things at once will be both exhausting and futile. Instead, they should pick one goal to focus on and one impulsive behaviour to manage. As they practise redirecting their impulsiveness, they'll get better and better at it.

And if they slip, that's no reason to give up. It's just a slip—a completely natural thing to happen along the way. If they're determined, instead of using the slip as an excuse to give up completely, they'll refocus and keep going.

Part Seven

BATTLING SELFISHNESS

When it came time to title this section of the book, I sent my editor, Kate, an email saying, "Can I name this section 'Selfish Assholes'?"

Kate wrote back: "Hahaha. No!"

Some people are selfish, plain and simple. They think they are more important than anyone else. They will not put themselves out in any way. With little or no regard for the needs or feelings of other, selfish people are concerned only with themselves. Yup, it's all about them.

I'm not sure how selfish people get away with dominating their relationships. I've had selfish people in my life and am often astonished at what they get away with. They seem to have no idea that they're leaving unhappy, disappointed, and angry friends and family in their wake. Or it may simply be that they do not care.

Psychologists would argue that we are all selfish to a greater or lesser extent. Selfishness is inherent in children who, until the age of about eight, are only concerned with having their own needs and wants met because, developmentally, they cannot yet put themselves in another's shoes. Some psychologists theorize that selfishness develops because a person's early needs were not met and they became stuck focusing on themselves and their needs. Others believe that selfishness hides a fear of inadequacy. Linked to both a lack of empathy and a tendency to manipulate, extreme selfishness can be pathological.

You need only look at the synonyms for "selfish"—egotistic, self-absorbed, narcissistic, inconsiderate, self-centred, mean, self-serving, stingy—to see just how much of a problem selfishness can be. Those aren't words you would want used to describe you, but they may be words you've used to describe someone in your life.

You may have a friend who shows no appreciation for whatever effort you put into the relationship and demands more. You may have a mate whose needs always seem to come before yours. You may have a sister who becomes moody, even angry, when the spotlight is not on her. Or a brother who always seems to be in competition with you. Maybe you have a parent who finds it very difficult to forgive any misstep you make, because they see those mistakes as purposeful strikes against them.

If you have an SA in your life, I'm sorry. I wish I had a magic solution for you to keep your lovie without being used as a doormat. I'll make some suggestions but, well, selfishness is its own reward.

37 • I'M BETTER THAN YOU

Daria was the eldest of four sisters. Because she had always been a prima donna, her younger sisters were used to Daria hogging all the good stuff for herself. She convinced her parents to give up the master bedroom in their home because Daria needed more space for her stuff than they did. And when her youngest sister's cellphone broke, Daria convinced her mom to give Tammy Daria's older phone so Daria could get the latest model for herself.

Daria's mother wasn't sure what to do about Daria's sense of superiority. Daria had always been a petulant child, and her mom found it easier to give in to her than to battle through a tantrum, particularly when the children were younger and she had four children under seven.

During her four years at university, Daria used up almost all the money her mother and father had set aside for the girls' post-secondary schooling. She refused to work during the school year. "You don't want me to fail, do you? If I have to work, too, my grades will suffer." She only worked part-time during the summer. "I work hard all year at school. I deserve some time off." And when her sister, Stacy, took an overseas credit course as part of her environmental studies program, Daria insisted her father also pay for her to go away, "somewhere warm so I can recharge."

There are people in the world who genuinely believe they are better than their siblings, their parents, their friends, and their mates. They insist on the lion's share of the resources, be it the faster car, the bigger room, the larger portion, or the newer and shinier toy. Absorbed in their own needs and wants, they couldn't care less who has to do without so they can get what they want. And their sense of ownership over things that actually don't belong to them can be quite astounding.

When Daria moved in with her boyfriend, Evan, she decided to redecorate his condo. She wanted cream carpets, cream furniture, and a king-size bed. She took Evan shopping with her but he had no say in anything they purchased. He paid for everything. And when she came home late one afternoon and found Evan's dirty boots by the front door, she forbade him to wear his work clothes home. Despite the fact that it was his condominium and he paid for everything, including a $250 a week allowance to Daria, he was to shower and change his clothes before he came home.

It is unclear why the people in Daria's life complied with her every demand. But they did. Through sheer force of personality, she succeeded in taking far more than her fair share of everything. In the process, she treated all the people in her life as if they were barely good enough to sweep up her dust.

Everyone is responsible for his or her own relationships. Those who choose to be users will gravitate towards those who choose to be used. The givers will seek takers. You cannot make other people rewrite the relationship dynamics they choose to play out. As hard as it may be to watch, that's all you can do.

If you are unfortunate enough to bear witness to the person who, by force of personality alone, gets everyone to do her bidding, you will also notice that while the people around her complain about her, they continue to do as she wishes. They pick up after her, support her, and encourage and love her, even as she treats them with disdain. And there isn't too much you can say to them that will change their minds about how lucky they are to have her in their lives.

If you try to intervene, you will likely succeed only in having yourself declared *persona non grata*. Until each person falls out of her thrall, they will continue to support and nurture her even as she drains the last bit of energy from them. Sadly, you won't be able to do a thing other than watch. It's a hard reality.

SEEING FROM ANOTHER'S PERSPECTIVE

1. If your lovie thinks love is the glue that binds, point out that this love lane is one-way, since he or she isn't showing you the care or empathy that's usually associated with love. Ask him or her, "How would you react if I . . ." [describe a selfish behaviour]. Or suggest that dude keep track of just how often his opinion is disregarded, his feelings shunted aside in favour of Selfish Sally's.

2. If lack of self-esteem seems to be at the root of your lovie's willingness to be a doormat, remind him or her just how terrific they are, and how hard it is for you to watch as they are taken advantage of. Reverse the tables by asking, "If you saw Trev . . . [describe a specific selfish behaviour], what would you think?" Pulling your darling one out of the shoes he or she has grown used to may help put things in perspective.

3. Help your lovie visualize what life might be like down the road. "How many times will you put up with buddy . . . [describe a selfish behavior]?"

4. Describe the lessons the selfish behaviour may be teaching other people your lovie cares for. "As Jeanette grows up, do you really want her emulating the way Sally treats you?"

38 • SELFISH IS AS SELFISH DOES

Adam and Sonia had been together for six years when they decided they wanted to adopt. It was a long process. And expensive. Adam was the major breadwinner in the household and travelled a lot for business. Sonia did most of the paperwork and follow-up for the adoption. She couldn't wait to be a mommy.

After baby Lillia arrived, Sonia decided to stay home full-time. She found it impossible to imagine handing this sweet little angel over to a daycare. Besides, Adam made more than enough for the family.

Soon they were running into financial problems. Sonia couldn't figure out why. She'd done a budget before the adoption, and even with the debt they'd taken on to get Lillia home, they should have been able to manage. Money kept disappearing from the joint account. When Sonia asked Adam where the money was going she was told, "Hey, I work hard for the income, the ONLY income, in this household. I shouldn't have to account for every penny I'm spending."

Sonia was taken aback. What the hell had happened? Adam had never been like this when it was just the two of them.

"I thought you wanted this baby as much as I did," she said to Adam.

"I thought I did too," said Adam. "I didn't realize our lives would change so much. We never go anywhere anymore, and without your income, it's really hard to have all the things we used to have."

"Like what?" asked Sonia, genuinely surprised by Adam's attitude.

"We used to eat out all the time. I loved spending time with you. But now we just sit home, trying not to wake the baby up. And last week we were invited to a weekend up at Sue's cottage. But Lillia was sick and we couldn't go."

"So, the baby is cramping your style?" asked Sonia.

"Don't try to make me look bad. You're the one who has turned into a total baby freak. You don't think of anything BUT the baby."

"What are you talking about? Last weekend I made us dinner and your favourite dessert. And I rented that movie you've been wanting to see."

"Which we watched in pieces because the baby woke up, cried, and you rushed up to her room time and again. Don't you think you should let her learn to settle herself?"

They looked at each other in silence for a minute. "So, let me get this straight. You're spending money behind my back because you're jealous that I'm spending too much time with OUR baby?"

"You're making me sound like a jerk," Adam said.

"Then you're spending money behind my back why?" asked Sonia

"First off, I'm not spending money behind your back. I just forgot to tell you about those transactions."

"What did you spend the $600 on? That wasn't exactly a small transaction."

"It was a deposit on a Rolex."

"What?" Sonia was astounded. Adam had been talking about getting a Rolex watch forever, but Sonia had always thought of it as a pie-in-the-sky dream. "You bought a Rolex?"

"Yes, well, I put the deposit down. I'm picking it up in a couple of weeks when I've got the rest of the money together."

"And where are you going to get that money."

"We got all that money from our parents."

"You mean the money they gave us for Lillia?" Sonia said slowly. "You want to spend Lillia's money on a frickin' watch?"

"Lillia doesn't need money. I'm working to support her. What good is that money doing just sitting in the bank?"

Sonia shook her head. She could not believe how selfish Adam was being.

Sometimes we like to use the word "selfish" to guilt the people in our lives into giving us our way. Identifying true selfishness can be tough because the word is applied to so many different behaviours. From the mom who chooses to work to the sibling who always expects things to go his way, we're faced with lots of opportunities to haul out the word "selfish" and apply it liberally. And we do.

I offer you this as a guideline: **It's not selfish to put your needs before another person's wants. It is selfish to put your wants before your loved one's needs.**

To go out and spend money on nice-to-haves with no consideration of your family's financial security is selfish. To insist that the things you want—you call them needs, but they are actually wants—always come before others' wants is selfish. To get angry every time things don't go your way is selfish. And if you act like a spoiled child, fail to understand other family members' needs, or act helpless to get your way, you're being selfish.

Having a nice wardrobe at the expense of enough life insurance to protect your family is selfish. Insisting on taking vacations with no money set aside for emergencies is selfish. Resenting that money is being set aside for the future because you would rather spend it now is selfish.

It can be difficult to watch as your grown children or siblings behave selfishly and their young children have to do without as a result. It can be even harder to wake up and realize that you're in a relationship with someone who is so selfish they can never see beyond their own desires.

Carmen and Antonio were married, with three children. Antonio was worried because Carmen had expectations he knew he'd never be able to meet. She wanted a bigger house. She wanted a newer car. She wanted, she wanted, she wanted. Antonio spent most of his money supporting the family. Carmen spent her money on herself: beautiful clothes, the latest toys, a beauty regime to rival that of a starlet.

When he married Carmen, Antonio enjoyed how she turned herself out. He was the envy of all his friends because his wife was stunningly beautiful and always looked like she'd just stepped off the pages of a magazine. Every day, Carmen would leave the house at six thirty to hit the gym before work. That meant Antonio had to get the kids up and off to his mom's. Carmen was supposed to pick them up by six, but often she'd head off for a drink with her girlfriends, and Antonio would end up getting the kids at eight when he was off work. Thank God for his mom. She would have the kids bathed and fed so he just had to roll them into bed.

A couple of times, Antonio had raised the issue of starting educational savings plans for the kids. Carmen just laughed. "Hey, I had to put myself through university," she said. "I'm still paying for it. No way are my kids getting a free ride." Antonio's parents had helped him with school, and he knew how much pressure that had taken off him. But Carmen wouldn't budge. She had the equivalent of two years' worth of tuition in shoes and handbags. But it was never enough.

People fall in love with selfish jackasses all the time. Some assume that they can love the other person out of their selfishness. Some think that their partner will change. Some have been in a relationship with a selfish partner for so long they think it's normal to always be on the giving end.

If you live with a person who takes for granted that you'll be there regardless of how selfishly they behave, you could very well be part of the problem.

If you have, up until now, refused to acknowledge the evidence that your mate, your mother, your sister, or your best friend is a selfish piece of work, you've opted for illusion instead of reality. It doesn't matter that the sex is great, that you both enjoy the same books, that you're on the same page when it comes to religious beliefs, or that you see eye to eye on almost everything. If that person always puts his or her wants before yours (or the children's), you've got Selfish on your hands. If their win results in your loss, you're dealing with Selfish. And if they manipulate you or show no concern for the impact they are having on your life, you're living with Selfish.

The first thing to do is to tell your mate, your mother, or your child just how their behaviour is affecting you. Do NOT label the behaviour as "selfish," since that'll just get their ire up. "You know what? When you leave me to do all the home care after I've worked a full week—same as you—I feel overwhelmed."

Next, give examples of their behaviour and how you felt as a result. "Remember when we planned to rent a cottage for two weeks last summer? The kids were really looking forward to it. So was I. But then you bought a new car, so we couldn't go." Or "A month ago when I was working on a Saturday, you promised you would take the kids to the school fair. Then you found out the game was on and everyone had to stay home so you could watch it."

You might want to set up a verbal signal that lets you indicate the behaviour your mate needs to change. It must be a word that you seldom use in daily life and that has no emotional connection. So, "asshole" is out of the question. Pick a neutral word. Then, when you see evidence of the behaviour, use the word to draw attention to that behaviour so your mate can learn to recognize it. Immediately explain how that behaviour is having a negative effect on whomever it is directed towards. "Stalagmite. Listen, hon, when you promise the kids one thing and then don't deliver, you show them you're not reliable, and that you don't love them enough to follow through on your promises. Is that the message you want to send?"

You can't always fix Selfish. You'll have to decide if you're prepared to live with it or not. You might suggest counselling if you think your mate will be open to that. Or you might just cut bait and move on. Only you can say how negatively the other person's selfish behaviour is affecting you and your family. It'll be a tough call either way.

DEALING WITH SELFISH

1. Decide if you even want to have a relationship with this person. Is the effort you will have to put in worth it to you?

2. Tell your friend, sibling, parent, or mate that their behaviour is having a negative effect on you. Very often, selfish people are completely unaware of the impact their selfishness has on others.

3. Use specific examples to demonstrate how the behaviour affects you. "I listen patiently when you want to rave about work, but when it's my turn you won't spend the time to

listen. Yesterday when I asked what you thought I should do, you were very dismissive and told me I was lucky to even have a job."

4. Come up with a verbal signal you can use to heads-up your buddy when Selfish rears its head. Be consistent in using the signal.

5. Deal with the behaviour. Don't get angry and start casting aspersions. Instead of saying, "You're a selfish bitch and I'm not putting up with it for one more minute," try "I know you don't want to hurt me, but when you ask me to babysit, and then won't return the favour, you're taking advantage of me and I don't like that."

39 • I MARRIED A MONEY
MORON. NOW WHAT?

When Charlotte met Hugo they were both still living at home. Charlotte was paying off her student loans as fast as she could. She and her mom had been on their own since Charlotte was six, and they were a good team, sharing the cleaning and cooking. Charlotte's mom said, "As long as you're getting that student debt paid off, you don't need to pay rent. Once the loans are gone, we'll talk about it."

Hugo's mom was doing his laundry and cooking his meals. Like Charlotte, he wasn't paying rent, but he had no student loans. His parents had paid his way through college. Now that he was working full-time, he had heaps of money for a new car, a huge TV, and all the other toys money could buy.

Charlotte and Hugo dated for several months. Hugo always picked up the tab. He was the man, after all. When Charlotte went to his house— well, technically his parents' house—she was amazed to see his mom fetch and carry for him. The only boy in a family of five, Hugo had it good.

He proposed on her next birthday and Charlotte was over the moon. They started planning the wedding. With her student loans almost gone, Charlotte asked her mom if it would be okay for her to focus on saving for the wedding instead of paying rent. Her mother agreed. "Is Hugo also saving for the wedding?" she asked.

"He's paying for the hall and the meal," said Charlotte. "I'm doing everything else."

"Sounds like a good plan," said Charlotte's mom. She liked Hugo. He was polite and kind to her daughter. What more could a future mother-in-law ask for?

The wedding went off without a hitch. Charlotte and Hugo moved into a lovely two-bedroom condo. That's when Charlotte found out that Hugo had put his share of the wedding on a line of credit. Oh, and by the way, he also had a couple of credit cards with balances. And, yeah, he was in overdraft. It was fine, though, cos he always made his minimum payments and had a great credit score. Charlotte wanted to scream.

There are some telltale signs that can be translated into "wrong way" when it comes to choosing a partner who is sensible about money. There's the young (or not-so-young) lad or lass who still lives with Mommy and Daddy but doesn't have a penny saved to show for it. Worse yet is the chick or dude who lives at home, doesn't pay rent, and depends on the 'rents to take care of everything. Hello. This is a child, regardless of how old she or he may be. Unless you're looking to adopt, run and hide.

If your dearly beloved needs to borrow money from you, from family, from other friends all the time, get out now. No cash flow management skills and the sense that other people are happy to help out are a sure sign that you're going to be left holding the bag down the road. And that bag won't be full of chocolates and roses no matter how showered in gifts you are right now.

Boyfriends or girlfriends who don't have bank accounts and choose to use a cheque-cashing service—or worse, a payday loan service—may be either uneducated or stupid. You'll have to find out which. If your attempts to educate them on a better way go unheeded, let that be the red light on your relationship.

Then there's the prince or princess who has a part-time job or a very modest income but wears the latest everything. If your sweetheart is a fashionista and you're wondering how he or she can possibly buy so much stuff on a small income, don't buy their "I'm a smart shopper" crap. Rest assured, there's a ton of debt lurking in your future.

Charlotte decided to take the bull by the horns and have the money conversation she should have had with Hugo before they got married. He seemed willing to listen. They talked about sharing expenses, and he agreed to a joint account. They talked about how much Charlotte hated the idea of being in debt, and Hugo nodded. He'd get those balances paid off quickly. He made good money. It would take him just a few months.

A few months came and went and things seemed to be going okay. When she checked in with him, Hugo said that he was putting $800 a month towards the balances. That sounded good to Charlotte. He was on track. But the reality was that Hugo would pay off $800 and then charge another $800 or more, so the balances were still growing. When he finally hit the limit on one card, he transferred the balance to a new, lower interest credit card. He told Charlotte about the new card and she seemed happy. What she didn't know was that Hugo was rebuilding the balance on the first card again.

Things hit a wall when Charlotte found out she was pregnant. In preparation for her maternity leave, she sat down with Hugo to see how they were doing, and how much they could start setting aside for the baby and to help cover her maternity leave. The debt had ballooned. Hugo now had four credit cards and the line of credit was at the maximum. And he was behind on a car payment. Charlotte was furious.

It's a funny thing about people and their unwillingness to change. Even after they understand the damage they are doing to themselves, the ability to behave differently seems to elude them. Even with the best of intentions old habits die hard, and the need to deal with having less money to spend means people can't put into action the very things that would make their lives so much better.

Some people end up in relationships where they are very badly matched when it comes to the money. One is a saver while the other spends like there is no tomorrow. One thinks about the future while the other can't see past next Tuesday. One is conservative while the other loves living on the edge.

If you're counting on your mate to do the things necessary to keep your financial boat afloat and he or she doesn't, you may have to accept that you're sailing the ship alone. If you love your mate, that may mean accepting them for who they are and getting on with the business of life. And if you have children, it may mean putting up a protective wall around yourself and your kids to make sure you are safe.

If you are living with a partner who is irresponsible with money, you have three choices:

- You can stay, fingers crossed behind your back, hoping for the best.
- You can leave, bearing the cost of the breakup both financially and emotionally. You better be dead sure this is the right step.
- You can accept that your mate won't change. Time to build a protective wall that isolates your partner's bad money management so you can keep yourself and your family safe.

COPING WITH A MONEY MORON

If you've begged, pleaded, cried, threatened, and even tried to walk away, maybe it's time to accept that this is who your partner is. If you can't live with their destructive behaviour, you know what you must do. If you can't live without this great love of your life, but don't want their storms to sink your ship, take these steps:

1. Make sure you are not on the hook for any of your mate's borrowing. That means no joint credit. No co-signing. No sharing of credit cards or bank accounts. Keep your cards and your PINs to yourself.

2. If you own a home together, accept that your home may not be around forever. Joint assets are at risk if your partner ends up in bankruptcy since those assets will be part of the proceedings. The only way to avoid this is if your partner's name is not on title. If it is, paying down your mortgage may be an exercise in frustration since whatever assets you build up may be affected.

3. Keep all the important must-pay bills in your name. Put all extraneous bills—cable, telephone, sports fees, et cetera—in your mate's name. If your buddy blows at getting the bills paid on time, you don't want it to affect the really important things or your own credit history.

4. Make sure you have a healthy emergency fund. The general rule of thumb is to have six months' worth of essential expenses. If you're married to a money moron, work at having nine months' to a year's worth of expenses socked away. (See Appendix 2: Creating an Emergency Fund.) Your partner's bad money management is an emergency waiting to happen. Be prepared.

5. Save/invest separately. Make sure he doesn't know where your money is and that he never has access to it. It doesn't exist as far as he's concerned.

6. Come up with a plan for the expenses. Your mate has to give you a specific amount every week to meet the family's needs. If she doesn't, then you're stuck with a freeloader and should reconsider your options. If she does, that money goes into an account that you use to make sure the essential bills are paid. The other stuff she can pay from her own account.

7. Keep your hand out of your pocket. This is the toughest thing you'll have to do. You cannot save your partner. You should not attempt to rescue him when he begs for help and promises to do better. It's part of the condition. Grit your teeth. If you fail at this part, you'll fail altogether!

This isn't about punishing your partner. It's about protecting yourself. And if you have children, they need your protection. Just because one member of your team can't see beyond his or her own nose doesn't mean the whole family should suffer. If you've got a partner who just doesn't get it, you've got some rough sailing ahead. Batten down the hatches!

. . .

If you live with someone who always puts their own needs before yours, if you have a relative or friend who doesn't give two whits about you, if you always feel like the guy who draws the short straw, I'm sorry. It's impossibly hard to love a body who only loves itself, or loves itself so much more than it is capable of loving anyone else.

There are all kinds of reasons you can use to justify holding on:

- The kids need their mom/dad. Ask yourself: What are they learning from a parent who always puts their own needs before the family's?
- Marriage is for life. Would you wish this kind of marriage on your children? What are they learning as they watch you be a doormat?
- I can't do any better. So, if you had rotten teeth that were causing you pain, would you keep them or would you have them pulled out and make do with soft food?

Sometimes it's hard to get perspective on the roles we play in our relationships, and whether they are fair to both sides. Pen and paper can help. Take a piece of paper and draw a line down the middle. On one side, write "What I Give"; on the other side, write "What I Get."

Only you can decide if you're getting enough from the relationship to justify what it's costing you. Just know that if you decide you're not and you choose to leave, it will be hard for a while. And then it will be a lot better.

If you can impress upon your lovie that their selfishness is a barrier to your long-term happiness together, you can help him or her grow.

But sometimes you can't.

I once knew a woman, let's call her Beth, who was as selfish as they come. Beth had a less-than-charming childhood; sometimes even her most basic needs weren't met. As she grew, she learned how to manipulate like a master. Her mate, her friends, her family all seemed to be drawn to her selfishness like moths to a flame. Her brother adored her (his wife did not.) Her best friend forgave Beth after two years of being shunned for something the friend didn't really have any control over. Her husband loved her to the point of refusing to leave her side when she demanded he stay home, even when it cost him every friend and activity he enjoyed. Beth was a piece of work.

Beth always saw herself in competition with the people around her. She showed off her handiwork like a three-year-old parading her accomplishments. She always had a better recipe, was more proficient with her crafts, or had read a better book. She threw hissy fits to get her way, once going so far as threatening to shoot herself. Her young daughter—Terry—listened intently as Daddy explained why he had to rush home. "Your mother has my gun and is saying she'll shoot herself. I've got to go." Terry thought, "Will she?" She didn't. It was yet another play for attention.

It turned out the cost of Beth's selfishness was her daughter. Having watched her mother's selfish gyrations for years, Terry eventually decided enough was enough. After ten years of not speaking, they reconnected for a brief time, during which Terry realized just how much she did not miss her mother's manipulations.

Terry felt the loss deeply, mourning for her mother (and her father) as if they had died. Eventually she realized that it was what it was and she moved on. During the brief reconciliation, Terry was overjoyed to reconnect with her father; her mother was there in the background. When her mother could no longer stand being sidelined and tried to push in on the relationship Terry was re-establishing with her dad, Terry called a halt. She realized that letting her mother back into her life would bring so much pain and confusion it simply wasn't worth the trouble.

Breaking up with someone selfish isn't easy. The cost may be huge. But you must weigh that cost against the cost of maintaining the relationship. Things do not have to remain as they are. You choose to keep them that way. Or not.

I wish you luck.

Part Eight

TAKING BACK POWER
AND CONTROL

Psychologists have spent thousands of hours trying to unravel the issues of power and control: why some people have it, why others do not, and how to get it. Turns out self-worth and a sense of autonomy are cornerstones of personal power. When we feel positive about ourselves—when we feel the locus of power is within us—we maintain control. The opposite is also true: when we feel that power rests externally with other people or with our circumstances, we feel out of control. And when we sense that others have control over the things we need and want, that makes us afraid. And that's when the power shifts.

Nowhere are the complexities of power and control more clearly seen than in our relationships. Some people voluntarily give up their power to others. Some have their control wrenched away. Whether a body has low self-esteem, lacks assertiveness, fears rejection, or needs the love and approval of others to feel happy, that body may be willing to give up control to avoid being abandoned. In a sad cycle, the person who assumes the control then feels more powerful and actually begins to see the person from whom they've taken control as little more than an object in their life. Power strangles empathy; whatever good feelings there once were are overtaken by contempt.

It's an easy thing to say: "Take back your power." Actually asserting yourself is scary hard. But failing to do so will not end well. As the person against whom you feel powerless gains more and more control, their contempt and disdain will grow, increasing the likelihood of the relationship ending badly. You can spend years—even decades—being trampled, only to be tossed away like an old mat. Or you can insist on being treated with kindness and respect. The relationship might still end, but you won't have given over your whole life to maintaining the illusion of a relationship.

If there is someone in your life who needs to assert him or herself, convincing them to do so can be a challenge. That's not to say you shouldn't try. And it's not to say you can't. It is to say that if you don't do it by the end of next week, you haven't failed.

The thing about power is that other people can't take it if you don't let them. If you've suffered at the hands of a controlling partner, friend, or parent, you have to learn to stand up for yourself. You need to recognize—say it out loud—that you are worthy of the power that is rightfully yours. Surrounding yourself with people who love you will help.

The first step is being honest about the fact that you're being trampled. I know it's embarrassing. I know you don't want to share your shame. I know you think you're the only one. You're not.

I've met heaps of people just like you. Let me introduce you.

Jan was working in a retail store as she tried to finish her degree, but school was taking longer than she'd hoped. It was frustrating. She barely made ends meet and sometimes thought she should just give up and get a better job. But she wasn't sure what that better job would be.

Tim was a pilot. He made great money but spent it almost as quickly as he got it. When he dated, he knew how to show a girl a good time: champagne, dinners out, flowers, gifts, and weekends away.

When Tim met Jan he was completely besotted, convinced he'd met his soulmate. She was as soft-spoken as he was bombastic. He loved her gentle spirit and her unassuming ways. He was used to women who demanded so much from him; Jan asked for nothing and was always thrilled with the simplest of gifts.

Six years and two children later, Jan was starting to show some wear and tear. As a child services worker, her job was very stressful. And because Tim was the major breadwinner, Jan stayed out of the finances. As she said to her best friend, Nancy, "He's making the majority of the money, so he should say how it's spent." But that didn't leave Jan very happy.

She knew they had some debt; she wasn't sure how much. She felt queasy as Tim blew money on a new SUV, clothes, and the tab for dinner with friends. One Thursday morning while grocery shopping, her debit card was declined due to insufficient funds. Jan was so embarrassed she thought she would die. "It must be a mistake," she said quietly to the cashier, as she fumbled in her wallet for some cash.

When she told Tim about the overdrawn bank account, he said it was just a mistake and wouldn't happen again. The SUV payment had come out the day before his pay went in and the account went into the red. When Jan told Tim she wasn't happy being in the dark—that she'd made a mistake giving him all the responsibility—he retorted, "I tell you everything. I told you I was buying that SUV. Why are you making a fuss now?" She told him in her soft, quiet voice that she'd rather be consulted than informed.

"I don't understand why you think you have to right to question my spending," he barked back. "I bust my ass to make money to support this family. Don't you think I should get to say in how it's spent?"

It's an old story. One person makes most of the money so a) won't be held accountable for spending, and b) thinks they get to make all the big decisions without consulting their partner. Meanwhile, the other refuses step up and insist on being an equal partner when it comes to how the family's money is spent, either because they don't think they have the right, they are intimidated by money management, or they feel the other person is better qualified.

One of the biggest mistakes couples make is allowing one person all the power over financial decisions because that person is the primary breadwinner. It's the "he or she who makes the most has the most say" game, and it's a game no one wins.

While the best cook usually gets to make dinner, it's a wise cook who checks to see what the other person wants to eat. And it's the same with money. One person may make more, or be better at the details of money management, but the other will soon grow resentful and angry if he or she is never part of the decision making. Any partner who says, "I make more,

I get more say," is making a straight-out power play. It's like saying, "I cook the food so I say what we eat. Too bad if liver makes you wanna hurl!"

Couples who consult each other—and the budget—before heading off to make a purchase are less likely to end up going off-plan when it comes to how the family's money is being used. But no member of a couple should have to ask permission to buy something.

If you are in a relationship that is based on love and mutual respect, neither partner should have more say in how the family resources are used. Money discussions should end in mutual agreement. And if you can't agree because you see things very differently, then negotiate your way to a resolution. Pulling a money power play is incredibly disrespectful of your mate.

If you are living with someone who insists on controlling the purse strings and you're not happy with how the money is being used, you must do something about it. In the best of all circumstances you will sit down with your partner and talk about what's on your mind. If he or she is unwilling to listen to your concerns, counselling may help. If your mate refuses counselling, you'll have to take more drastic steps.

What are you doing that your mate counts on? Cooking? Laundry? Housekeeping? Schlepping the children to and from daycare? STOP.

You have the right to an equal say in how the money in your family is being spent and saved unless you're prepared to never know. Or you're ready to shut up and stay out of it from now until forever. You're not? Then you must do something to get your partner's attention and make it clear that things are going to change.

If the kids go to daycare, be the first to leave for work so buddy has to drop them off and make it clear that you expect your mate to pick them up on time because you've made other plans for after work. (I'm a mother. I know this will be hard. But if you aren't prepared to put your foot down and claim your fair share of the decision making, stop whining. As long as you allow disrespect to continue, it will.) What if your mate doesn't get the kids? Really? Aren't the kids his (or hers) too? If you cannot trust your mate to take over the daycare schlep, it's time to move on.

If you are the primary cook, stop cooking. Until you've been over the finances together and figured out your respective roles in an equal relationship, you don't put a pot on the stove. Make it clear that if he or she isn't home in good time, the children will go to bed hungry because you're not cooking another piece of toast until you're sharing the financial responsibility. (Hey, sounds harsh, right? Do you really want your children to grow up watching you being treated like a second-class citizen in your own home? What message does THAT send?)

If you're contributing all or part of your income to the family coffers, open up a separate account and redirect your paycheque to the account that is in your name only. Until you're fully informed and involved in the financial decision making, buddy can manage without your paycheque.

Ultimately, only you can decide the lengths to which you'll go to make it clear that the status quo isn't working for you anymore. It won't be easy, particularly if the precedent set has been in place for a long time. But you can do it if you're serious about becoming an equal partner in your relationship.

CLAIMING YOUR VOICE

1. Having realized that giving up all the decision making was a mistake, you must now explain your change of heart to your mate. Assuming your mate is willing, sit down and talk about where the family stands financially and what you want your role to be moving forward.

2. If your mate tries to distract or dissuade you, be firm in your resolve. Insist on being included in the decision making. If your mate still makes decisions or spends money without your input or knowledge, suggest the help of a counsellor to work out this inequality in the relationship.

3. If your mate refuses to seek help or minimizes your importance (or your ability) in contributing to decisions, you have three choices:

   - Leave. Leaving may be a tad drastic at this point, but it's an option.
   - Suck it up and live like a second-class citizen in your own home. Hey, lots of people do it and continue to be miserable for the sake of _____ [you fill in the blank].
   - Take steps to get your partner's attention:
     - Open a new bank account and direct your payroll deposits to the new account. Explain that once you know what your shared costs are, you'll be happy to contribute your fair (not necessarily equal) share.

- Do no more than your fair share of household maintenance: cooking, cleaning, laundry, schlepping the kids. Refuse to be relegated to the role of support staff in your own home.

41 • WHAT SHE DOESN'T KNOW CAN'T HURT HER

Penny was madly in love with Colin. They met while they were both on a teaching exchange in Australia and got married within a few months of getting home. She knew he was a little impulsive, but that was okay. She loved his spontaneity, loved how adventurous he was. He pulled her along with him, making her try things she would never have tried on her own. The first time he convinced her to jump out of an airplane, she had thought she would die. But she didn't. They'd been skydiving a half-dozen times since. Ditto the first time he talked her into scuba diving. Penny would never, in a million years, have done it without Colin's encouragement.

Now, six months into her first pregnancy, Penny was a little worried about Colin. Without the high-rush activities they had done together, he was looking for thrills in other places, including poker games. Sometimes he wouldn't get home until three or four in the morning. Other times she'd wake up to find him playing poker online. When she asked him if everything was okay, he assured her that things were fine, just fine. She never pushed it. She really didn't want to know.

When people are keeping financial secrets there are often warning signs. Many people choose to ignore those signs, revelling in the "peace at home" that comes with ignoring the elephant in the room. But ignoring a problem never makes it go away; ignoring a problem just makes it become more of a problem.

How might you know there are money secrets at home

that need to be uncovered?

- Has there been unusual activity on financial accounts? Unaccounted-for withdrawals means cash going places buddy doesn't want to talk about.
- Does your mate change the topic whenever money issues come up? Deflection is a major tool in the secret keeper's kit.
- Does your partner want to assume all control? Is he or she unwilling to show you the financial records? While having separate bank accounts and credit cards is healthy, sharing the balances and what you're doing with your money should be part of your regular communication.

Colin was in debt. There was the line of credit. There was the vehicle loan. Oh yeah, and the overdraft he seemed to live in. Colin wasn't sure how he'd let things get so out of hand, but now all his credit cards were maxed out. Colin had a problem and he wasn't sure what to do next. But telling Penny was out of the question.

When Colin showed up at his brother's house asking for a $5,000 loan, he said it was for an investment tip that he knew would pay off. His brother, Devon, said he didn't have that kind of cash available. But he asked about the investment. "Well," Colin laughed, "it's actually an investment in my marriage. If Penny finds out how much debt I've got, she'll flip a kidney."

"How much debt do you have?"

"It's pretty ugly," said Colin, skating the question. "I was actually hoping to get in on a poker game and make some money to get back to even."

"You were going to borrow $5,000 from me for a poker game?" Devon asked incredulously.

"Hey, man, desperate times call for desperate measures." Colin laughed, seemingly unaware of just how ridiculous he sounded.

"You better go home and fess up to Penny," said Devon.

"Are you crazy?" said Colin. "What with her all hormonal and stuff, she'll just blow it out of proportion."

People use all kinds of excuses for keeping secrets. From "I don't want to upset her," to "I'm afraid he'll leave me," to "I'm trying to protect him," to "She won't understand," there are dozens of ways to justify not telling mates, friends, parents, siblings, and anyone else who asks the truth.

Have you ever gone shopping, brought home an item, hidden it from your mate, and then brought it out like you've always had it? How about telling people you paid less for something than you really did? Ever ripped tags off new stuff in the hope that it'll blend in with your old stuff? Hey, if you have to lie about what you're buying, doesn't that send a signal that maybe you shouldn't be buying it?

Most people who keep secrets do so because they're afraid of what will happen when the truth comes out. Like children who lie to keep themselves out of trouble—"No, Mom. It wasn't me who ate the cookies"—these people think that by obfuscating, they can keep their missteps from becoming common knowledge. What's a little sleight of hand if it means one less argument, right?

They never think about these two big questions:

1. Is it really worth losing your partner's trust to keep them in the dark about your debt, your bad habit, your shop-

ping, or whatever it is you're holding close to your chest?

2. If your partner lied to you about money, would you be able to trust them about anything else?

Telling the truth about how you have messed up—whether it is because you've got a gambling problem, an impulse-control problem, or a past-mistakes problem—takes courage. Are you such a big chicken that you can't tell the truth like a real grown-up?

Living a lie about anything, including money, brings with it enormous amounts of stress. Inevitably, the mental anxiety of keeping secrets or anticipating being caught is harder to deal with than the fallout of telling the truth.

Devon called Penny. "Colin was just here trying to borrow $5,000 off me. I think you need to have a conversation with him."

"What?"

"Listen, I know he's my brother and I should keep his secret, but I just don't see how that's going to lead anywhere good. Promise me you won't freak out on him."

"Do you know why he wanted to borrow the money?"

"Yes, I do." Devon hesitated.

"You're in it now. You might as well tell me."

"His gambling put him in the hole."

"I knew there was something wrong. He has been so tetchy lately. Do you know how bad it is?"

"No. He wouldn't tell me. But he was going to try and gamble his way out."

"Crap!" Penny paused to pull herself together. "Okay, thanks for calling me. I know this must have been hard. I really appreciate the heads-up."

Colin walked into the house two hours later. Penny was ready for him.

"Hey."

"Hey."

"So, Devon called."

"What! I'll kill the fink."

"Seems you have something you want to tell me."

"No, I have something I don't want to tell you. I'll take care of it."

"Or you can remember that I love you and we can work on the problem together. We're a family," she said. "And if you need me to listen, I will."

So, what do you do if you've been keeping a secret and you think it's time to come clean?

1. Don't try to anticipate how the person you are confessing to will respond. You'll be wrong. You might overestimate their reaction. You might underestimate their response. And all that energy spent in trying to guess will be wasted. Be prepared for anger and disappointment, but don't waste time trying to guess how bad it'll be.

2. Pick a date and time and make it clear that you need to have a talk. Don't procrastinate. It's easy to find excuses not to follow through on your decision to come clean. Stop wussing out. Get it over with.

3. Lay out the problem clearly. If you're in debt, have copies of your statements. If you've been hiding your shopping, bring out your receipts or the items you've hidden. Show and tell will make it real.

4. Have a plan of action for how you're going to solve whatever problem you've created. It's not fair to bring your

problem to light only to lay it at the feet of your mate and say, "Okay, I told. Now you solve my problem." Taking responsibility means having potential solutions at the ready to show you're serious about fixing whatever you've broken. "Penny, I know I've created a huge problem by gambling, so here's what I'm going to do. First, I've joined a support group and I promise, no more gambling. Second, I'm going to take an extra job on the weekends for the next several months to get this debt paid down before the baby comes."

5. Give your partner a chance to respond. You've been thinking about this for days, weeks, months, even. This may all be brand new for your trusting partner. They'll need a little time to respond and get how they are feeling off their chest. Don't take anything they say in anger as gospel. Acknowledge their feelings and keep moving towards solutions. Do not become defensive. Apologize, ask to be forgiven, and keep talking about your next steps.

Benny didn't tell Nola about the debt he had before they got married. Benny claimed that the debt was his debt and he'd take care of it himself.

Nola didn't tell Benny that three weeks after they got back from their honeymoon, her employer called her into his office to tell her that the department in which she worked was being closed down and she'd be out of a job. Nola thought that she'd be able to get another job quickly and transition without Benny having to know about her losing her job.

Nola was two weeks into unemployment. She still got dressed every morning and left the house. She'd head to the coffee shop, get a paper, and look for jobs. She'd been to a few employment agencies, but nothing had come up yet. Now her next paycheque was due, and she wasn't sure how to tell Benny there wouldn't be one.

Meanwhile, Benny was counting on Nola's share of the money going into their bank account so he could follow through on the debt repayment plan he'd created.

The caca was just about to hit the fan.

Communication is job one in the survival of any relationship. If you can't bare your financial soul to your partner, and if you can't trust that person to tell you the truth, you should not be hooked up. It doesn't matter how conflict-averse you are, if you're rationalizing why you don't have to be honest about money—"What she doesn't know can't hurt her"—you're on a slippery slope. Financial secrets inevitably come to light and, when they do, they can destroy trust and torpedo your relationship.

Whether you've racked up your credit cards because you find it tough to walk past a great deal, or you got a raise you didn't bother to tell your mate about so you'd have extra money in your pocket, it's time to tell the truth. The whole truth.

If you're the partner receiving the confession, you need to give your mate the space to get it all out without bursting into tears or going on a rampage. Sure, you weren't prepared for whatever came out, but if you're committed to keeping your relationship, you'll need to demonstrate the desire to understand what happened.

Know that the secrets being kept may have deep roots. If you've been ignoring—or worse, enabling—your mate's deceptive behaviour, you bear some responsibility for finding a new way to communicate. Think back to the day you decided to become a team. Do you remember why you did that? Can you put yourself back in those shoes and use that frame of mind to find the way to a new beginning?

Ask questions. Don't let the confessor gloss over the details. You want to know how the problem arose, why she felt the need to keep it secret, and what she's planning to do to solve whatever problem you now face as a couple. Stress that you're going to deal with this together. The secret keeper may be doing most of the heavy lifting when it comes to fixing the mess, but you're in it together.

You must both follow up on the plan you've agreed upon together. Just sticking your head in the sand with an "It's his problem to deal with," won't get the best results. But neither will taking on the role of helicopter parent. Don't insist on being kept up to date on every small step. Instead, agree on a date for your next discussion and what will be accomplished by that date. Then wait patiently. You have to demonstrate that you trust your mate if you want him to know you believe in him.

Establish a communication routine when it comes to your money so there's no opportunity for future secret keeping. Set a regular date for discussing incomes, reviewing expenses, and catching up on progress for your individual and joint short- and long-term goals. Pull your credit histories every six months and share them so you each know what credit accounts exist and where your credit stands.

If your mate fails to follow through, you may want to seek

professional help in terms of laying out a plan together or protecting yourself financially, whichever you think is more appropriate.

Don't expect the journey back to trust to be an easy one. Having been betrayed, you may find it very difficult to trust your friend or partner again. Honest effort is obvious. Further obfuscation should not be tolerated. If you can learn to communicate honestly and build transparency into your financial dealings, if you speak openly about how you're feeling and are determined to resolve issues together, you stand a chance.

COMING CLEAN YOURSELF

1. The next time you catch yourself not telling the whole truth, ask yourself why you're holding back. Imagine how good it will feel to finally be free of the falsehoods so you can truly be yourself.

2. Set a date for coming clean. Find a private spot and be ready to show and tell.

3. Lay out the problem clearly. Do not hide even the smallest details. If you have debt, make a list of who you owe, how much, for what, the interest rate, and the payment required to get it gone by a specific date. If you have a shopping itch you've been scratching, show your credit card balances, the last 10 things you bought, and explain why you think your shopping is a problem. Whatever you are sharing, provide plenty of details. This shows you're serious about acknowledging your problems and coming clean.

4. Have a plan of action for how you're going to solve what-

ever problem you've created. How will you pay off the debt? How will you change your shopping behaviour? This is your problem and you're going to fix it. Be clear on how.

5. Be prepared for anger, tears, and recriminations. You deserve it because you've been lying. Suck it up and let it pass. If you think no more progress can be made that day because your mate is too upset, say something like, "I know I've disappointed you and I'm very sorry. I am going to make this better. But maybe you need a little time before you can hear anything else I have to say. I'm going to run to the store and pick up something for dinner. Then after we eat we can talk again, okay?"

GETTING SOMEONE ELSE TO COME CLEAN

1. If you think your friend, sibling, or mate is keeping a secret that is hurting them (and potentially you), you've got to take the bull by the horns.

2. Sit as close to them as is comfortable for you. People are less likely to lie when you're in close proximity. You should be about 18 inches to two feet away, with your arms uncrossed and your palms in your lap, and be as relaxed as possible.

3. Ask your mate or friend to tell you the secret they have been keeping. If you know the secret, say so up front but reinforce that you want your pal to tell you in their own words. Maintain eye contact and be confident when expressing yourself. You want the truth.

4. Many people keep secrets—or out-and-out lie—to keep themselves out of trouble. Explain that you're not interested in flipping a kidney or punishing your pal, that you

want to get to the heart of the matter. You must convince your mate that nothing will change, that there will be no negative consequence, to telling the truth.

5. Talk about how you will resolve the problem as a team. That does not mean you're willing to take on the heavy lifting . . . that's the other guy's job. But you will be there to support and love them through whatever it is they have to do to fix the problem.

Lucas grew up with parents who had very different views on money. While his mom was very frugal, his dad was the "good guy," buying toys and planning vacations. They fought often about money because his mother's dread of being in debt often came up against his father's desire to have a great life. His parents ended up divorced, and Lucas decided then and there he'd never fight about money. Having lived with his mother for a good part of his formative years, he had adopted her sensible spending habits.

When Lucas met Elania he was immediately taken with her spontaneity and joy. Where he was careful and deliberate, she was reactive and unrestrained. He loved the way her face lit up at even the smallest of gifts. And she loved his careful attention to detail. She was in something of a financial mess when she and Lucas decided to live together, but Lucas was patient and helped her figure out how to deal with her student debt and credit card balances.

When they decided to get married, they both agreed that the wedding should be small and intimate. Lucas suggested they each make a guest list and a wish list of how they wanted their wedding to look and then sit down to compare lists. He was somewhat horrified by Elania's list. She wanted to invite 130 people to a full dinner and open bar. "Do you have any idea what this would cost?" he asked her.

"You were the one who said to 'blue sky,'" she laughed at him. "It's all up for negotiation." Then she took a look at Lucas's list. He had a guest list of 15, wanted to have an afternoon wedding with a light lunch, and then head off immediately for the honeymoon, which he thought they could book last minute so they'd get a great deal. Elania sighed.

She had married her father.

Elania came from a single-parent home with three siblings and a father who worked two jobs to make ends meet. Her mother had died when she was just three and her father was always pinching pennies. While Elania had big dreams for her career and her life, her father had always harped on her to be realistic. "You have to live within your means," he said. "You have to know your limits," he said. "You have to be careful with money because it's hard to come by," he said.

And now here she was, marrying a man who thought so small it made her want to cry. She loved Lucas to bits, but she didn't know if she could live a life in which she had to be careful to colour within the lines.

There's an old saying that girls marry their fathers and boys marry their mothers. It goes way back in literature, a story told again and again, as if in warning to those of us who might follow the same path. There's no question that our early lives with our parents have an impact on how we use money.

Did you have a controlling father who always had to have the last word? Was your mother totally dependent on him for every decision made in the household? If your mate shares characteristics with your dysfunctional parent and you're being cast in the opposite role, you could very well have brought to life the archetype so often retold in our mythologies. If you don't want to unconsciously follow a pattern that could be destructive, you must be aware of how your history is impacting your present.

Tanishia was a style hound. She liked to look good. She only bought quality. She was determined to have the best of everything. When she and Zane married, he was stunned as he watched boxes upon boxes of clothes, shoes, hats, handbags, and jewellery come into their new home. He loved that she always looked beautiful. When he entertained clients over dinner, Tanishia's style made a great impression. But he had not been prepared for the sheer volume of her stuff.

Tanishia couldn't let go of anything. She had come from very limited financial circumstances, wearing hand-me-downs most of her life. Her mother had ingrained in her the need to care for her things and never waste anything. Now that she earned her own money, she was never going to wear anything but the best. But she also couldn't part with anything she'd spent good money on. So, all her life—she was 30 now—she had "invested" in good pieces and now she had enough stuff to fill their basement.

"Where are we going to put all this?" asked Zane as the piles of stuff were carried into the house. "Y'know, I always wondered why it seemed like you never wore anything twice. Now I can see why."

Sometimes our money styles come not only from what our parents said but also from how we responded to our early lives. While our parents may have been careful with money, we may be sick and tired of always watching the pennies. If our parents were constantly fighting debt, we may never want to repeat the stress and conflict that came with that debt.

Your mate's money attitudes and behaviours have a lot to do with how he or she responded to early experiences. If you don't talk about those early experiences—and the ensuing attitudes and behaviours—you might be in for a shock later on.

Once you've identified the fact that your money styles are different, you'll have to find ways of addressing those differences. Here's one way:

Alex said to Brett, "I think before we go any further with this wedding planning, we should sit down and talk about how we both feel about our money. I know we're going to have different attitudes, so let's talk about them."

Brett thought that was a great idea. They made a date for the following Saturday night and Brett said he'd cook. Alex went to the library. There were a lot of books about money, so Alex focused on finding information they could use to help them uncover differences in their styles. The result: six statements they could respond to and discuss to see how similarly or differently they felt about various money issues. (See Appendix 3: Alex and Brett's Talking Points.)

"Here," Alex said, handing Brett two sheets of paper. "Rank each of these statements from one to five, depending on how you feel about the statement. One means you strongly agree. Five is the one you agree with the least. Then we'll compare our answers and talk about why we answered that way."

As they talked about their differences, Brett realized that his frugality felt like chains to Alex. Alex realized that money in the bank was important to Brett because it helped him feel more confident in their ability to cope with whatever life threw at them.

"So, if we work to build up an emergency fund, that'll make you feel better?" Alex asked.

"Yes," Brett said. "Having a healthy stash of cash will go a long way towards making me feel safe. But I know you want to be able to have fun too. So, how do we balance the two?"

"Well, how about we set a goal of having the emergency fund in place by a specific date? Would that help you?"

"Yes."

"Then we can also give ourselves an allowance for fun so that I don't feel like you're trying to save all the money."

"I like that idea. How much do you think it should be each month?"

"You write your number on a piece of paper and I'll do the same. Then we'll negotiate to somewhere in between."

Brett wrote down $100. Alex wrote down $250. They had some talking to do. But they were talking.

Some of us come to new relationships with bizarre or irrational attitudes towards money. Unconsciously carrying emotionally charged memories from our youth, we don't even realize how our past is shaping our future.

If you and your mate polarize over money, each defending your territory to the death, you're going to have a miserable relationship. If you can find a way to use each other's strengths to make the family unit stronger, you're much more likely to have a happy and peaceful life together. Planners can help dreamers make their dreams into goals. Dreamers can help planners come up with ideas they may never have been able to generate on their own. Spenders can help savers learn to have fun. Savers can help spenders set aside a little sumthin' sumthin' so they have options in the future.

Ultimately, being able to talk about your differences and negotiate to a common ground are the most important skills to have. If you can't talk about money you shouldn't even bother trying to have a relationship. And if you don't love each other enough to do the give and take a relationship requires to survive, don't even bother to pretend that you're making a commitment to each other. When we always put our own needs and wants first, we're not really in a relationship, so why pretend?

43 • I AM NOT A BULLY!

Holly and Jackie had been roommates for two years before Holly realized what a bully Jackie was. If Jackie didn't get her way, she'd stamp her size six foot and toss her mane of black curls. She'd slam doors. She'd throw things. Over time Holly realized it was easier just to give in.

When Jackie was late with her share of the rent for the third time, Holly decided to put her foot down. This was ridiculous. "Jackie, what makes you think I want to always be the one covering your share of the rent?"

Jackie laughed. "Hey, hon," she said, "you always come through for me, don't you?" Holly saw red.

"Not anymore," she said. "If you can't come up with your share, you'll need to find another place to live."

Jackie realized Holly was serious. Her eyes clouded as she said, "Don't you even try to make me move." She pushed past Holly, heading to Holly's bedroom. She went to the closet and started pulling out clothes, tossing items onto the floor.

"What are you doing?" yelled Holly as she followed the rampaging Jackie into her room.

"You borrowed my black jacket last week. I want it back." Jackie kept pulling things out of the closet and throwing them to the floor.

"Stop, Jackie!" Holly shouted. Jackie didn't. Six items later, she found what she was looking for. She ripped the jacket off the hanger and threw the hanger at Holly, narrowly missing her head.

Bullies come in all shapes and sizes. Being a bully has less to do with height and weight and more to do with a person's determination to get their way. Sweet as pie one minute, a bully can turn on you with startling speed and ferocity. Sometimes bullies are loud. Sometimes they are so quiet it's scary. Ultimately, their goal is to get you to back away from whatever it is you want so they can have whatever it is they want.

We all have different communication styles. Some of us have no problem with confrontation, while others are quick to rush in and smooth things over to avoid conflict of any kind. If you want a money talk to work, regardless of your communication style, you have to find a way to move to the middle. No, the tough talk won't evaporate, and if you're a "smoother," you'll have to fight your own desire to make things less conflict-ridden to get your buddy to meet you halfway. With practice—this doesn't happen overnight—you'll both learn to manoeuvre to the middle ground where you can meet.

When Olivia met Ed she knew she'd found her happily ever after. He was charming. He took such good care of her. But the first time she criticized his rampant spending, he turned on her. "I work hard for my money," he said, his growl reverberating through the room, "and you're NOT going to tell me what I can or can't do with it." Olivia was actually frightened by Ed's body language and tone. An hour later it was as if nothing had happened. The next time she watched Ed drop a pile of money on motorcycle gear and thought about saying something, she decided to hold her tongue.

The biggest flag that you are dealing with a bully is that you change your behaviour in order to please (or not anger) the other person. You should be able to discuss—even argue about—money without feeling intimidated. If asking a simple question, like "What did you spend this $75 on?" brings an emotionally laden response that leaves you breathless, you're likely living with a bully.

Sometimes bullies are demeaning, as in, "If you weren't so stupid, you'd realize that I have to . . ." Sometimes they are disdainful, as in, "I'm don't answer to you. You're in no position to question my actions." And sometimes they explicitly threaten, as in, "If you keep on me about this, I'm leaving."

No one has the right to make another person so uncomfortable that they actually change their behaviour to avoid getting into a situation where they feel unsafe. Sometimes bullying happens without the bully even realizing what they're doing.

There are people who enjoy conflict. They like a good brawl from time to time. They find themselves fixing for a fight. It's how they work out their anger and frustration. Pair them up with someone who hates conflict of any kind and you've got a bully/bullied situation in the making.

Often the high-conflict individual doesn't even recognize the pattern. But with each conflict won, they are reinforced to dominate the next encounter. Over time, they take for granted that it's their way or the highway. You're either with them or against them; there's no grey area.

Fixing a bullying relationship doesn't happen quickly. And sometimes you may need the help of a good friend or counsellor to come up with strategies for dealing with bullying behaviour. If you think your relationship is worth it, you'll both do whatever it takes.

DEALING WITH A BULLY

1. After a bullying incident, once cooler heads prevail, ask the bully why he or she felt so strongly and acted with so much vigour during your last conflict.

2. Describe how you feel when your friend's bullying behaviour shows up. Are you intimidated? Sad? Diminished? After the next conflict, write down exactly how you feel so that you can share your feelings once the conflict has passed.

3. Make a declaration that you will not be bullied anymore. You have to be determined to end the cycle, or resolve yourself to living a bullied life forever. Your statement might be something like, "I know you love me, and you may not realize you're doing it, but you're bullying me. You are determined to get your own way and it doesn't seem to matter how your behaviour hurts me. Well, it matters to me. Either you want me in your life or you don't. Tell me now so I know whether you're serious about helping to fix this problem."

4. If your bully denies being a bully, say, "It doesn't matter that you don't think you're being a bully. The fact that I feel bullied means we have a problem. Do you want to have this relationship or not?"

5. You may need to use a code word to help the bully recognize when he or she is slipping into bully mode. Pick a word you don't use often and pull it out at the first sign of bullying. Explain the exact behaviour that made you use the word. "Chartreuse. When you just said you don't much care what I think, that was your bully speaking. Do you really not care what I think?"

I DON'T WANT TO BE A BULLY

If you're a bully, you may have assumed this role because doing so gets you what you want. Or maybe everyone seems willing to let you get away with being pushy or belligerent. Perhaps you were bullied yourself, and this is all you know. Regardless of how you came to acquire this destructive behaviour, you have to decide if it's how you want to continue on in your life. Demanding that other people always give way grows old soon enough, and if you don't want to end up alone, you'll have to take control of your behaviour.

1. Listen to the things you say to the people you claim to love or admire. If those things were said to you, would you feel hurt? If so, apologize.

2. Ask your friends and family to give you a signal when they see signs of your bullying behaviour. Having established this bad habit, you may not even be aware when you pull the hammer out. A code word—one that has no purpose other than to identify your behaviour—can help.

3. If you're determined to get your own way, and bullying is the only way to make that happen, ask yourself why. Are you being a lazy communicator? Do you lack the skills to make yourself understood? How are you going to get those skills?

4. Seek professional help. An impartial helper can point out the impact your words or body language may be having on those around you. And a professional can help you develop strategies you can use to stop the bullying behaviour.

When Leslie met Sam she had just come out of a bad relationship and had thoroughly mucked up her money. With several credit cards run to the limit, she didn't know how she was ever going to get out of debt. Sam was not only handsome and charming, but he seemed to have it all together. When he suggested that Leslie move into his house so she could focus on getting her debt paid off, she was thrilled and relieved. As an accountant, Sam was used to money and seemed very comfortable with it. He had systems in place for everything from paying bills to investing for the future. Leslie was happy to just let go the reins of her financial life and let Sam take over. They opened a joint account into which Leslie directed her paycheque.

Sam paid all the bills and took care of everything else to do with the money. They each got a weekly allowance of $100 for things like lunch and entertainment. When Leslie said she needed a new car, Sam arranged everything and presented her with a cobalt blue Mini Cooper on her birthday. She was over the moon.

Leslie and Sam travelled. They ate out often. And they loved to go to the theatre and see concerts together. But when Leslie said she wanted to put a sunroom on the back of their home so she could "garden all winter," Sam hesitated.

"Is there a problem?" asked Leslie.

"No," said Sam quickly, "I'll just crunch some numbers." Then Sam agreed to the addition. Everything was perfect. Well, almost perfect. Leslie, having gotten her feet back under her—and having a sense that maybe it was time to stop acting like an ostrich—realized that she wanted to know what was going on with the money.

Leslie said, "You know, I don't have a clue how much money we have in the bank. I'm really not comfortable with that anymore. I want to understand how we're doing."

Sam responded, "It's fine, sweetheart. You don't have to worry." She let him brush her off. But the next time the credit card bill came in she opened it and was surprised to see a hefty balance.

When Sam came home that night she showed him the bill and asked why there was a balance. "You're opening my mail now?" he growled at her. "I take care of the money and I'll take care of this."

"Please, can we sit down and go over where we stand? I know I came into this relationship financially wonky, but things have changed and I want to help," said Leslie.

Sam took a deep breath. "Sure, let's go over it next weekend." But next weekend was the trip to Sam's mom's cottage. And the following weekend they were busy entertaining Leslie's sister who was in from Chicago. And the following weekend . . .

When Leslie's best friend announced she was getting married in Aruba, Leslie thought it would be great if she and Sam stayed for a few extra days to get some sun and a break from winter. For the first time in their lives together, Sam said no. "We went to Punta Cana last year so the travel fund is empty. We can't go."

Leslie got angry. "That's ridiculous. Bev's my best friend. Of course I'm going."

"Well, I don't know how you're going to pay for it, because there's no money."

"What do you mean there's no money? We both have great jobs, and the last time I asked you if we could sit down and talk about the money you told me not to worry my pretty little head about it. We'd better sit down now, hadn't we?"

"No," said Sam. "I'll figure something out."

Leslie felt steam coming out of her ears. "Why do you keep brushing me off? What is it that you don't want me to know?"

"I've got to go to the office," said Sam as he brushed past her and headed for the door. As he slammed the door and left, Leslie felt tears spring to her eyes. She slammed her mug onto the counter, splashing coffee everywhere. And the dam broke. She burst into tears as she reached for a cloth to clean up the mess. How was she ever going to get Sam to talk to her about the money? She wasn't an idiot. She had made mistakes but those were behind her. Or were they?

Most people want to have some control over their lives. Some people want to control the other people in their lives too. Taking control over others usually happens slowly, and it may be a while before one mate notices that he or she doesn't get to make any of the big decisions.

Sometimes people relinquish control because they feel the other person is better at the job. Sometimes it's because one partner doesn't want to be bothered with the worry and the details. And sometimes it's because one mate is afraid to lose the other. Each time they give in, more of their control territory is eroded.

Giving up financial control may feel good—who wants to have to worry about the money, after all?—but it's a baaad idea. A really baaad idea. It implies that you don't care about the money. And not staying involved puts you in a vulnerable position. If disaster strikes—death, job loss, illness, or divorce—you'll rue having taken a back seat on your finances.

If you've willingly given over the money management to a mate, or it has been wrangled from you over time, you need to take back some semblance of control over your money and your life.

"Sam, I really want to find out what's what. What if something happened to you?"

You should expect some pushback. It may be in the form of guilt or a challenge.

"What, you don't trust me to manage the money anymore?"

Don't get embroiled in an emotional tussle. Stay focused on the issue.

"It's not that I don't trust you. I don't think it should be all on your shoulders. We're a team, right?"
"It was good enough for you when we got together and you couldn't dig yourself out of all that debt you'd racked up."

Expect your compliance in giving up control to be thrown back at you. You deserve it for the holiday you took from responsibility. But don't let it deter you from pushing forward to regain an equal financial footing.

"That's true. I did let you take over. And that was a mistake. If we are partners, then we share the good stuff and the stuff that just has to get done. And I'm determined to be part of the financial decision making moving forward together. So, let's gather up everything right now and take a look at what's what."

If your mate tries to distract you—this works on babies, puppies, and ostriches—smile and stand your ground.

"Okay, but let's do it this weekend. I've got a meeting in half an hour."
"Go to your meeting. I'll be here when you get back and we can do it then."

Your objective is to get all the information out in the open where you can both look at it together. You want to know

- how much money you earn as a family;
- what you're spending on fixed expenses like mortgage and property taxes or rent, utilities, vehicle loans, cell and Internet, insurance, and child care;
- how much you've been spending as a family, on average, each month;
- how much you owe and to whom, and what the debt repayment plan looks like;
- if you own a home, whose name is on the title, how much you owe, and what the current terms of the mortgage are;
- how much you have saved for retirement and where it is invested;
- how much life and disability insurance are in place for each of you;
- what accounts have been set up beyond your retirement

savings: regular savings, unregistered investments, Tax-Free Savings Accounts, and Registered Education Savings Plans if you have children; and

- whether you have wills and powers of attorney in place and where those documents are kept.

It may take a couple or more reviews to get your head wrapped around your current financial position. Take your time. You're not just looking at the paperwork to get a general understanding; you want to really know what's going on. And that can take time to process. Slowly and steadily work towards full financial awareness. Once you know what's what, set a regular date (at first once a month, later once a quarter) to review as a team exactly what's happening with the money. If the plans you've laid have to be tweaked, do it together.

I've met couples where one partner won't let the other in on a thing. They don't know how much money comes in every month. They don't know where the money is going when it flows out. And despite repeated attempts to garner some information and have a say in the family finances, nothing ever comes of it. It's unhealthy. Assuming your situation has not gotten to the level of abuse, if you're done being an ostrich and you're ready to put on your big girl or big boy pants, there's no time like the present.

TAKE BACK CONTROL

Faced with reclaiming control over the money, take these steps:

1. If you are not currently working, get a job. Even a part-time job. You need some money of your own.

2. If you are working and your paycheques are going into a joint account, open a new account and change the deposits to that new account. Do not share the account information with your mate. When it comes to shared expenses, explain that once you know what they are, you'll be willing to contribute to them proportionate to your income. Until then, your money stays in your bank account.

3. Insist that if your partner wants to maintain the relationship, you both must share all the information relative to the money. If your partner threatens to leave, acknowledge that he or she has the right to do that. You must mean it if you expect that response to have any real impact on your mate.

4. If your partner threatens to a) throw you out, b) cut you off, or c) take the children, know that the legal system is as much on your side as on your spouse's. Don't be intimidated. You have a right to know what's going on and you're not going to settle for less than 100% disclosure. Seek legal guidance immediately.

5. Stop doing anything that requires care of your mate: laundry, cooking, and the like. You are not their maid, slave, or parent. You are their partner, and if your mate wants what you have to offer, he or she must be willing to give you want you need to feel part of a healthy relationship.

6. Once your partner agrees to share information and control, have the money conversations you've not been having. You may need several conversations to get up to speed. It doesn't matter how long getting caught up takes, how hard it is, or how confused you feel. Don't give up. At the

end of each money talk, set the date and time for the next one, and establish what actions you will each take between now and then. Follow through.

7. If you falter in any way, your mate will likely see that as an opportunity to turn back the clock to the way things were before you demanded financial equality in your relationship.

8. Find someone you can talk to and bounce ideas off as you move through this process to ensure you're thinking clearly. You can also use this person to practise what you're going to say to your mate so you can get some experience being the new you.

45 · WHEN CONTROL TURNS INTO ABUSE

"I don't think you understand," said Jackson in a low, menacing voice. "You're stupid, so you don't get to make any decisions. Just do what I tell you."

Tanya flinched. Things were getting worse. Jackson seemed hell-bent on making her life as miserable as possible, and she just couldn't see her way out of the mess.

When Tanya met Jackson he was a delight. After leaving the home of her very controlling parents, Tanya was relieved to find a partner who asked her opinion on everything—even something as simple as where they should eat.

"Dinner out tonight?" asked Jackson.

"Oh, I'd love that," said Tanya. "I hear there's a lovely little Vietnamese place that just opened up next to Little Tony's."

"Vietnamese? Jezus, Tanya, why would you want to eat that stuff?"

"I dunno," she replied, her voice dropping. "Just for something different, I guess."

"Well, okay, maybe next time, but today I really feel like a pizza. Little Tony's is a great idea."

"Okay." Tanya brightened. "I had a pretty good lunch, so I really should stick with a salad tonight anyway." And they were off to dinner, both in agreement.

Now Jackson and Tanya had been living together for almost nine years. Her first pregnancy had been difficult, requiring bedrest for the final month. Jackson had been fabulous, bringing her magazines to read and making her meals. He told her he would take care of her forever. He wanted her to stay home with the baby indefinitely because that's what children deserved. Having come from a divorced home, he'd spent hours alone at home while his mom worked to support their broken family. That was never going to happen to his kids.

Baby Jon came along two years later. Tanya was getting itchy to go back to work but Jackson pointed out that between daycare costs and the other money they'd spend because Tanya was working, expenses would more than eat up all her income. What was the point of that?

Over time Jackson got tighter and tighter with the purse strings. First he told her that they only needed one account and would save on banking fees. Then he put her on a weekly allowance of $200 to run the house. It usually wasn't enough for anything other than food, cleaning supplies, and the odd T-shirt or new set of socks for the kids.

Tanya and Jackson were sitting over breakfast when Tanya asked if it would be okay for her to buy a new set of drinking glasses. "Half the ones we have are broken," she said, "and I saw a set of eight on sale for $20."

"Don't you have any money?" he asked.

"Well, I only have about $5 left from my allowance, and that'll have to do me until Friday."

"Well then, you'll have to wait until next week."

"Jackson, this isn't just for me, you know. This is for the house, for all of us."

"Last week it was boots for Mitzi. The week before that you claimed Jon needed a new coat. Now you want glasses. It never ends, Tanya."

"Gosh, Jackson," Tanya said. "It's not like I'm spending the money on myself. The kids needed those things, and when your mom and sister came for lunch last week I was embarrassed when we served them water in mugs. If it's a money thing, maybe I should get a job."

"You barely manage to get meals on the table and keep the house clean now!" Jackson shouted. "How the hell would you manage a job? Besides, who would hire you?"

"Shhh," said Tanya. "I don't want the kids to hear us fighting."

"Then don't give me your crap. I give you $200 in cash every week. Make it work."

"Jackson, don't be unreasonable. That's to buy groceries and whatever else I can squeeze out of it. I can't clothe the kids and myself on that too."

"Shop second-hand. Don't waste so much money on rubbish like glasses. How much did you spend on Mitzi's boots?"

"They were only $35. I got them on sale."

"I gave you $50. Where's the rest?"

"I bought her a new pair of jeans too."

"See, that's what I mean. You said you wanted money for boots and then you go and buy jeans. THAT'S why I don't trust you with the money."

Tanya sighed and turned away. It was never-ending. She'd pleaded for a debit card on the account so she could get what she needed for the kids, but Jackson was adamant that her having one would lead to confusion and an overdrawn account. And whenever she had to ask him for cash, he put her through twenty questions before he'd give her the money, if he even did.

While she'd thought about leaving, Tanya simply couldn't figure out how to take the kids and go without putting them all on social assistance. She was stuck between a rock and a hard place. Besides, Jackson was a great dad. He took Mitzi skating every weekend in the winter and he'd started to teach Jon woodworking skills. Jon loved to spend hours in his dad's workshop. How could she take their father away from them?

It's often difficult for people to identify the moment in time when their partner's controlling behaviour turns to abuse. Sadly, it happens more often than most of us realize. People live with the erosion of their financial control and suck it up for the sake of the kids, to keep the relationship, or to avoid the conflict inherent in disagreeing with their mates.

How do you know if you might be in a financially abusive relationship? Does your partner

- give you a limited allowance and watch what you buy closely?
- demand receipts and accountability for every penny you spend, without full disclosure being reciprocated?
- insist your money be put into a joint account but deny you access to the account?
- refuse to let you see the financial records: bank accounts, credit card statements, and the like?
- ask you to sign financial paperwork without reading it?
- become angry if you buy something for yourself?
- block your attempts to get a job or improve your education or skills?
- insist you work in the family business for little or no pay?
- refuse to give you enough money to clothe and feed yourself, while spending money on his or her own entertainment or pleasures?
- belittle your ability to understand and deal with financial matters?

The first step is to acknowledge that you're in a financially abusive relationship. I know this step is very hard. Change feels impossible, and you'll have to prepare yourself for some very tough months if you decide things must change.

Recognize that financial abuse—the extreme of financial control—hardly ever stops there. As one partner gains more and more control over the other, the tendency is for the abuse to escalate. If you feel trapped because you're afraid your partner may seek revenge, you will need to get resources on your side before making a move. Family and friends may help. Or you may need to seek professional counselling. Above all, remember that your mate's behaviour is not your fault. You are not responsible for someone else's actions. And you have a right to be treated with respect and to share the financial knowledge in your relationship.

I'm not going to give you a scenario for how to open up the conversation and gain some ground because I don't believe it will help. Once financial control moves to the arena of abuse, it's not likely that your mate will change enough to resolve the problem without you taking drastic action. As the victim of the abuse, you aren't the problem. Your mate is. Until your partner seeks professional help, there isn't much hope that things will change.

This situation is so much harder if you love your mate and just want things to go back to how they were before it got so bad. Wishin' ain't gonna make it so.

If you are ready to take steps to change your life, you've got some preparation to do. You'll need money. And you'll need support systems like the numbers for local shelters, family members, and friends, and perhaps your spiritual leader's support. Gather a full supply of any prescription medication you are taking. Gather your legal identification. Then make a plan for when you will leave and what you will take. Contact a divorce specialist beforehand to find out the rules and the best way to make the change.

· · ·

How is it that some people seem to control their own destinies while others feel as if they are at the whim of the fates? I have long been told how lucky I am. I have a blessed life. I know I am both lucky and blessed, but that's not what makes my life as wonderful as it is. It is my sense of control over my own outcomes that makes my life so satisfying. But the control wasn't given to me, and I've had to fight hard to keep it.

Sometimes people give up their power slowly. Over time, it seems to erode like the banks of a rushing river, little bits falling away until, finally, huge chunks drop into the angry, powerful waters.

Sometimes people come into relationships with no power of their own. They hitch themselves to a personality that seems capable and in control, and they are content to be caught up in their mate's slipstream.

Sometimes people have their personal power ripped away.

It doesn't matter how a body gets to the place where they feel like they are no longer directing their own life. To stay in that place means to give up.

If staying is dangerous, if staying is demeaning, if staying is painful then you must work up the courage to take back the power and control you should have, or change your circumstances completely so you don't have to fight with your bully anymore.

You only get this life. Never mind all the ones you may have lived before or the better place to which you may be going. This life is the only one you have right now. Don't give it over to someone who doesn't value it as much as it should be valued. And don't take it for granted.

You are as strong, as worthy, and as capable of being in charge of your own life as you want to be.

Want to be.

CONCLUSION

Talking about money is harder than talking about sex, religion, politics, and even death. Survey after survey tells us that couples enter relationships without saying word one about their expectations for dealing with financial issues together. Every Valentine's Day brings a slew of articles on why having that money talk is important, and yet few people have it. We find it easier to tell our partner what makes us feel good sexually than what makes us feel safe financially.

Parents refuse to talk to their kids about money, using words like "privacy" and "tacky" as their excuse for ignoring a life skill their children will need to be successful. Instead, they look for ways to off-load the responsibility—on to teachers or financial advisors—so they don't have to feel uncomfortable or answer questions that are challenging.

If you accept the premise that money is simply a tool—it saves us having to throw a goat over our shoulder when we head out to do our shopping, lopping off pieces as we go to pay for the goods and services we buy—then why have we loaded money down with so much baggage? Why have we spent generations sidestepping questions about how much we make, how we should split the dinner bill, or how much we'll give to each of our children to help them get through school? And why do we let others use money like a two-by-four to manipulate us into doing what they want?

No one should allow money—how much they make, how much they spend, how much they keep—to define who they are. A person who makes $320,000 a year as a TV personality isn't better than someone who makes $32,000 as a child and youth care worker. A person who lives in a $2-million home isn't better than a person who rents a one-bedroom apartment. And a person who drives a late-model foreign sports car isn't better than the person who drives a 10-year-old domestic jobbie. What defines us is our ability to live a truthful life, a life that adds value to our community, a happy life.

It's time for us all to accept responsibility for how we choose to see and use money. It's time for us to make it clear to the people in our lives that if they respect us as much as we respect them, they will not ask us to do things that go against our core values. And they will not ask us to put ourselves in harm's way—financially or emotionally—to save them.

It's also time for us to stop buying the garbage that talking about money can ruin relationships. Relationships in which you cannot talk about money are already weak.

If you can't tell your mate how much you owe, that speaks to your fear of being judged, your lack of trust, or the fact that you know your mate is going to blow a gasket because you're a money moron and you don't want to have to change your behaviour.

If you can't talk to your children about money, it is your sense of ineptitude, your belief that money defines you, or your lack of a financial strategy that's stopping you. If you truly want your children to have lives that aren't sabotaged by a lack of money skills, you'll figure it out so you can teach it to your children. (You'll be better off for doing so too.)

If your parents won't talk to you about their plans for retirement, how they want their care to be managed, and where they keep their wills, it's because they don't trust you. Or they think you're an idiot. Or they don't want you to lose respect for them because they've made a right wet mess of their money.

But not talking about money—and all the underlying things that lead us to blame money for our problems—isn't going to get us to a better place. To start the journey of taking control of our money and our lives, we have to throw open the windows and doors, dust out the secrets, and treat money like rice or bread or beans. We have to know how much we have, how we plan to use it, and how long we've got until we need to get some more. We have to be honest, sincere, and open about money and the role it plays in our lives. And we have to stop using money as the excuse (or the two-by-four) in our relationships.

We have to accept that it is our attitudes towards, and behaviour with, money that need to be addressed. And the way to do that, is to talk, Talk, TALK.

No matter how much you may wish otherwise, there may be people in your life that you can't help. Recognize that they are bound by their fears and anxieties. The mess they've made may not yet be frustrating enough, painful enough, dangerous enough for them to overcome their fears of not having what they want, not being able to keep up with their friends, not appearing to be cool.

The best you can do is to continue to challenge their thinking and wait for the moment when you can step in to show them a better way. Until then, just don't get drawn into enabling their delusions or, worse, being harmed by them. Never lend them money; every dollar you hand over is a gift. Stop supporting their delusions. "No. I know you can't afford to give me a gift so I'm not willing to accept this from you." Show them by your own actions that you are aware and that awareness comes with great joy, not a sense of having to give up a life full of fun and spontaneity.

You know the old saying "You can lead a horse to water but you can't make him drink." It's absolutely true. And until that horse is thirsty enough, all the cold water of reality won't make a scrap of difference. Just be ready when your pony wants to take a slurp.

ACKNOWLEDGEMENTS

The HarperCollins team is the best in Canada. From sales to marketing to editorial to publicity, they are so committed to their authors it takes my breath away. They have welcomed me into their family and treated me with care.

David, I will miss you.

Every time I write a book I say thank you to my agent, Curtis Russell, and my editor, Kate Cassaday. Thank you is not enough.

Without Curtis none of the books I've published in the last six years—crap, Curtis . . . them's a lotta words!—would have been written. When Curtis first approached me about writing a book I was less than enthusiastic. Having had several bad experiences with other Canadian publishers, I was determined never to write another book. When he expressed interest in repping me, I was profane. He was not deterred. A kind and thoughtful man, Curtis is made of tough stuff. I didn't scare him away (thank heavens), and from the very beginning he diligently negotiated some pretty sweet deals for me. And I LOVE that he thinks I'm funny.

And now to Kate, my darling Kate, who puts up with my roaring and arguing, my unusual telephone style, my passionate tirades. Winsome, determined, and kind, Kate has this remarkable ability to get me to see things from another perspective. Every single project we have worked on is better because of her keen insights and eye for detail. Although I sigh at her never-ending questions and her penchant for shuffling the pages of my books, she is, without question, my favourite editor. I love how she always makes my work better. Thanks, babe.

To my kids: Thank you for the love and the lessons. You are my air.

A special thank you to my daughter, Alexandra, who listened to every word as I wrote it, giving me encouragement and direction, and keeping me honest. "Really, Mom, would anyone say that?" I've never written this much dialogue before and between Alex and Kate, I think the voices I wanted you to hear ring true.

And thank you to the many people who watch, listen, write, tweet, and comment daily. You are a loyal and kind audience and I hope you've learned enough through the books and TV shows to build your own strong personal economy. Now I pass the baton to you. You have friends, family, and communities that need your knowledge and wisdom. Please share yours as I have shared mine. YOU can make all the difference in the world. Teach one person. Then ask that person to pay it forward. Don't get frustrated over the people who slip away, who don't follow exactly the road you intended, or who miss a few steps. That is their journey. Whatever you can do to help, do.

APPENDIX 1: BUILDING A BUDGET

Over and over again people tell me they don't know how to make a budget. It doesn't matter how many articles they read, how many worksheets they download off the Internet, how many times they try. They just can't do it.

Once I started doing the TV show *Til Debt Do Us Part* and introduced the jars, people headed out to buy their own. But they still couldn't figure out how much money to put in the bloody things. (Actually, a whole bunch of viewers wrote to me to ask why I wasn't selling those jars so they could buy them. Rinse out your jam jars, people. Don't waste money buying jars.)

I've covered the building-a-budget issue in detail in some of my other books. If you need more detailed instructions than I give here, get your hands on a copy of *Debt-Free Forever*.

The most important step in figuring out your money and how to take control of it is to complete a spending analysis. And it's the step most people want to skip. If you don't know where your money is going now, how can you ever hope to know what you may be overspending on?

Here's an example of what I mean. Let's say you're building your budget and you decide to allocate $600 a month to food. Off you go to the supermarket. You shop as you always do, come home, cook. You buy more food, cook, eat. You do it all month. At the end of the month you add up all the money you spent on food and the total comes to $879.63.

"See," you say triumphantly, "budgets don't work."

It wasn't the budget. It was YOU.

By not doing a spending analysis, you had no idea how much you were spending on food. You kept doing what you'd always done and spent what you always spent. What a surprise!

If you want your budget to work, you have to first see how you've been spending your money. Only by knowing where your money has been going can you make conscious decisions about whether you're satisfied with how you're spending your money and what you'll change to make your money work better for you.

So, the first step in making a budget is completing a spending analysis. If you aren't prepared to take this step, embrace your financial ignorance and move on.

If you're ready to face your reality, gather up six months' worth of all your statements: bank statement(s), credit card statement(s), line of credit statement(s). You're going to break every transaction out so you can see EXACTLY where your money has been going. (I've done this for all the families who have appeared on all my shows, and six months works best to get the clearest picture of what you've been doing. If you shortcut, the results won't be accurate.)

Use your common sense when it comes to deciding which categories to put stuff in. For example, if you pay someone to cut your grass, that's home maintenance. If you pay for monthly massages for health reasons, not as a self-indulgence, put it under "medical," not under "beauty." But don't lie!

If you have a whole bunch of transactions in department or discount department stores that you can't break into categories, simply enter them into the "department store" category.

Making a budget is a bit like doing a puzzle. Once you've done a spending analysis you have all the pieces and you just have to get them into the right place. You may not get it right on the first go. Sometimes you have to move those pieces around a few times to make it work.

Make an Excel spreadsheet (or you can use pen and paper), and put your net income—how much goes into the bank—at the top.

Next come your expenses. Start by subtracting the money you should be saving for a) emergencies, b) retirement, and c) kids' educations, if you have children. These savings amounts should not be afterthoughts; they go into the budget right off the bat. If you have consumer debt, you need to deduct your debt repayment amount as well.

Plop the monthly averages from your spending analysis into the budget. Then set to work to make your spending plan balance.

You may have to adjust the amounts you are spending

on your variable expenses and your nice-to-haves downward until the budget comes out even. If you've cut those categories to the bone and the budget still doesn't balance, fixed expenses come under the knife. Will you find a cheaper form of transportation? Will you move to cheaper digs? What are you going to change to make the budget balance?

Resist the urge to *pretend* you're making a balanced budget. Don't leave out categories like clothing, home maintenance, fun, family gifts, medical, and car repairs. It makes much more sense to make a plan that will work than to set your plan up to fail. Yes, you may need to adapt on the fly if your "car repair" money hasn't built up enough to cover the cost of the new tires you have to buy. But it's unlikely that you'll have to buy new tires, repair the roof, buy the kids new shoes, and cover a birthday all in the same month, so as long as you have enough money in your planned-spending account, your budget will work.

Your planned-spending account is where you keep all the money you plan to spend that hasn't gone out yet. If you budget $100 a month for gifts, you'll accumulate that money in your planned-spending account. Ditto your annual home insurance, property taxes, vacation, clothing—anything you budget for monthly but pay for less regularly. Track each category and the amount you are accumulating on a spreadsheet or in a notebook.

There are no hard and fast formulas for what you should spend on your variable costs like food or transportation; it's a matter of what each person or family needs. While one family may be able to survive spending just $100 a month on gas, another may have to spend three or four times that. There's no right-amount rule for any category. It's a matter of need and available income.

The bottom line is that you can't spend more money than you make. If you can't get the budget to balance you either cut costs or make more money. Debt has to be repaid. And you have to save something both for emergencies and for the long term.

It's your money. You can do anything you want with it EXCEPT spend more than you make.

APPENDIX 2:
CREATING AN EMERGENCY FUND

The rule of thumb is that you should have enough cash to cover six months' worth of essential expenses: rent, utilities, basic food, and the like. Cash in the bank means you have options so you can deal with whatever life throws at you. No cash, no options!

People often can't wrap their heads around the idea of accumulating a huge pile of money for an emergency. The concept of saving that much money is overwhelming. Instead of trying to imagine an enormous number, take it one expense at a time.

Go over your budget with a highlighter and highlight the expenses you'd have to keep paying even if your income disappeared. These are your essential expenses.

Now go back over your list and cut out anything you've kept that's not essential. If you've just gone from two incomes to one, or you have no income at all, you can suspend your cable, telephone, entertainment, and everything else that falls into the wants category. You can also trim your other expenses back. Remember, this emergency fund is to see you through tough times. You don't eat steak in tough times.

Write in the monthly amount you would budget for each of your essential expenses in tough times. Put six check boxes beside each amount. Pick the first expense you want to have covered. Most people pick shelter or food.

How much can you save every month? Ten dollars? Twenty-five? One hundred? Open up a high-interest savings account. Have the amount you've designated automatically deducted from your regular account into your emergency fund account every month.

Most people have expenses they can trim to boost the money going to their emergency fund. Do you buy coffee every day on the way to work? Calculate how much you're spending, cut it in half, and save the difference. Go out for a drink with your friends after work? Buy your lunch? How quickly could you build your emergency fund if you focused on being safe as opposed to being satiated?

Once you've got a month's worth of food covered, put a check mark in one of the "food" box. There, you've done it. One month's worth of food money at the ready. Keep going.

APPENDIX 3:
ALEX AND BRETT'S TALKING POINTS

Rank each of the statements in the following categories on a scale of one to five, with one being strongly agree and five being strongly disagree. Compare your answers with your mate's and talk about why you think you answered as you did. If you're on the same page, great. If there are areas where you see things differently, you'll have to negotiate to a common ground. These talking points should get you started on a conversation you'll be having for the rest of your relationship.

1. Saving
a) ___ I think savings are important but I don't have as much as I should.
b) ___ I have a hard time saving money. There's always something to buy.
c) ___ The more money I have saved, the more in control of my life I feel.

d) ___ Having lots of money in the bank makes me feel important.

e) ___ Saving is the most important thing; spending on anything other than essentials must always take a back seat.

2. Spending

a) ___ I shop around so I know I've gotten a good deal.

b) ___ I love shopping sales. When something's a good deal I can't pass it up.

c) ___ I feel great when I buy something new. I love that feeling.

d) ___ I only buy the best. Name brands are investments.

e) ___ I hate shopping. Every time I have to spend money I feel angry or scared.

3. Gifting

a) ___ I'd much rather give a beautiful gift than buy myself something.

b) ___ It's important to give expensive gifts or people will think you're cheap.

c) ___ I would never regift; that's just tacky.

d) ___ I buy expensive presents because I want people to know I appreciate their friendship/love.

e) ___ I'm against spending money on gifts. What a waste of money.

4. Debt

a) ___ I don't see any problem with putting a vacation on a credit card and then paying it off when I get back.

b) ___ I'm not debt-averse, but I know what my limits are.

c) ___ As long as I'm keeping up with my minimum payments, my credit score is fine.

d) ___ Life is for living. What's a little debt?

e) ___ No debt, no debt, no debt, no debt.

5. Acquisition

a) ___ I don't want to own a lot of stuff because I think it's just a waste of money and space.

b) ___ I love shopping. I can always find a place to put something new.

c) ___ People judge me by how I look. I've got to keep up appearances.

d) ___ Needs always come before wants, but some wants are good too.

e) ___ I only spend on things I plan to buy and have researched carefully.

6. Money Management

a) ___ I want to know where my money is going. I track my spending.

b) ___ I don't like making the financial decisions. It's all so confusing.

c) ___ It's important that I be able to pay my own way. You should too.

d) ___ Money is for spending. What's the point of money if you can't enjoy it?

e) ___ I don't have a problem borrowing money from friends or family when I run short. I just pay them back.